CONTENTS

SHAKESPEARE
SET FREE

TEACHING

HAMLET

•

HENRY IV
Part 1

PEGGY O'BRIEN, GENERAL EDITOR
JEANNE ADDISON ROBERTS, SCHOLARSHIP EDITOR
MICHAEL TOLAYDO, PERFORMANCE EDITOR
NANCY GOODWIN, CURRICULUM EDITOR

•

Teaching Shakespeare Institute
Folger Shakespeare Library
Washington, D.C.

WASHINGTON SQUARE PRESS
PUBLISHED BY POCKET BOOKS

New York   London   Toronto   Sydney

"Up Jack" from *The Beautiful Changes and Other Poems*, copyright 1947 and renewed 1975 by Richard Wilbur, reprinted by permission of Harcourt Brace & Company.

A WASHINGTON SQUARE PRESS *Original* Publication

A Washington Square Press Publication of
POCKET BOOKS, a division of Simon & Schuster Inc.
1230 Avenue of the Americas, New York, NY 10020

Shakespeare set free: teaching Hamlet, Henry IV, Part 1 / Peggy
    O'Brien, general editor . . . [et al.]. —Washington Square Press New
    Folger's ed.
        p.   cm.
    "Washington Square Press original publication"—T.p. verso.
    ISBN 0-671-76048-3
    1. Shakespeare, William, 1564–1616—Study and teaching.
2. Shakespeare, William, 1564–1616. Hamlet. 3. Shakespeare,
William, 1564–1616. Henry IV. Part 2. 4. Henry IV, King of
England, 1367–1413—In literature. 5. Historical drama, English—
Study and teaching. 6. Tragedy—Study and teaching. I. O'Brien,
Peggy.
PR2897.S44 1994
822.3'3—dc20   94-13796
                                                        CIP

First Washington Square Press printing September 1994

10 9 8 7 6 5 4

Cover illustrations by Kinuko Y. Craft

Printed in the U.S.A.

SHAKESPEARE

SET FREE

Also from the Teaching Shakespeare Institute

Shakespeare Set Free: Teaching *Romeo and Juliet, Macbeth,* and
A Midsummer Night's Dream

Published by WASHINGTON SQUARE PRESS

ACKNOWLEDGMENTS

Shakespeare Set Free belongs to the Folger Shakespeare Library's Teaching Shakespeare Institute, a program born with the enduring faith and to the high standards of Carolynn Reid-Wallace. Each time I open a letter from a teacher or have a phone conversation with someone about her fourth-period class, I give thanks to the National Endowment for the Humanities, which continues to make the institute's work possible.

This volume owes much of its life to the collective genius of the faculty and participants of "Teaching Shakespeare's Language" who were in residence at the Folger Shakespeare Library during the hot summers of 1988 and 1989:

Andrea Alsup, *Woodstock, Vt.*
Tom Berger, *Canton, N.Y.*
Susan Biondo-Hench, *Carlisle, Pa.*
Stephen Booth, *Berkeley, Calif.*
Kathleen Breen, *Louisville, Ky.*
Susan Cahill, *Sparta, N.J.*
Carlos Castillo, *Denver, Colo.*
Martha Christian, *Kingston, Mass.*
Barbara Crabb, *Helena, Ark.*
Donna Denizé, *Arlington, Va.*
Ellen Diem, *Inola, Okla.*
Judy Dill, *Columbia, S.C.*
Susan Donnell, *St. Louis, Mo.*
Judith Elstein, *Somers Point, N.J.*
Lynn Frick, *Madison, Wis.*
Nancy Goodwin, *Clinton, Okla.*
Martha Harris, *Golden Valley, Minn.*
Diane Herr, *Lansdale, Pa.*
Tony Hill, *Stratford-upon-Avon, U.K.*
Judith Klau, *Groton, Mass.*
Michael LoMonico, *Stony Brook, N.Y.*

Jerry Maguire, *Columbus, Ind.*
Mary Beth Maitoza, *North Providence, R.I.*
Russ McDonald, *Greensboro, N.C.*
Diane Mertens, *Madison, Wis.*
Barbara Mowat, *Washington, D.C.*
John Murphy, *Claremont, Calif.*
Louisa Newlin, *Washington, D.C.*
Skip Nicholson, *Los Angeles, Calif.*
Suzanne Peters, *Tucson, Ariz.*
Mary Winslow Poole, *Washington, D.C.*
Christopher Renino, *New York, N.Y.*
Randal Robinson, *East Lansing, Mich.*
John Scott, *Hampton, Va.*
Susan Snyder, *Swarthmore, Pa.*
Annie Stafford, *New York, N.Y.*
Everett Stern, *Toledo, Ohio*
Robin Tatu, *Washington, D.C.*
Pat Thisted, *Colorado Springs, Colo.*
Michael Tolaydo, *Washington, D.C.*
George Wright, *Minneapolis, Minn.*

During those summers, institute members received bountiful support from Lauri Lewis, Heather Lester, and Mr. Freddie Lindsay. During the 1988–89 school year, hundreds of students in classrooms all across the country contributed greatly to this project.

From that summer to this day, this series has benefited from the enthusiastic and wise direction of Jane Rosenman at Washington Square Press.

The Folger Shakespeare Library, under the direction of Werner Gundersheimer, continues both to celebrate and to incite the work of teachers and students. Director of Museum and Public Programs Janet Alexander Griffin embraced these books with the same enthusiastic support that she gives to all the library's education programs. Barbara A. Mowat and Paul Werstine have provided us with brand-new editions of the New Folger Shakespeare, enabling us to work with fresh and exciting authoritative texts.

Directly and indirectly, the staff of Museum and Public Programs has contributed immeasurably to this volume, just as it contributes to every bit of the library's education work. Jane Bissonnette, Janice Delaney, Stephanie DeMouche, Bill Fecke, Anna Flye, Saskia Hamilton, Katy O'Grady, Susanne Oldham, and Chris Shreeve are smart, talented, dedicated, hardworking, and hilarious. They make all things possible on a regular basis.

Shakespeare Set Free: Teaching Hamlet *and* Henry IV, Part 1 has enjoyed the unmatched expertise, devotion, and perfectionist eyes of the Folger's small and sturdy education staff. Evidence of Louisa Newlin's work as a fine teacher and a fine scholar can be found not only in her essay on *Henry IV, Part 1* but also on many pages of the curriculum section. Ever the high-spirited manager and teacher, Molly Haws has propelled herself into an allegorical phone booth from which she has emerged as *Super-editor*, a hero bent on continuity and correctness.

The Reading Room staff—particularly Betsy Walsh, Rosalind Larry, and LuEllen DeHaven—provided assistance in all aspects of this work. *Shakespeare Quarterly* assistant editor Mary Tonkinson continues to serve as our fearless dial-a-grammarian, willing to set English teachers straight about matters of usage at a moment's notice.

I remain in debt to the "Folger Net," the family of Teaching Shakespeare Institute alumni that continues to stay family, and in particular to members of the class of 1993, who with one excited whoop last summer let me know that these books are indeed a good idea. I am grateful to head scholar Russ McDonald, who continues to hold the institute to his own high standards and to enrich all of its efforts with his prodigious intellect, energy, and wit.

As ever, Jeanne Addison Roberts remains a teacher's teacher, continuing to inspire the work of the institute and the lives of all of us who are a part of it. Like many institute members, I want to be Jeanne Roberts. Her intelligence, courage, insight, and support are reflected in every page of this book.

Shakespeare Set Free is a monument to the vision, grit, and sheer belief of Nancy Goodwin. As curriculum editor, she put much of this book together with her usual brilliance, honesty, persistence, and humor, leaving those she edits only grateful for her attention and insight. She is aided in this work by Michael LoMonico, a man whose immense wisdom is born of inspiration and practicality, whose dedication to this series is unwavering, whose generosity and humor are legend. And he can cook.

I am grateful to the students in my family and extended family, all of whom are every kind of smart and who talk to me—some have been doing this for most of their lives—about what and how and why they are learning or not learning, in school and out. I am a good listener. I am their student. These teachers are Jake Mutrie, Jordan Barnett, Jon Goldman, Tim Mutrie, Megan Hester, Maura LoMonico, Whitney Barnett, Evan Keeling, Barbara Barnett, and Kate Mutrie.

Then there is my ongoing debt to Beth O'Brien and John O'Brien. We share the most mammoth education project of all—growing up. About learning and about life, they are full of insight, warmth, humor, and above all, wisdom. They are extraordinary teachers, and I am learning as fast as I can. Their enthusiastic spirit is the magical floating backdrop behind all of my work.

P.O'B.

"Do I Have to Read This Again? We Did This Last Year."

❧

A LETTER FROM PEGGY O'BRIEN

Shakespeare Set Free: Teaching Hamlet *and* Henry IV, Part 1 is the second round in the Folger Library's series on teaching the plays of Shakespeare. Writing the Introduction to this volume sticks me tight between my desire to say flat-out things that need to be said and my horror of repeating myself. For teachers new to the *Shakespeare Set Free* series, I want to lay on some essentials about teaching and about teaching Shakespeare. But if you are already our friend and colleague, I run the risk of doing the unthinkable—wasting your time.

So here are a very few old things and a couple of new things about *Shakespeare Set Free* and how these books came to be, about teaching literature in general, about teaching Shakespeare in specific. Breathe deeply and stay perky, even if you've taken this ride before.

The Teaching Shakespeare Institute is the dynamite combination of a remarkable research library and a bunch of real people with real voices at work on Shakespeare and the business of teaching Shakespeare. The Folger Shakespeare Library houses one of the world's largest and perhaps the most significant collection of materials pertaining to Shakespeare and the English and Continental Renaissance. The Folger is also the center of a great deal of education work, and all of that work is based on a few deeply held, well-tested beliefs. I feel that I have been talking about these beliefs for a long time. They are laid out pretty completely in *Shakespeare Set Free: Teaching* Romeo and Juliet, Macbeth, *and* A Midsummer Night's Dream. Here is a quick recap, along with a few late-breaking additions:

1. **The most significant work in the entire world goes on in schools. Period.**

2. **The people who know most and best about teaching are the folks who do it every day with real kids in real classrooms.**

3. **Shakespeare is for all students of all ability levels and reading levels, every ethnic origin, in every kind of school.**

4. **Shakespeare wrote more than four plays, and many of those other thirty-four plays are terrific for students.** The Big Four are fine plays, even though I get impatient about the fact that many students' entire Shakespeare education never moves past this very, *very* short list. I get more than impatient when forced to dwell on the fact that

the women in these four plays are silenced in one way or another; they die, they go mad, they disappear, or like Portia and Calpurnia, they never had much to say in the first place.

Histories and comedies are splendid, and all kinds of students really like them. The *Shakespeare Set Free* series is straightforward in its intention to seduce teachers in this direction, pairing a Big Four play with a comedy or history taught less frequently. The myth that tragedies are "easier to teach" or "easier to learn" than histories or comedies is *myth*. Ask anybody who has ever taught *Twelfth Night, Henry IV, Part 1, Much Ado About Nothing,* or *Richard III.*

5. **The teaching of literature has not changed much in a hundred years.** A series of studies published by the Center for the Learning and Teaching of Literature tells us that Shakespeare is taught in 91 percent of American secondary schools. One study that focused on methodology leads us to the notion that in roughly 70 percent of American schools the predominant method of literature teaching is still teacher-led discussion of text.

The teaching of writing, of course, has been completely revolutionized within the last decade or so. The teaching of writing is all about *process,* and we know that learning happens in the course of that process. The majority of literature teaching, however, seems to be all about a *product*—student answers to text-based questions posed by the teacher.

Take a look at these lists of "study questions":

1. What does Romeo say of himself and his melancholy?

2. What news did her mother communicate just before the feast began? Describe what occurred.

3. Describe the parting of Romeo and Juliet.

4. Give an account of the battles in which Macbeth and Banquo had been engaged prior to the opening of this drama.

5. How does the character of Macbeth differ from Lady Macbeth's?

6. What happens to the Thane of Cawdor?

1. Why is Romeo filled with melancholy?

2. Describe Juliet's response to her mother's announcement that Paris wishes to marry her.

3. As Romeo and Juliet are about to part, how do they differ in their views of the future?

4. What does the Captain tell King Duncan about Macbeth's battlefield deeds?

5. Contrast the characters of Macbeth and Lady Macbeth.

6. What happens to the Thane of Cawdor?

All of the questions in the right column are from an extremely popular American anthology published in 1991. The list on the left is direct from the vaults of the Folger

Shakespeare Library. The questions on *Romeo* are from the Collins School and College Classics published in 1879. The *Macbeth* study questions were published in the London Series of English Texts somewhere close to 1900.

You get my point here. Not only are students still being asked fairly dull text-based questions, but in many cases they are being asked the *same* dull text-based questions that were asked a hundred years ago. Are these kinds of questions getting students to think? Or just to remember?

6. **Shakespeare study can and should be active, intellectual, energizing, and a pleasure for teacher and student.** This is not about *acting*. It's about *doing*. When students get his language in their mouths and take on the work of actors, directors, and scholars, they find themselves engaged in the very best kind of close reading, the most exacting sort of literary analysis. They begin asking questions and positing answers. They know a play from the inside out. This is the learning process. This is also *very* good teaching.

So how do we get students to think about literature? Well, here at the Folger we have good evidence that students who learn Shakespeare through the *process* of performance and through the *process* of a collaborative investigation of the play with their teacher and their classmates have a much greater understanding of Shakespeare's language than students who sit and have things explained to them—like theme, imagery, and what happened to the Thane of Cawdor.

Advancing and celebrating that process, *Shakespeare Set Free* is the sum of these beliefs and forty-five rather amazing people. Since 1984, groups of scholars, actors, directors, and junior and senior high school teachers have gathered during the summers for a month of rigorous Shakespeare exploration roughly divided into three geographies: scholarship, performance, and curriculum. We talk, listen, act, react, argue, question, explicate, perform, write curriculum, and rewrite curriculum. A special institute was convened during the summers of 1988 and 1989 to tackle the problems of teaching Shakespeare's language. From the collective genius of this group comes *Shakespeare Set Free*—conceived, shaped, taught, reshaped, taught some more, refined, then entrusted to a single person to teach yet again, then to re-edit in a single voice. In this volume, the sections on teaching *Henry IV, Part 1* and *Hamlet* represent the comprehensive knowledge of many fine working teachers and the practical journeys of two.

Andrea Alsup and Pat Thisted kept on keeping on, each teaching full-time high school English while taking up the challenge of this labor. They worked with curriculum editor Nancy Goodwin, who taught high school in Clinton, Oklahoma, as she rode herd on the editing process. Mike LoMonico did his editing while teaching Long Island high school students full-time and college students part-time. Yes! These people are living proof that a good teacher can do *anything*.

Shakespeare Set Free is for the life of your mind, both in and out of your classroom. For many summers, Tom Berger, Stephen Booth, Louisa Newlin, Susan Snyder, and Jeanne Roberts have proposed new ways to look at old plays, offering us a revived and enlarged view of Shakespeare's words and of our own minds at the same time.

Their articles here include topics that past institute members have found insightful and sometimes revolutionary—food for your own thoughts. Similarly, actor-in-residence Rosemary Walsh offers a dynamite collection of activities that for a decade have energized institute participants and their students. Actor-director Michael Tolaydo has worked up for Eastcheap and Elsinore two more pieces of "the Tolaydo method," the direct and simple way for students to work with and discover a piece of text.

Contributors to *Shakespeare Set Free* are scholars, actors, teachers. We come from different places headed for the same destination—your classroom. This book reflects true learning, no single way to travel. That's why you'll find in this book a fresh dialogue in which contributors variously support and contradict one another. You'll find scholarship turning up in the curriculum plans, teaching strategies talking back to performance pieces, and language study everywhere.

This book is by teachers, for teachers—for *all* teachers. And although the methodologies in this volume are the work of high school teachers, both plays and methodology are utterly possible in elementary school or a college classroom. We urge you to extrapolate these teaching strategies up and down the learning curve. The strategies for teaching *Henry IV, Part 1*, for example, are aimed at students who have "done" Shakespeare before. Yet I will never forget the day an incredibly "regular" tenth grader reading Shakespeare for the first time pounded up my front stairs to pronounce *Henry IV, Part 1* "the perfect play!" Shakespeare's plays are divinely flexible and can be understood and appreciated on many levels.

Is *Shakespeare Set Free: Teaching* Hamlet *and* Henry IV, Part 1 "right"? Is it the definitive way to teach this stuff? I'm a good teacher and an old teacher, so I'm a little skeptical about definitives. I do know, however, that this is a *good book*.

Use this book. Use it to nurture your own mind. Use it to charge up your teaching. Write all over it like a favorite cookbook. Mark it up with your own better ideas or new thoughts that *Shakespeare Set Free* might spark. Add your genius to this book and then tell me what happens. I hate to miss anything, and I sure hate to miss anything I need to know about good teaching.

PEGGY O'BRIEN
Folger Shakespeare Library
December 1993

Thinking About the Plays

·

JEANNE ADDISON ROBERTS
EDITOR

Fathers and Sons (And What About Mothers and Daughters?)

JEANNE ADDISON ROBERTS

THE AMERICAN UNIVERSITY

The two all-time favorite characters of Shakespeare's plays are Falstaff and Hamlet, and it is exciting to have the opportunity to read together the plays that these two superstars inhabit, *Henry IV, Part 1*, and *Hamlet*. At first glance the characters and the plays may not seem to have much in common. One play was originally called *The Historie of Henrie the Fourth . . . with the humourous conceits of Sir John Falstaff* and the other *The Tragicall Historie of Hamlet, Prince of Denmark*. Falstaff is billed as a secondary character in a history play and distinguished for his "humourous conceits"; Hamlet is the central figure of a tragedy. Falstaff is old ("inclining to threescore," 2.4.438)[1] and fat; Hamlet is young and glamorously athletic (we feel we know this even though the text identifies Hamlet's age as 30, 5.1.152–153 and 5.1.167, and his mother worries about the duel because her son is "fat and scant of breath," 5.2.313).

What is there, then, about the two of them that audiences have always found so intriguing and so memorable? Perhaps the strongest quality they share is an insatiable addiction to language. Both are witty, quick, articulate, fascinated by turning words over to play with meanings; both are fluent in verse and prose. In sheer linguistic volume, both loom large. In addition, both characters occupy positions peripheral to the establishment and can comment on conventional society from wry outsider perspectives that everyone sometimes shares. Both have a flair for the dramatic and like to score in personal power struggles.

Even more important is the complexity and ambiguity of the characters. Both are appealing in their wit, their humanity, and their underdog positions, but each is also revealed as capable of cruelty, deception, childish irresponsibility, and even criminal behavior. No two experiences of the plays ever evoke precisely the same responses to Falstaff and Hamlet, and no critic ever has the last word about either.

Unforgettable as the two characters are, however, they are only parts of the complex appeal of their plays. Probably written within three years of each other (*Henry IV, Part 1*, in 1596–97; *Hamlet* in 1600–1601) when their author was in his early thirties, shortly after the death of his only son, both plays deal with aspects of one of the most

---

[1] Except where otherwise noted, all references to Shakespeare's works are to the New Folger edition (New York: Simon & Schuster, 1992–   ).

important of human relationships—child to parent, youth to authority. In these two plays, of course, the focus is on sons and fathers—Prince Hal and Henry IV in one case, Hamlet and his father and uncle in the other. Both plays introduce secondary father-son relationships, but Hamlet might be thought of as a kind of archetypical "son" and Falstaff as a type of imagined benign "father." Both plays explore the young male's struggle to become "king" (both literally, over a kingdom, and metaphorically, over himself), to achieve an independent but relational identity, and to find justice in an unjust world.

Each play sets a young man in a troubled kingdom ruled by a guilty king who reached his position by violence and maintains it precariously. Each young man must attempt to achieve kingship over himself and his country by negotiating between his absolute ideals and the gray realities of the world. As Henry V, Hal succeeds gloriously, if briefly, as a military leader, while Hamlet's bloody revenge costs him his life. The paths of both winner and loser should be of immediate and engrossing concern to the adolescent male faced with comparable problems.

Prince Hal, understandably resenting the overt hostility of his disappointed father, who actually wishes that Hal were not his son (1.1.85–89), is rebelliously drawn to the unprincipled and hedonistic charms of Falstaff. While his father is teleologically obsessed with the demands and judgments of history, Falstaff is absorbed with the mundane charms of successive days, and especially nights. It is easy to see why Hal is put off by the cold, self-justifying postures of his father. (Try to make sense of Henry's first speech. Does it make you want to hear more?) We can also imagine why the peace established between them is uneasy, even after the superficially "happy" ending of *Henry IV, Part 1*. But Falstaff too gradually reveals himself as an unsatisfactory "father," misusing the money for enlisting soldiers and shamelessly appropriating to himself Hal's victory over Hotspur. Only when Hal adopts the Chief Justice as his intellectual "father" in *Henry IV, Part 2*, does he successfully achieve "kingship." Other minor but illuminating father-son relationships occur between King Henry and his son John, between Northumberland and Hotspur, and between Glendower and Mortimer, adding resonances to this central theme.

Like Hal, Hamlet is haunted by his father—not by his faults but by his imagined perfection. The suggestion of Freud and Ernest Jones that Claudius and the elder Hamlet are two aspects of one father and that young Hamlet identifies with both seems to me a useful insight. Hamlet remembers the elder Hamlet as a mythical giant, the titan Hyperion, loving but not lustful. He discovers in Claudius the lecherous satyr of avid and repulsive sexual engagement. (Children rarely believe, in spite of being the evidence, that their parents could be sexual beings.) Hamlet can neither become the perfect father nor kill the imperfect one, although he repeatedly chides himself for prolonging delay. When he does act, it is to cause the death of Polonius, an essentially harmless old man (and a father) and two relatively innocent bystanders, Rosencrantz and Guildenstern.

Like Hotspur, Fortinbras and Laertes offer complementary examples of sons who delight in action, but their actions are no guarantee of success. We know that after a period of calculated delay, Prince Hal as Henry V invades France with dubious legitimacy and having won a glorious victory, leaves a son who will lose all that his father has gained (Epilogue, *Henry V*). Hotspur and Laertes die, and Fortinbras's success in battle does not seem to qualify him to bring order to the chaos of Denmark.

Father-son reconciliation often requires painful compromise, and the consequences may be far from satisfactory. Reconciliation may be impossible. But however they end, the problems of resolving generational conflict are as relentlessly recurring as generations. Drama does not solve such problems, but it opens them to empathy and exploration. The father-son struggles seem as immediate today as they must have seemed to Elizabethan audiences.

You will have noticed that I earlier used the word "humanity" in regard to Falstaff and Hamlet as if it were a universal term, but how valid is such a concept? Specifically, how does it relate to women and other minority groups in these two plays (women may not be a numerical minority, but like other minorities, they continue to be underrepresented in power structures)? It is hard to think of a Shakespeare play in which women are as peripheral to the action as they are in *Henry IV, Part 1*. Most of the men seem to have neither mothers, wives, nor daughters (Hotspur, Glendower, and Mortimer are technically exceptions). We have brief glimpses of Glendower's daughter, now Mortimer's wife, but she speaks and sings only in Welsh. Mistress Quickly puts in appearances primarily as an ignorant innkeeper who fractures the language and is exploited and mocked by Falstaff. Hotspur has a witty and assertive wife, but her assertiveness does her little good. Her longest speech is a description of her husband (2.3.39–67). Eleven of her sixteen speeches are one-liners, and she appears in only two scenes.

The women in *Hamlet* are peripheral in a different way. Ophelia seems to be a model of the role for women advocated by Elizabethan advice books—that they should be chaste, silent, and obedient. She is obedient at the expense of her own feelings. She has little to say; her best speech is a description of Hamlet in happier days (3.1.163–175). And she is probably chaste (unless possibly she is pregnant by Hamlet, as she is in one of the sources, and her mad songs are certainly suggestive). She is also passive, even in the face of death. Gertrude has more lines, but they do not establish a self. She seems to be rather a figment of her son's fevered imagination than a developed female character. Like Hamlet, we do not know for sure whether she has been adulterous, whether she was an accomplice in murder, whether she goes back to Claudius's bed after her son's injunction to stay away, or even whether she drinks the poisoned cup knowingly and deliberately or merely because she is thirsty. Actors are rarely able to bring the character to life.

So how should women and other minorities read these plays, which seem so centered on the experience of the elite white European male? It is, of course, absurd to stigmatize Shakespeare, an extraordinarily open-minded writer but a man of his time, as a male chauvinist pig or to dismiss him as a dead white European male, but it seems to me important to read and watch his works resistingly, remembering that they are the product of an age very different from our own.

Lyn Mikel Brown and Carol Gilligan, in *Meeting at the Crossroads* (Harvard 1992), have reported on the development of a group of adolescent girls who between 10 and 14 changed from independent, assertive, creative children to repressed, timid, passive, and compliant women. The authors attribute this change to the long-standing and still powerful model of "femininity" that continues to prescribe chastity, silence, and obedience as the crucial qualities for young women. Obviously the sample was small, and there are, increasingly, exceptions to this pattern, but we must be aware of the danger of constricting our daughters and sensitive to ways in which reading Shakespeare might enforce stereotypes. In fact Brown and Gilligan found that Shakespeare might be used to combat stereotypes. They found that learning and speaking the lines of important male characters was empowering to their female students.

If we are to study examples of traditional social models, which show the dire consequences of violating conventional imperatives (and study them we must if we read traditional European literature), we have a responsibility to study them critically and to avoid being seduced into simplemindedly or absentmindedly accepting their patterns as unalterable. Although I focus on women, the same imperatives apply for other minorities.

In other Shakespeare plays, women are sometimes actively involved in politics, war, murder, and social upheavals. Particularly in the comedies, they may even be leaders in love. But in these two plays, audiences are forced to focus on men. If they look critically, they will see a world not wholly unfamiliar in this respect. Power struggles ignore women; machismo breeds dissensions; women are primarily sex objects; and even Hotspur, who has a lively wife, expects her to be silent and obedient—chastity is taken for granted. In *Hamlet*, as we have seen, woman is either a powerless victim or (to Hamlet) a nauseatingly lustful seductress. Where, then, is a modern woman to find connections with these plays?

Fortunately for the survival of Shakespeare, in spite of outmoded gender roles, there seem to be elements in his work that engage audiences so powerfully that it is tempting to entertain the possibility of a few "universals." Some struggle between the young and their parents of the same sex is probably as unavoidable for women as for men. Experiencing the struggle dramatically in the present climate may actually have special meaning for a girl who wants to radically modify traditional expectations. If, like Hal, she does not want to replicate exactly the life of her parent, she may well learn to become a "king" as he does, by experimenting with a series of "parents." Or her inability to reconcile opposing models of adulthood may lead, like Hamlet's, to tragedy. Her reconciliation with her mother may be as uneasy as Hal's with King Henry or as impossible as Hamlet's with his two "fathers."

Women may also deserve some credit for the enduring popularity of Falstaff and Hamlet. Perhaps surprisingly, the "good ole boy" Falstaff may have a special appeal for women. His unapologetic enjoyment of the body, his nurturing rather than judgmental attitude toward Hal, his disregard for honor, and his ability to relish the pleasures of the moment without much regard for the future are all qualities often linked, rightly or wrongly, with women and minorities. As early as 1786, a female actor played Falstaff on the London stage, and other women have since succeeded in the part. Black actors too have adapted easily to the role.

Of course, most of what we know of critical attitudes toward Falstaff comes from white male critics. Attitudes have varied with the temper of the times. Dr. Samuel Johnson, in the late eighteenth century, saw the dangers of a "will to corrupt" combined with "the power to please," but other critics were more tolerant. In the same period, Maurice Morgann argued that Falstaff could not be a coward because he evokes feelings of affection and admiration rather than revulsion in the audience. The romantics found Falstaff heroic *because of* his excesses. A. C. Bradley, early in the twentieth century, denounced the rejection of Falstaff as "horrible." Modern women and other minorities can probably relate to all these responses, drawn to but also fearful of the determined outsider. A recent addition to the critical response has actually been a consideration of the character's androgynous quality, a proposal to entertain the idea of Falstaff as mother. The movie *My Own Private Idaho,* an adaptation of *Henry IV,* shows that homosexuals too may have a personal identification with Falstaff. Somehow he transcends usual limits.

Women have always been drawn to Hamlet, and female actors such as Sarah Bernhardt and Judith Anderson have assumed the role with some success. Women can relate perhaps even better than men to Hamlet's sensitivity, volatility, brilliance, his relatively powerless "outsider" status, his enigmatic fascination, and even his failure. Women and other minorities may have a special sense of the "rottenness" of their own private Denmarks and the difficulty of setting their worlds right.

Not long ago I saw a production of *Hamlet* in which the roles of Hamlet, Laertes, Horatio, and Rosencrantz were played by women as women. Ophelia and Guildenstern were male. To my surprise, all the men transformed to women were perfectly credible and as engaging as ever. The friendship of Hamlet and Horatio was essentially unaltered. Rosencrantz was still an unremarkable cipher. Laertes was a convincing activist returned to avenge her father's death. Scenes between Hamlet and Gertrude still worked well in spite of an altered dynamic that now played two women off as rivals for husband-father. Hamlet was an Electra figure now more powerful than her diminished rival, the reincarnated but enfeebled Clytemnestra. Male or female, Hamlet was the central figure, and Gertrude remained shadowy and unclear. The one character that could not be accepted was the male Ophelia. Some talented male actor might succeed as an Ophelia, but this actor clearly hated the role, and the audience simply could not accept a male in a part so fragile, so passive, and so traditionally "feminine."

If there is a message about universality in these two plays, the hope clearly lies in the male characters. Falstaff and Hamlet and the issues of their plays seem to hold some clues. Dramatic characters are not "people," and drama is not life, though we inevitably imagine for the moment that both things are true. But the enduring popularity of Falstaff and Hamlet suggests that among all Shakespeare's "characters," these two possess a complexity and an immediacy that connect them with a broad spectrum of audiences. They may indeed approach the "universal." And as long as families survive, the issues dramatized in their plays can hardly avoid some relevance, even if only to give us the opportunity to rethink them.

Tampering with Shakespeare's texts in ways that change genders, settings, and situations is very disturbing to some people, but productions and interpretations have always tampered. Indeed, we do not know what the "essential" Shakespeare might be. What we have depends too much on scribes, printers, actors, directors, and audiences. For the modern theater, tampering with the text is one way of testing its universality. For women and minorities, it provides an opportunity to see limitations more clearly and to investigate subtleties, possibilities, and "modern instances" in ways that strictly traditional productions (whatever that might mean) do not. All actors imbue their roles with their own unique presences, and all audiences are limited by their own time and place. Why try to set limits to the search for "humanity"? The miracle is that Shakespeare survives the whirligigs of time as other playwrights do not. And so we keep on trying to find out why.

These two plays provoke us to explore those ills we have and perhaps even to fly to others that we know not of, and to have a very good time in the process. The essays that follow suggest some ways of thinking about these plays, and the performance section and lesson plans offer some ways of promoting understanding and creative interpretation in students.

"Who's There?" Talking to Others and Talking About Yourself in Shakespeare

SUSAN SNYDER

SWARTHMORE COLLEGE

That Shakespeare's language was different from ours is evident when editors provide glosses for words in his text that are no longer current or that have altered in meaning. But the difference has more subtle dimensions that don't show up in footnotes but nevertheless affect meaning in important ways. For one aspect of this difference we may look at how characters talk about themselves and how they address someone else. Modern usage in this respect is fairly straightforward: "I" is the way to refer to oneself; "you" is the way to address another person. Shakespeare's language had more options, however, so that in his dialogue these apparently simple conventions become complicated. Given a choice between forms, the one chosen has significance, often accentuating or qualifying our sense of personal situations and relationships.

First, talking to another person. The "you" so universally applied today was at an earlier stage of the development of English a plural form used in talking to more than one person; for singular address, the form was "thou." Simple enough. But by Shakespeare's time, "you" was already beginning to take over. It was not only the standard plural but also the accepted way of talking to a single person if that person was not in an intimate relationship and was felt by the speaker to be his social equal or superior. "Thou" was still the norm in certain situations—a rather disparate set of them.

The key to some of them is intimacy. "Thou" and its other forms, "thy" and "thee," were appropriate between lovers, between husband and wife. On the other hand, one also used "thou" when formally petitioning God or a god. Such prayers may or may not be accompanied with feelings of intimacy, but "thou" is probably felt to be right here principally because it is unusual, a departure from standard human-to-human speech. (Invoking the deity as "thou," the only vestige of older usage that has survived into modern English, seems likely to disappear like the others; modernizations of ritual favor "you.")

Presumably it's because of this connection with the supernatural that Shakespearean ghosts are addressed as "thou." Macbeth always called Banquo "you" when he was alive, but when Banquo's bloody ghost comes to his banquet, he uses "thou":

9

"Never shake / Thy gory locks at me" (Macbeth 3.4.61–62). There is no question of intimacy between the terrified Macbeth and the ghost of the man he had murdered; rather, his "thou" marks this Banquo, walking after death, as a supernatural visitation. When the Weird Sisters later show him a vision of Banquo's descendants who will rule in Scotland, Macbeth again calls the individual apparitional kings "thou." In *Hamlet*, the ghost at issue is, or was, also a king. When he was alive, both his son Hamlet and his subject Horatio would have addressed him with the respectful "you," but when he returns from the grave, he is "thou" to both of them.

If Hamlet's "thou" to his father marks his ghostly status, Old Hamlet's "thou" to his son is quite usual. A parent talking to a child normally used "thou," and that was also the mode for talking to a servant. While intimacy is sometimes implicit in either situation, the main operative factor here is the lower social status of the person being addressed. Child or servant did not answer in kind but used the more formal "you." Again, it's the transgressions that have impact. Using "thou" to someone who would normally be called "you," for example, can be a calculated insult, imputing that person's inferiority and the speaker's contempt. In *The Merchant of Venice*, Antonio has to ask for a loan from a man he despises. He calls Shylock "you" when he's asking but slips into "thou" when he's reminded of his habitual disgust at Shylock's usury.

> I am as like to call thee so again,
> To spet on thee again, to spurn thee, too.
> If thou wilt lend this money, lend it not
> As to thy friends, for when did friendship take
> A breed for barren metal of his friend?
> But lend it rather to thine enemy.
>
> (1.3.140–145)

Antonio's speech specifically *denies* friendship as a condition of the loan. His "thee"s and "thou"s are hostile, a verbal attack equivalent to his spitting on Shylock; they signify not intimacy but its opposite.

"Thou" might express love or contempt, awed distance or intimate closeness. As for "you," in some situations it was standard good manners; in others, a signal of distance and displeasure; in still others, a sign of new status. Shifts between "thou" and "you" often enact the ins and outs of a relationship, as in the first scene between Oberon and Titania in *A Midsummer Night's Dream* (2.1). They begin with the habitual "thou," though already angry with each other, but when the Indian boy comes up, the object of their quarrel, they start calling each other "you." Brutus and Portia, in their scene before the assassination (*Julius Caesar*, 2.1), go the other way. Portia protests at the distance he has recently created between them, his failure to confide in her, and even while Brutus denies her accusation, he inadvertently affirms the distance she complains of by calling her "you." In fact, he hasn't told her of his fears about Caesar's rise or about the conspiracy. When she compels him back to their old way of sharing secrets, he changes to the intimate "thou."

A live king, as opposed to a dead one like Hamlet's father returned in ghostly form, was always addressed as "you," being everyone's social superior. For a subject to call him "thou" was totally out of order, a gesture either presumptuous ("The king is my buddy") or seditious ("Down with the king, who is no better than I am!"). Falstaff's mistaken trust that Prince Hal will go on being his jolly drinking companion when he is Henry V is underlined when he uses the presumptuous "thou" in calling to the newly crowned Henry: "God save thy Grace, King Hal! my royal Hal!" (*Henry IV, Part 2*, 5.5.41).[2] "Thy Grace" sounds very peculiar because the ritual salute and regal titles clash with the familiar intimacy of "thy." This is, as will soon be made clear to a crestfallen Falstaff, no way to speak to a king. The comradeship is over.

Even Hamlet, himself a prince, is bound by the convention in addressing the king. Though he hates his uncle Claudius and frequently attacks him verbally, he usually accords this king the customary "you." That makes his sudden change all the more dramatic in the final duel scene. When Claudius's secret crime is finally exposed, Hamlet is free not only to punish him publicly but to degrade him dramatically with the demeaning "thou."

> Here, thou incestuous, murd'rous, damnèd Dane,
> Drink off this potion. Is thy union there?
> (*Hamlet*, 5.2.356–357)

This is a version of the seditious "thou," the subject rebelling against the monarch. The illicit ruler, Claudius, has been calling the shots since before the opening of the play, and now at last Hamlet moves into that dominant position, forcing his uncle to drink the same poison that killed his father, and to choke on the "union" that once made Gertrude's son so sick with disgust. Informing Hamlet's assertion of authority over the exposed king is something of the same moral contempt that Antonio conveyed in his "thou" to Shylock. If the usurer and extorter is unworthy of normal address, how much more the regicide.

Calling a king "thou" gains other kinds of resonance in *King Lear*, where the monarch goes from total autocratic power to a powerless state of exile and madness. In the first stage, when Lear in heedless rage banishes his only deserving daughter, Cordelia, his friend and courtier Kent is frantic to stop the injustice. His protest bursts out in direct, homely language as he tries to break through the layers of formal manners and court flattery to make Lear listen.

> Be Kent unmannerly
> When Lear is mad. What wouldst thou do, old man?
> Think'st thou that duty shall have dread to speak
> When power to flattery bows?
> (*King Lear*, 1.1.162–165)

Kent knows this is no way to talk to a king, but his is not the contemptuous "thou" of Hamlet to Claudius. Rather, he hopes to shock by his rude speech, called forth by the extremity of Lear's blindness: "To plainness honor's bound," he justifies himself

---

[2] *The Riverside Shakespeare*, ed. G. Blakemore Evans (Boston: Houghton Mifflin, 1974).

in the same speech, "When majesty falls to folly" (165–167). Later in the play, when Lear is mad and destitute, another former courtier devoted to Lear calls him "thou," but this time in pity rather than anger. When the blinded Gloucester, now a match for Lear in pathos, meets his king again, he greets him with great emotion:

> O ruined piece of nature! This great world
> Shall so wear out to naught. Dost thou know me?
>
> (4.6.149–150)

Even while Gloucester likens Lear's fall to the end of the world, he speaks in the intimacy of compassion—not only pity but compassion in its original sense of "feeling *with*," for he too has suffered.

If people had to decide how to talk to kings, kings had to decide how to talk about themselves. The monarch in current political theory was not only "I" but "we"; not only the "body natural," subject to weakness and finally death, but the "body politic," joined with his land in a kind of mystic ongoing corporate existence ("The King is dead, long live the King!"). Queen Katherine, in *Henry VIII*, gets them both into one sentence: "Sir, / I am about to weep; but thinking that / We are a queen . . . my drops of tears / I'll turn to sparks of fire" (2.4.69–73).[3] "We" for her public identity as coruler; "I" for the private, suffering self.

Shakespeare's monarchs don't often combine "I" and "we" in the same breath; rather, they use one or the other according to the situation. King Henry, in the council that begins *Henry IV, Part 1*, speaks in the royal "we" when considering public affairs—plans for a crusade, troubles with the Welsh and the Scots. When the talk turns to Hotspur, however, Henry shifts to "I." He now speaks less as king than father as he measures the achievements of that young warrior against the perceived worthlessness of his son. Even when the king turns back to public events, he continues to use "I" in talking of Hotspur (though not when disposing of other issues like the Jerusalem expedition), perhaps still betraying a personal investment in this paragon of valor who he wishes were the son of his blood.

Later in the play (3.2), in a strained encounter with the unsatisfactory Hal, Henry's alternations between "I" and "we" map the course of their confrontation. Estranged from his son while he faces the threat of rebellion against his rule, Henry is caught between angry incomprehension of Hal's conduct and a desperate need to have his heir at his side. While struggling with personal ties and his own guilt and fear (is God punishing his usurpation of the throne by making the Prince of Wales a wastrel?), Henry speaks with the personal "I." He shifts to the royal "we" when he turns to the rebellion that threatens "our throne," but then immediately back to "I" as he bitterly suspects that Hal, his "nearest and dearest enemy," is so alienated that he will enlist with the rebels to fight against his father rather than support him. Henry's language operates to make the political uprising seem a personal rejection, conflates the waywardness of his son with the waywardness of his subjects (led by the very Hotspur

---

[3] *The Riverside Shakespeare*, ed. G. Blakemore Evans (Boston: Houghton Mifflin, 1974).

whom he had wished to have as his son). It is only when Hal ringingly declares his adherence as son and champion that Henry can, at the end of the scene, resume his royal "we" and his confidence as leader.

Claudius, the murderer-king in *Hamlet*, greatly favors "we," countering with outward assertions of royal authority his inward knowledge of how false that authority is. As Hamlet comes to that knowledge his psychological attacks on his uncle tend to destabilize Claudius's royal pronouns. After the play within the play has exposed his fear and made his nephew seem even more dangerous, a jittery Claudius, talking to Rosencrantz and Guildenstern about his dangerous Hamlet, jumbles the person and the ruler:

> I like him not, nor stands it safe with us
> To let his madness range. Therefore prepare you.
> I your commission will forthwith dispatch,
> And he to England shall along with you.
> The terms of our estate may not endure
> Hazard so near 's as doth hourly grow
> Out of his brows.
>
> (3.3.1–7)

As Claudius's royal "we" repeatedly slips into "I," we can see how private panic keeps contaminating what he wants to present as reasons of state.

In some ways, Claudius is an early study for Macbeth—another murderer-king subject to fears and attacks of conscience whose pronouns can give him away. In Macbeth's first appearance as king (3.1), he leans heavily on the royal "we" in talking to Banquo and the other lords. In a more private conversation that follows soon after with two subjects he will suborn to kill Banquo, he speaks as "I." He makes a few attempts at the royal stance, but for the most part Macbeth, unlike Claudius with Rosencrantz and Guildenstern, doesn't try to present eliminating Banquo as necessary for the public good. He does indeed work to provoke in them a hatred of Banquo to match his own, but his end is apparently to distance and dilute his own personal guilt ("I"), not to present the murder as a public service ("we").

In Macbeth's next public scene (3.4), he outdoes Claudius in pronoun breakdown. He opens the banquet with the royal plural—"ourself will mingle with society" (3.4.4)—but this secure corporate identity proves impossible to keep up as one of the murderers comes in reporting the dispatch of Banquo but generating new fears about Fleance. And before long, even the assurance that Banquo is out of the way is shaken. Macbeth repossesses the royal pronoun only to wish hypocritically for the presence of "our Banquo," and then goes to pieces when his wish is answered. Crazed with personal guilt and fear, he speaks as "I" not only to Banquo's ghost and to his wife but to the thanes in general, when he can remember they're present. With the disappearance of the ghost, Macbeth can say, "I am a man again" (3.4.131). He has more difficulty speaking like a king again.

After this point, only midway through the play, the royal "we" drops out entirely from his speech, although he remains king of Scotland until his death in the last scene.

For Macbeth as for Claudius, that royal "we" is something gained by stealing, an alien style that can't be worn in comfort because it doesn't fit, like the kingship it expresses. In the words of Angus, one of his Scottish subjects now in revolt against him,

> Now does he feel his title
> Hang loose about him, like a giant's robe
> Upon a dwarfish thief.
>
> (5.2.23–25)

Whether and when the king uses "we" or "I," then, can tell us about his degree of legitimacy and security, his skill at public relations, his emotional condition, the state of his conscience. The plays I have talked about, like most of Shakespeare's histories and tragedies, take monarchy as a system for granted. The issue is often "Who is the rightful king?" but not "Should we have a king?"

In *Julius Caesar*, though, that is exactly the question as Caesar grows too big and powerful for the republican structure. He turns down the crown offered to him in a public ceremony, but apparently there will be another offer in the Senate on the Ides of March. Certainly he sounds like someone practicing to be king—hearing petitions, posturing, asserting his sovereign will, and even breaking out in a royal "we": "What touches us ourself shall last be served" (*Julius Caesar*, 3.1.8). While this happens only once, another habit of language much more widespread asserts in a similar way the speaker's preeminence among men and elevation above personal frailty. Dismissing the bad omens on the day he will be killed, he says, "Caesar should be a beast without a heart / If he should stay at home today for fear" (2.2.45–46). "Know," he later loftily instructs a petitioner, "Caesar doth not wrong, nor without cause / Will he be satisfied" (3.1.52–53). He refers to himself in the third person rather than the first, and uses not a pronoun but his name. There are many other instances, but the ones I quoted bring out particularly his use of the name where we would expect "I" when he is identifying with Roman ideals of honor, steadfastness, and contempt for danger. This way of presenting himself as a public entity parallels the royal "we" in that it discards the single "I" for a corporate identity that involves the clan and the state. Not "Gaius" or "Julius," but "Caesar"—his family name, his Roman name.

There is more to this reifying of the name than Caesar's posturing. Others do it: Cassius, Titinius when he's committing suicide (significantly, a very Roman act), even Portia—she too in a context of asserting her stoic Roman virtues. Brutus does it most of all, as often as Caesar. Family name in his case has a more specific weight than for Caesar because he especially reveres his republican ancestor Junius Brutus. When Cassius and the other conspirators invoke that ancestor and the republican cause, Brutus responds less as "I" than as the self-consciously Roman "Brutus." "O Rome, I make thee promise, / If the redress will follow, thou receivest / Thy full petition at the hand of Brutus" (2.1.59–61); "Brutus had rather be a villager / Than to repute himself a son of Rome / Under these hard conditions . . ." (1.2.182–183).

It is this public persona that can assent to killing Caesar, as opposed to the individual self whom Caesar has loved and favored: "I know no personal cause to spurn at him, / But for the general" (2.1.11–12)—that is, the public good. Antony harps on this violation of the personal tie in his funeral oration, and part of the satire is his constant repetition of the name Brutus, which is overused as much as "honorable man." But this reifying of the name unexpectedly likens Brutus to his adversary and supposed opposite, and suggests that the popular, modest-seeming statesman is as arrogant in his way as the protodictator and presents himself as similarly exempt from human frailty and fallibility. In talking about themselves as public institutions of courage and rectitude, Brutus and Caesar are disturbingly alike.

Easily ignored in reading or even performing the plays, characters' ways of talking about themeselves and talking to others can tell us a great deal. To get at these meanings, we have to consciously probe and evaluate for meaning what Shakespeare's audiences registered automatically, subliminally. But the questioning can be fruitful.

Couples in Shakespeare; or, Two's Company, Three's a Crowd

Thomas L. Berger
St. Lawrence University

According to one of the editors of this volume, I once delivered a lecture on "Couples in Shakespeare" to a group of secondary-school teachers at the Folger Shakespeare Library. I do not remember having done so. My memory has failed me. Again. I find this particularly dismaying because according to the aforementioned editor, the lecture was "not bad." No fool, I take "not bad" to mean "all right," and it is an easy flight in the heat-seeking missile of my self-esteem to go from "all right" to "damn good."

Puzzling over this on my way home from a Shakespeare Association of America convention in Kansas City, Missouri (coupled, indeed twinned, with Kansas City, Kansas), I moved into the suppositional. Let's suppose I did give such a lecture. Whatever would I say in such a lecture? Would what I have to say, and would what I said be of any value to someone trying to tease a meaning or two out of a couple of Shakespearean texts?

My flight landed at the Dallas–Fort Worth airport, where I was to change planes for the brief hop to Austin, Texas. Insofar as one has to walk roughly halfway to Austin at the Dallas–Fort Worth airport to get on a plane to travel the remaining halfway, I had time to ponder this whole business of coupling as I strolled from gate 4 to gate 46. Ahead of me at one point was a most attractive couple, a man and a woman in this case, and for a moment I took some interest in them. Who were they? Were they married? Where were they headed? Why didn't they take their children along? Were they returning to their children? If so, they had precious few presents for those children, thank you very much. Why was she wearing heels that made her significantly taller than her husband? I wondered if he was wearing a tie. He'd better be if he's married to a woman like that.

I had to abandon my musings when the woman strode on ahead of the man, as, alas, it turned out that for a moment or two, they just happened to be walking next to one another at roughly the same pace. So much for them as a couple.

When I got to gate 46, I checked to see if indeed American Airlines had recorded my status as a "frequent flyer" (the best reason, as far as I can tell, to go to conventions) and then sat down in the smoking section of the waiting area. The elder of the two men sitting opposite me was puffing on a pipe, the younger on a cigarette. Why would a right-thinking father encourage his son to smoke? And the son, why would he . . .

Am I the only person who constantly engages in such activities? Must I constantly create relationships where none exist? And why do I never do it with threesomes and only occasionally, almost exclusively with middle-aged women at upwardly mobile restaurants, do it with foursomes? Still in the suppositional, let's suppose that my fancy is not unshared, and let's suppose that Shakespeare knew that among his audience were people very much like me. Using the plays under consideration as examples, permit me to create couples in *Henry IV, Part 1* and *Hamlet* and to read those couples in ways not unlike the ones I used on the unsuspecting souls in the Dallas–Fort Worth airport.

Upon entering a theater in late-sixteenth-century London, a playgoer, my playgoer, would see first an empty stage. Then he or she would see that stage peopled perhaps by a single actor, perhaps by a pair of actors (a couple), perhaps by three actors, perhaps by four or more actors. This playgoer, if he or she were anything like me, would respond to many things: the costumes, the music, the poetry, the action itself. This playgoer would also respond in some way to the number of actors-characters he or she saw on the stage.

Hamlet's "now I am alone" would strike a respondent note in this playgoer, trained to recognize and expect a certain range of dramatic activity from a solitary figure on the stage. Hamlet is perhaps Western literature's most solitary figure, alone on stage for six soliloquies (1.2, 2.2, 3.1, 3.2, 3.3, and 4.1). But then, he is not alone in 3.1, with Ophelia left on stage and Claudius and Polonius spying from behind an arras. Nor is he alone in 3.3, as the would-be penitent Claudius fails in attempts to have his thoughts reach heaven. Simply by virtue of their speaking alone on stage, Ophelia (3.1) and Claudius (3.3, 4.3) will link themselves in my playgoer's mind with Hamlet. All three are isolated, with Hamlet stuck between the guilt of Claudius and the innocence of Ophelia.

Prince Hal pulls no punches in his first soliloquy (1.2), outlining for my playgoer what he is doing (upholding "The unyoked humor of your idleness") and what he intends to do ("imitate the sun"). Later, in 5.3, Hal thinks (as does my playgoer) he is alone when he addresses the dead Hotspur and moralizes the scene. He thinks (as does my playgoer) he is alone when he discovers and addresses the "dead" Falstaff and moralizes over the supposedly lifeless colossus of sack. But Falstaff is very much alive, as my playgoer discovers when "Falstaff riseth up" to deliver the last of his five soliloquies. The first of these, a disquisition on the state of military recruitment, occurs in 4.2; the second, Falstaff's catechism on honor, occurs in 5.1; the third, delivered over the dead body of Sir Walter Blunt, combines the comments on honor with reports of the deaths of Falstaff's recruits; it occurs in 5.3, as does the fourth, a short reprise to the third. It is hardly surprising that Hotspur should have the only other soliloquy in the play (2.3), though one might expect King Henry IV, a man increasingly isolated, to speak alone. Perhaps his never being alone stresses his isolation.

But this is not an essay about soliloquies. When my playgoer saw two people on stage, he or she would invest those characters with another set of responses different from but analogous to the set he or she invested in the solitary figure. There are certainly many more scenes with couples than scenes with solitary figures, since two people conversing can deliver a good deal more narrative and dramatic information than one person speaking alone. Their conversations have about them an intimacy that is certainly lacking when other characters are on stage to hear them and to (mis)interpret their words. And while it is easy for a solitary figure to lie to himself, it is every bit as interesting dramatically to watch two people manipulate the truth in dialogue with one another.

Turning first to *Henry IV, Part 1*, there are by my count twenty-three segments of dramatic action where two people are alone as couples on the stage. We have been trained, perhaps rightly, to see the dialectics of *Henry IV, Part 1* as the pulling of various forces on Prince Hal in preparation for his inheriting the kingship from his father and becoming Henry V. We have been trained to see Hal in opposition to his father, to Falstaff, to Hotspur, taking from each what he needs to become the "perfect mirror of Christian kings" and rejecting what he thinks he does not need, what he thinks will be to his detriment. Such a scenic structure Shakespeare inherited from the morality plays and the moral interludes of his dramatic heritage. These twenty-three segments, these couplings, reveal that there's a lot more going on than we might glean from a cursory analysis. This always seems to be the case in Shakespearean texts.

Looking at the twenty-three couples, we see what we expect to see. And what we expect to see is done supremely well. But we see a lot more:

1. 1.2.1–111: Hal and Falstaff
2. 1.2.167–201: Hal and Poins
3. 2.1.52–103: Chamberlain and Gadshill
4. 2.2.97–101: Hal and Poins
5. 2.3.37–67: Hotspur and Lady Percy
6. 2.3.78–124: Hotspur and Lady Percy
7. 2.4.1–34: Hal and Poins
8. 3.2.5–166: Hal and King
9. 3.3.1–54: Falstaff and Bardolph
10. 3.3.211–216: Hal and Falstaff
11. 4.2.1–49: Falstaff and Bardolph
12. 4.4.1–41: Archbishop of York and Sir Michael
13. 5.1.122–127: Hal and Falstaff
14. 5.2.1–28: Worcester and Sir Richard Vernon
15. 5.3.42–59: Hal and Falstaff
16. 5.4.25–38: King and Douglas
17. 5.4.44–58: Hal and King
18. 5.4.59–75: Hal and Hotspur
19. 5.4.78–88: Hal and Hotspur, Falstaff "dead"
20. 5.4.89–103: Hal and dead Hotspur, Falstaff "dead"

21. 5.4.104–112: Hal and "dead" Falstaff, Hotspur dead
22. 5.4.113–131: Falstaff and dead Hotspur
23. 5.4.166–169: Falstaff and dead Hotspur

The scenes we like to think we remember best from *Henry IV, Part 1* are those involving Hal and Falstaff, and indeed the first 111 lines of 1.2 are taken up with those two as a couple—Hal berating Falstaff, Falstaff defending himself. After that scene, though, we see Hal and Falstaff as a couple only briefly in three scenes, once in 3.3 and twice in 5.1. The first of these, 3.3.211–216, may well be private, but it is largely informational:

> Jack, meet me tomorrow in the Temple hall
> At two o'clock in the afternoon;
> There shalt thou know thy charge, and there receive
> Money and order for their furniture.
> The land is burning. Percy stands on high,
> And either we or they must lower lie.

The second, 5.1.122–127, prepares us for Falstaff's catechismical soliloquy on honor (5.1.128–142). The final coupling between the two takes place later in Act 5, when Hal enters to demand a sword of Falstaff. Denied that, the Prince looks for a pistol and finds a bottle of sack. The first coupling opened 1.2 with Hal's "What a devil hast thou to do with the time of the day?" The last echoes the first: "What, is it a time to jest and dally now?" The coupling has come full circle. Hal has imitated the sun, reforming himself but hardly reforming his fat companion.

Hal and his father, Henry IV, couple only twice. Nearly the entirety of 3.2 is taken up with Henry berating himself and his son and Hal promising his father the reformation he had promised my playgoer at the end of 1.2. This reformation is held back from us in the next scene, however, when Hal reports to Falstaff: "I am good friends with my father and may do anything." That Hal is as good as his word to his father is demonstrated in their second coupling, on the battlefield at Shrewsbury in 5.4. After Hal enters to the King and Douglas and makes the Scot flee, the King tells Hal, "Thou hast redeemed thy lost opinion." Oddly, Hal responds by saying that if he had wanted the King dead, he could have let Douglas finish his father off and saved himself the trouble. Warmly, the King responds, "Make up to Clifton, I'll to Sir Nicholas Gawsey."

Immediately following this, as effect to cause, is the coupling of Hal and Hotspur, something for which my playgoer has been waiting a long time. Like high school heroes (or Greek and Trojan warriors), they taunt one another for seventeen lines. Before one can kill the other, Falstaff breaks up their coupling, entering to cheer on the Prince. It is only after Douglas enters and "kills" Falstaff, a deed the Prince will reenact at the end of *Henry IV, Part 2* that Hal can slay Hotspur. Hotspur's dying speech and Hal's response couple them again and contrast sharply and positively with their earlier boasts.

We respond to these final words in one way when we hear them, and the accompanying stage picture is emblematic—Hal standing between the dead Hotspur and the "dead" Falstaff, the emblem of moderation between the excess (and thus corruption) of honor and the excess of, well, excesses. But Shakespeare subverts our response (and the Hal-Hotspur coupling) when Falstaff rises. Falstaff and the world he represents are by no means dead; Falstaff lives as a comment on the dead Hotspur. His stabbing of Percy and his plans to claim that he killed him make Percy into food for worms indeed. Falstaff's coupling with Percy can occur only when one or the other is dead. Both living cannot occupy the same stage space.

So much for the couplings in *Henry IV, Part 1* that "matter." They matter even more when set against the other couplings in the play, couplings that in turn create meanings and worlds that contribute in their own way to the world of the play. In 2.3 my playgoer gets to see Hotspur and Lady Percy, the only married couple in the play, and excepting Falstaff and Mistress Quickly, the only functional heterosexuals. For all its sprightly wordplay, the couplings of Hotspur and his Kate reveal a marriage in which the husband pays little attention to the wife. Is Hotspur even listening as Kate describes to him his ills, his dreams, his lack of appetite? It is easy to say that rebellion has ruined this marriage. I suppose that is because it is true. In 3.1 Kate refuses to sing, refuses to acknowledge harmony, refuses to obey her husband.

If Hotspur's relation with his wife is over after 2.3, then Hal's with his companion Poins is over after 2.4. Poins exists very much as a plot device to assist Hal in exposing Falstaff and confounding Francis. Why is he dropped from the play after 2.4? Dramatically, he is no longer needed now that Hal has been called to his father and to princely responsibility. The rejection of Falstaff we can understand; the rejection of Poins is something else indeed. Does Shakespeare mirror in some comparative way the coupling of Hal and Poins with the coupling of Falstaff and Bardolph in 3.1 and again in 4.2, and does this mirroring explain implicitly the Prince's rejection of Poins?

Couplings alone do not a play make. But surely the number and variety of couplings in *Henry IV, Part 1* contribute to and make visually apparent the many dichotomies of the play. They clearly establish and hierarchize, simply in the order of their presentation and in their acts of visual exclusion, the play's various relationships.

Hamlet, a play perplexing, it seems, in every way a play can be perplexing, is no less perplexing when it comes to its various couplings. I count twenty-nine couplings in the play, moments in which only two characters are on stage:

1. 1.1.1–14: Bernardo and Francisco
2. 1.3.1–56: Laertes and Ophelia
3. 1.3.95–145: Polonius and Ophelia
4. 1.4.97–102: Horatio and Marcellus
5. 1.5.1–119: Hamlet and Ghost
6. 2.1.1–83: Polonius and Reynaldo
7. 2.1.84–134: Polonius and Ophelia
8. 2.2.187–237: Hamlet and Polonius
9. 3.1.64–162: Hamlet and Ophelia (King and Polonius behind arras)

10. 3.1.176–192: King and Polonius (Ophelia in "background")
11. 3.2.55–97: Hamlet and Horatio
12. 3.2.297–321: Hamlet and Horatio
13. 3.3.29–39: King and Polonius
14. 3.3.77–101: Hamlet and King (King at attempted prayer)
15. 3.4.1–10: Gertrude and Polonius
16. 3.4.11–27: Hamlet and Gertrude (Polonius behind arras)
17. 3.4.31–117: Hamlet and Gertrude
18. 3.4.118–156: Hamlet and Gertrude and Ghost (Ghost invisible to Gertrude)
19. 3.4.157–240: Hamlet and Gertrude
20. 4.1.5–33: King and Queen
21. 4.1.39–46: King and Queen
22. 4.5.80–103: King and Queen
23. 4.7.1–37: King and Laertes
24. 4.7.49–186: King and Laertes
25. 5.1.1–56: Two Gravediggers
26. 5.1.57–62: Two Gravediggers (Hamlet and Horatio observe)
27. 5.1.67–119: Hamlet and Horatio (Gravedigger digs)
28. 5.2.1–90: Hamlet and Horatio
29. 5.2.196–208: Hamlet and Horatio

But there are problems in such an approach. How, mundanely, is one to count Rosencrantz and Guildenstern? If we can conceive of them as one character, divided into Tweedledum and Tweedledee, then the number of coupling scenes increases significantly. But Rosencrantz and Guildenstern are sufficiently differentiated to be regarded as two similiar but individual characters. They are a walking and talking couple wherever they go. The two gravediggers form another couple, however briefly. They talk while Horatio and Hamlet observe them, and so strictly speaking, they are not alone on stage. Similarly, while Horatio and Hamlet discuss mortality after the departure of the second gravedigger, the first gravedigger remains on stage digging, leaving Horatio and Hamlet not strictly coupled. The King and Polonius hide behind an arras in 3.1 while Hamlet speaks his "To be or not to be" soliloquy, which is not really a soliloquy because Ophelia is on stage. Polonius is behind the arras again in 3.4, a place he doesn't want to be for the life of him. Most bizarre, Hamlet is coupled with his mother, Gertrude, and she with him, for the better part of 3.4. When the Ghost enters and Hamlet sees it, Hamlet and the Ghost and Gertrude form a threesome. Gertrude, however, cannot see the Ghost and thus remains coupled with her (fully lunatic, so she thinks) son.

"Who's there?" "Nay, answer me." And so begins the first coupling of the play, the exchange between Barnardo and Francisco. In this opening exchange, each character desires information that he can then use to obtain control over someone or something. This desire for control characterizes much of the coupling in the play. Unlike *Henry IV, Part 1*, where the impulses in one character to control another (Lady Percy and

Hotspur are examples) are present and functional, in *Hamlet* these impulses seem to have gone out of kilter as the characters seem continually to be duking it out for control over one another.

In their coupling scenes with Ophelia, both Laertes and Polonius attempt to control her, to prevent her sexual coupling with Hamlet. The motif certainly obtains in 2.1. The first half of the scene shows Polonius giving instructions to Reynaldo to spy on (and thus control) Laertes; while in the second half, Polonius hears Ophelia's report of Hamlet's melancholy and plans to use it to his advantage. When Polonius "boards" Hamlet in 2.2., he is attempting to obtain information, as Hamlet well knows and as his wordplay well demonstrates. Ophelia is made to couple dramatically with Hamlet in 3.1., with the King and Polonius in hiding, in order to obtain information that might be used against Hamlet. The two are never alone on stage. And a couple, the King and Polonius, evaluate it at the conclusion of the scene, coupled so that they virtually ignore the maligned Ophelia, who will go mad, who will die, who will never couple dramatically or sexually with Hamlet. As Gertrude strews flowers on her grave, she says to the dead Ophelia, "I hoped thou shouldst have been my Hamlet's wife; / I thought thy bride-bed to have decked, sweet maid, / And not have strewed thy grave."

Near the beginning of 3.3, Polonius couples with the King, who agrees to Polonius's plan to spy on Hamlet and Gertrude's conversation, just as Gertrude and Polonius couple at the beginning of 3.4 before Hamlet arrives at his mother's closet. Gertrude and Ophelia are linked in this scene, Hamlet talking with his mother, with Polonius behind the arras, just as Ophelia had talked with Hamlet, with Polonius and the King behind the arras. All want information from Hamlet, information he is loath to give. In his coupling with the King in 4.7, Laertes replaces his father. Instead of seeking information, the couple plot Hamlet's death.

It is the Ghost who seeks Hamlet and whom Hamlet seeks. Hamlet seeks the information the Ghost seeks to give. Both seek control. The Ghost revisits Hamlet when he is in Gertrude's closet to whet Hamlet's "almost blunted purpose." The Ghost's reassertion of his control over Hamlet strengthens Hamlet in his resolve to wrest Claudius's control of Gertrude away from him. The effects of the various couplings in 3.4 are seen, as so often in Shakespeare, at once, in this case in the very next scene, 4.1. Here Claudius, coupled with Gertrude, is about to decide what he must do with Hamlet now that Polonius is dead. The trip to England will be a mortal one for his nephew-son.

For all Hamlet's isolation, for all his aloneness, for all his soliloquies, Hamlet still has Horatio. In a world where everyone seems to be pumping everyone else for information, where every action is studied, read, and evaluated, how lucky Hamlet is (how lucky everyone else is not) to have in Horatio someone who is simply a friend, someone he can trust. They couple before the "Mousetrap" when Hamlet gives Horatio instructions to observe Claudius, and again afterward when Horatio assures Hamlet that he is correct in his assessment of the Ghost's words and Claudius's guilt.

Hamlet has Horatio in attendance throughout most of the fifth act. Though we hear it reported, we first see Hamlet in that act returned to Denmark in the company of Horatio. They talk not of stratagems and spoils but of the gravediggers. Hamlet couples with Horatio again in the next scene, first when he relates to Horatio, and to us, exactly what happened to him when he left Denmark for England, and then again after Osric has arranged the fencing match with Laertes, about which Horatio has serious misgivings. Hamlet assures him, "There is a special providence in the fall of a sparrow. If it be now, 'tis not to come; if it be not to come, it will be now; if it be not now, yet it will come. The readiness is all" (5.2.233–237). Hamlet dies in this same scene, having avenged his father and his mother. He dies in Horatio's arms, coupled.

By indirection find direction out. Each in its own way, all the Folger Shakespeare Library Teaching Shakespeare Institute sessions came to focus on Shakespeare's language, to focus on the words. And after all is said and done, it is from Shakespeare's language that I derive my greatest pleasures. Shakespeare's language is at once direct and complex. Sometimes it's easy; more often than not, it's hard. When it's at its easiest, it's at its hardest. Many high school students are put off by Shakespeare's language, and this is understandable. They often have no point of entrance into the language. They are thrown into the deep end and are expected to swim. Some can swim supremely well. Most cannot.

Let me invite my readers to throw their students into the shallow end of their explorations of Shakespeare—of his plays, of his stage, of his language, of his themes. Ask your students to look at the text and to determine which of the characters are alone on stage and which appear as couples. I said "look at the text." I did not say "read the text." Ask them then to look at the text and to determine how many of those characters who are alone on stage or who are alone as couples really are alone. Is there someone dead on stage with them? Is there someone just offstage, say, behind an arras, who is listening to every word?

Note, please, that you have not asked your students to "read" a single word. By now, though, in order to figure out the assignment, they will have had to read plenty. This determined, ask them to see if there is one solitary figure who is on stage alone more often than others and if his appearances have anything in common. Has the situation changed or remained static? Does he or she use the same or similar words? Which words of similar meanings does he tend to repeat? Which couple keep appearing in the course of a play? How does their relationship grow and change? What do they say to each other at the beginning that they no longer say at the end?

Your students may not be able to swim, but you've got them in the pool, paddling about, unafraid. By indirection find direction out.

Nice Guys Finish Dead: Teaching
Henry IV, Part 1 in High School

LOUISA FOULKE NEWLIN
FOLGER SHAKESPEARE LIBRARY

Shakespeare's English history plays are not, as Rosalind says of Phoebe in *As You Like It*, for all markets. It is hard to keep the characters straight. Too many are called by several names, and they tend to inherit, or grab, new titles: the "Bolingbroke" (a.k.a. "Harry Hereford") of *Richard II* is "King" in *Henry IV, Part 1* and isn't even the hero of his own play. Sometimes key people alluded to are dead before the play even starts—Gloucester in *Richard II*, Richard II in *Henry IV, Part 1*, for example. During a first reading, you need to keep looking at a genealogical table, and it helps to have handy a map showing England, Scotland, Wales, Ireland, and France.

Having issued that caveat, I will also say that most of my best students, and many of my worst, have enjoyed the histories tremendously. That they are about events that "really happened" appeals to those students with little taste for the fantasy worlds of *A Midsummer Night's Dream* or *Twelfth Night*. The histories are full of *action*, a quality beloved of high school students. Once they understand the issues, they realize that the political power struggles of the fourteenth and fifteenth centuries resemble, sometimes strikingly, the ones they read about in newspapers. While it is clear that Shakespeare was aware of the high price of war, there are displays of courage and heroism in the histories that even committed pacifists can find inspiring. In short, the English histories offer a lot that is relevant to young people's concerns.

In particular, *Henry IV, Part 1* is an absolutely wonderful play to teach to tenth, eleventh, and twelfth graders. The language of the principal characters, especially that of Falstaff and Hotspur, is rich, energetic, and immediate. Most of the time you don't even need to look at speech prefixes to know who is talking. Among the many subjects the play is "about" are ones that interest me as well as my students: politics and politicking, adolescence and coming of age, family relationships, courage and cowardice, loyalty and betrayal, the pursuit of duty and the pursuit of a good time.

Nothing energizes a class like a good argument, and my students argue a lot about whether Falstaff is fundamentally likable or fundamentally repellent and whether Prince Hal is a cool guy or a cold fish. (Is he a temporarily misguided young man who grows up to be an ideal Renaissance warrior-king leading troops to glorious victory at Agincourt or an ambitious and self-serving person who matures into an effective but dislikable war-seeking ruler?) Students watching their fellows perform the roles of Hal and Falstaff for the class can begin to measure the extent to which an audience's impression of character is shaped by an actor's performance, a variant I want them to keep in mind.

Finally, I like teaching *Henry IV, Part 1* because it is a "comedy" as well as a "history." In high school, Shakespeare's most frequently taught plays are tragedies. Students should have a crack at the comedies too and see that sometimes, even in required reading, foolish human behavior is forgiven and catastrophe avoided. The play is also a "comedy" in the sense our students understand the term best: it is often actually funny.

High school students particularly like *Henry IV, Part 1* because it offers them two young men, Hal and Hotspur, who have considerable trouble with authority figures; because Hal gets to spend a lot of time hanging out with an amusingly disreputable friend, a "villainous abominable misleader of youth" (2.4.479–480), and still turns out to be a hero in the end; and because Hotspur, the kid held up as an example by Dad, loses out. Interestingly, although my students often prefer Hotspur to Hal, they *identify* more with the latter, and what they like most about *Henry IV, Part 1* is that for them, it is in part about the process of growing up.

Perhaps even more than *Hamlet, Henry IV, Part 1* poses a riddle that is key for adolescents: What does "growing up" really consist of? Hal is always implicitly asking himself questions my students are trying to answer for themselves: What sort of person do I want to be? Do I want to fill the role my father and/or mother has decided I should fill? Can I be myself, separate from my parents, and yet have my parents' approval? Do I need their approval?

These questions cut right across lines of gender, race, geography, and academic standing. They allow girls as well as boys to identify with Hal—a necessary thing, since the paucity of good women's roles is undeniable. Kate is intelligent, charming, and prescient—but ignored. The earthy Mistress Quickly makes her presence felt but doesn't really "count" the way the men do, and Lady Mortimer doesn't speak, except in Welsh. That the women have no direct effect on what the men do, no matter how harebrained or destructive it is, is a subject worth discussing. It's worth noting that the male-dominated world of the play is one whose power center Prince Hal himself seems to have doubts about entering.

The hazards of the histories mentioned in the first paragraph notwithstanding, it isn't really necessary to spend much time introducing the play. Although students do need to know enough of the historical context of the action to render the play intelligible, a little fourteenth-century English history goes a long way. It is all too easy to get mired in the treacherous quicksand of background and important to get into the foreground—that is, into the play itself—as soon as possible. (Some kids, of course, really *enjoy* learning the details of the "real" history and will delight in filling in the genealogy charts on Handouts 6 and 7 in the *Henry IV, Part 1* curriculum section.)

The trick, of course, is to get students to care about the play, and they are more likely to care if they have a chance to "act it out," as they put it. Once students have had a chance to be Hal, Hotspur, or Falstaff for fifteen minutes, they have made a real investment in the proceedings. Ideally, they should hear aloud every word in the play, spoken by each other, preferably in action, as the unit plan in this volume proposes. If it is impossible to make room in the school year for twenty-four lessons on *Henry IV, Part 1*, however, one can settle for having students perform only five or six scenes. Those sections not performed can be read, or even summarized, and discussed.

The trouble is that to select certain scenes for performance, and therefore to empha-size them, is an interpretive and limiting act. While I feel obligated as a teacher to point out a path through the text's thicket, I dislike cutting off access to other routes that might lead to different destinations. Nevertheless, a teacher, like an actor, must make choices, and mine are described below.

I have said that for adolescents, *Henry IV, Part 1* is a play about growing up. Bruno Bettelheim, in *The Uses of Enchantment,* defines the maturing process as "coming to a secure understanding of what the meaning of one's life ought to be," and I usually focus on scenes that subtly or directly dramatize Hal's progress toward such an under-standing, which involves, among other things, accepting his father without imitat-ing him.

There is no one "right" place to begin; however, starting with line 1 of this play could be the kiss of death since the rhetoric and allusiveness of the king's long opening speech and his ensuing conversation with Westmoreland exemplify a lot of what some high school students find baffling and off-turning about Shakespeare. A better point of departure, since the parent-child conflict is apt to engage the class from the start, might be the king's speech (1.1.77–94) in which he compares his Harry to Hotspur ("sweet fortune's minion and her pride"), envies Hotspur's father, and wishes the two had been exchanged in their cradles.

> Yea, there thou mak'st me sad, and mak'st me sin
> In envy that my Lord Northumberland
> Should be the father to so blest a son,
> A son who is the theme of Honor's tongue . . .
> Whilst I, by looking on the praise of him,
> See riot and dishonor stain the brow
> Of my young Harry.
>
> (1.1.77–85)

The sentiments the king expresses are ones with which most teenagers are all too familiar.

Or one could instead begin with 1.2, with two students acting the parts of Hal and Falstaff. Even with minimal understanding of the context, it is perfectly clear to the class why Hal is down there at the Boar's Head. Falstaff is nothing if not fun to be with, and the king is no fun at all. The king takes the long historical view, often very gloomily, and Falstaff takes the moment as it comes, exuberantly. Hal needs to arrive at his own definitions of honor and courage, and the tavern is a safer place to do this than the court. A doting father-figure is more comfortable than a real father who puts pressure on you. However, how to take Hal's "I know you all" soliloquy at the end of this scene, in which he reveals his game plan, may be less clear to students than his reasons for avoiding his father.

> So when this loose behavior I throw off
> And pay the debt I never promisèd . . .
> My reformation, glitt'ring o'er my fault,
> Shall show more goodly and attract more eyes
> Than that which hath no foil to set it off.
>
> (1.2.215–222)

Is Hal just rationalizing his goofing off? If he has already made up his mind to reform in time, has he been manipulating his tavern friends for his own purposes? Is the speech unpleasantly calculating, or is the idea it expresses admirably practical?

The ambiguities of this speech notwithstanding, doing 1.2 first often makes 1.1 easier for students to deal with, although most eventually come to recognize Shakespeare's good judgment in ordering the scenes as he did. Working backward, they see plainly the parallels between Hal's filial rebellion and Hotspur's political one and between Hal's true father's theft of his cousin Richard II's crown and his "false father" Falstaff's vocation.

The next scene I ask the class to perform is 2.2, the Gad's Hill robbery, in which the theft motif is developed in a different key. Falstaff has been robbing the king of his son's company; here he robs Henry IV in another way by stealing the pilgrims' money destined for the royal exchequer. The spectacle of Falstaff being easily robbed in turn by Hal and Poins in disguise is highly comical, but although Hal is amusing himself, he is also making a serious test of his fat friend's honor and courage and finding them wanting.

In 2.4, after Falstaff has magnified the episode into an epic encounter in which he stoutly defended himself (as Poins predicted he would), Hal exposes Sir John as a liar and a coward. During the famous "play extempore" later in the scene, it is as if Hal, seeing Falstaff impersonate the king, is struck hard by the contrast for the first time: "Dost thou speak like a king?" he asks. It's hard to think of any actor making that line sound anything but unkind. After he and Falstaff exchange roles and Hal has his turn to play king, he makes it cruelly clear that in time he will, in Falstaff's words, "banish plump Jack." At the very end of the scene, Hal tells Peto he will go to court in the morning and that the stolen money "will be paid back again with advantage." He is starting to repay the "debt he never promised."

Someone like the president of the school's honor council will surely remark at this point that it's obvious that once Hal is chief of state, he will have to get rid of Falstaff. This is probably true. But students should examine closely Hal's behavior in this scene. Do they like what he's doing here? Does he really need to prepare so publicly for the inevitable rejection of his old friend? Shakespeare hardly ever makes things too easy for an audience. He doesn't allow us to have the warm and fuzzy feelings about the prodigal prince that we would like to have. This disconcerts many students—a good thing, in my opinion.

It is usually not Hal but Hotspur who really stirs adolescents, who makes them feel as they like to feel about heroes. Yet students can recognize how Hotspur is a foil for Hal and why he rather than Hal will end up dead. Hotspur is tremendously appealing, a figure of wild chivalry, passionate imagination, immense honor and integrity. What he lacks is political judgment. This is brilliantly demonstrated in an eminently actable part of 3.1, lines 1–150, where Hotspur, Glendower, and Mortimer plan the way they will carve up the kingdom. Hotspur becomes increasingly irritated by Glendower's posturing and baits him mercilessly, pushing him to the point where his uncle and brother-in-law take him aside and give him avuncular advice about the wisdom of not alienating your allies.

Hotspur's teasing of Glendower lacks the sly and nasty edge that Hal's remarks to Falstaff often have. But Hotspur does not know when to hold his tongue, and Hal does. Hal hangs fire where Hotspur would explode. Hotspur would not do well on the campaign circuit; Hal would.

This becomes apparent in the scene in which Hal acknowledges the error of his ways (3.2). While the king is berating him, Hal listens patiently as the king goes on scolding him for nearly a hundred lines, allowing himself only one meek two-line interruption: "I shall hereafter, my thrice gracious lord / Be more myself" (3.2.94–95). The dramatic imbalance between father and son makes the scene difficult to enact, and students, whose antipathy to this sort of parental lecture is strong, often find nearly everything the king says excruciatingly boring. But I like to have them perform and discuss this dialogue, usually with some of the king's lines cut, because it shows Hal to be in control of himself and politically astute. Besides, it is a key turning point in the play; by its end, Hal is reconciled with his father and accepts the responsibility of going to war with him. As he later tells Falstaff, "I am good friends with my father and may do anything" (3.3.192–193).

Before meeting the ingenious suggestions provided elsewhere in this volume for staging the Battle of Shrewsbury in a high school classroom, I restricted myself to two manageable and important segments from it, a practical if slightly faint-hearted approach. The first is Falstaff's famous soliloquy on honor (5.1.128–142). "What is honor? A word. What is in that word 'honor'? What is that 'honor'? Air. A trim reckoning. Who hath it? He that died o' Wednesday." After discussing it, by way of contrast, students can go back to 1.3 and hear what Hotspur has to say on the subject:

> By Heaven, methinks it were an easy leap
> To pluck bright honor from the pale-faced moon,
> Or dive into the bottom of the deep,
> Where fathom line could never touch the ground,
> And pluck up drownèd honor by the locks,
> So he that doth redeem her thence might wear
> Without corrival all her dignities . . .
>
> (1.3.206–212)

It is between these two extreme conceptions of honor that Hal is finding his own position.

The second "scene" is the part of 5.4 where Hal and Hotspur share the stage for the first time, meeting each other on the battlefield while Falstaff lies nearby, playing possum. Hotspur's dying speech reinforces the notion that Hotspur should have been the hero.

> O Harry, thou hast robbed me of my youth.
> I better brook the loss of brittle life
> Than those proud titles thou hast won of me.
> They wound my thoughts worse than thy sword my flesh.
> But thoughts, the slaves of life, and life, time's fool,
> And time, that takes survey of all the world,
> Must have a stop.
>
> (5.4.78–85)

Harry Percy, at least for us romantics, outshines Hal, as Mercutio outshines Romeo. But once again Shakespeare doesn't let us get away with putting the two Harrys into tidy categories. Hal too has the sheen of chivalry upon him in his generous tribute to the dead Hotspur:

> Fare thee well, great heart.
> Ill-weaved ambition, how much art thou shrunk!
> When that this body did contain a spirit,
> A kingdom for it was too small a bound,
> But now two paces of the vilest earth
> Is room enough. This earth that bears thee dead
> Bears not alive so stout a gentleman.
>
> (5.4.89–95)

Hal's detractors will say it is easy for winners to be generous. Maybe so, but not all of them are. Hal deserves credit for being a survivor who has found a middle ground that allows him autonomy and scope. His own sense of honor is keen but modified by pragmatism. On the battlefield, he is both brave and skillful. Hotspur is always spoiling for a fight; Hal does not go to war until he needs to. (Falstaff, true to form, goes only under duress.) Hotspur feels most at ease in a military context; Falstaff is at home in the Boar's Head; Hal can move easily between different milieux. Hal is able to waste time enjoying life, as Hotspur cannot, but unlike Falstaff, Hal knows when it is time to get serious.

And it is time to get serious at Shrewsbury, where all the worlds of the play meet and show their true colors. The king shows himself as courageous, reliable, and honorable, in contrast to Northumberland, who lets *his* son down at the crucial moment. Falstaff proves as cowardly and unreliable as ever. Yet although Hal moves closer to his father's pole of "rule" and rescues him from death at the hands of the Douglas, he is not yet ready to go cold turkey and part with "misrule," with the fun, wit, and freedom from time and history that Falstaff embodies. When Falstaff puts forth his absurd claim to having killed Hotspur, Hal rescues him from disgrace by not denying it: "For my part, if a lie may do thee grace, / I'll gild it with the happiest terms I have" (5.4.161–162).

The play is done, but the story of Hal's growing up is not. Whenever time allows, I ask students to read and stage the last scene (5.5) of *Henry IV, Part 2*. (This helps to content those who have been haunted by the fear that they are reading only half a play.) It is a scene so difficult for audiences to watch that many eighteenth- and nineteenth-century productions shuffled scenes around or cut lines in order to make it easier to bear.

As the coronation procession passes by, Falstaff, all eagerness, calls out to the new king, "God save thy Grace, King Hal, my royal Hal! . . . God save thee, my sweet boy!" (5.5.41–43).[4] Henry V does not at first even speak directly to his old friend:

> KING   My Lord Chief Justice, speak to that vain man.
> CHIEF JUSTICE, (*to Falstaff*)   Have you your wits? know you
>   what 'tis you speak?
> FALSTAFF   My King, my Jove! I speak to thee, my heart!
>
> (5.5.44–46)

No stage directions tell us that Falstaff is behaving in an unseemly way or that he merits the chilling rebuke that follows:

> KING   I know thee not, old man, fall to thy prayers.
>   How ill white hairs become a fool and jester!
>   I have long dreamt of such a kind of man,
>   So surfeit-swell'd, so old, and so profane;
>   But being awak'd, I do despise my dream.
>
> (5.5.47–51)

As if this were not enough, the king goes on in these cold cadences for another twenty-four lines. As one of my students remarked of the king when we watched this scene on the BBC video, "He's talking just like his daddy." Mistress Quickly will say of Falstaff in *Henry V*, "The King has kill'd his heart" (2.1.88).

As many others have noted, it is one thing to accept the rejection of Falstaff intellectually, to acknowledge that it is essential if Henry V is to be a respected sovereign, and even perhaps to agree that the new king must make the break so complete and so public that he will be invulnerable to temptation and to rumor, but it is quite another to accept this rejection emotionally when we see it performed. Students may feel that Shakespeare should have left well enough alone at the end of *Henry IV, Part 1*.

At the start of *Henry IV, Part 1*, Hal seemed, like Holden Caulfield, reluctant to become an adult, for some pretty good reasons. By the end of *Henry IV, Part 2*, he has become if not actually a "phony," someone Holden would probably have trouble liking. The questions I leave my students with are something like these: How do you feel about King Henry V's rejection of Falstaff? Is he simply being mature and responsible? Is this the way "good leaders" must behave? Must Hal, in order to banish fat Jack and his lawlessness, banish good humor, compassion, and warmth—"all the

---

[4]*The Riverside Shakespeare*, ed. G. Blakemore Evans (Boston: Houghton Mifflin, 1974).

world"—as well? Is the price of "growing up" really rejecting Falstaff and all that he represents?

The way my students answer those questions depends partly on how they look at the world. To help them see it more clearly, I like to show them the superb 1989 film of *Henry V,* directed by and starring Kenneth Branagh. This gets them arguing all over again.

The Coherences of *Henry IV, Part 1* and *Hamlet*

Stephen Booth
University of California at Berkeley

Literature is different from all the other arts in that literature alone has for its raw material elements that appear to have been created only as means of transporting information from one mind to others: words.

Common sense says, therefore, that the value of literature must derive from what it tells us.

Common sense is wrong. After all, as the physicist Percy Bridgman observed half a century ago, common sense is something that tells us the world is flat.

In the case of the value we place on literature, not only is common sense wrong, but we all know it to be so. Remember that I am talking here about what we do value literature for, not what we should value it for or what we might be more comfortable believing ourselves to value it for. Remember too that aside from the fashionable (I suspect only temporarily fashionable) puzzle literature of the twentieth century (literature designed to be deciphered), what we study and teach is popular literature of the past: Shakespeare, Mark Twain, Marlowe, Jane Austen, Steinbeck, Milton, Dickens, Swift, Bernard Shaw, and so on. Saying that we value those people's fictions for what they tell us is comparable in its blind complacency to saying that customers for comparable twentieth-century fictions come to them for what they show or tell us about human nature; or about human society; or about the history of philosophy; or about contemporary mores; or about their creators' psyches—comparable, for example, to saying that we value Alfred Hitchcock's movies as the revelations of Hitchcock's private neuroses that they undoubtedly are or that we value the works of Steven Spielberg as recent chapters in the history of the romantic infatuation with sentimentally misconceived childhood or that we value *Murphy Brown* for its politics, sexual or otherwise. Saying that we value this or that Shakespeare play for what it shows or or tells us is like implying, as so many ad campaigns once did, that we value ice cream because it is chock-full of vitamins, minerals, and protein.

What we value in literature is obviously the pleasure it gives us. And that pleasure is in the experience—in minutes or hours spent reading or in observing the two hours' traffic of a stage.

There can be, I grant, an easily exaggerated pleasure in discovering in the reports of artists and their characters confirmation of one's own responses to human situations and the common phenomena of life. Joy in liberation from imagined uniqueness is particularly valued by young people, but I find it hard to believe that for anyone of any age, such discovery is ever more than secondary, is ever more than a nice little intellectually comforting lagniappe to an experience sought out for its own sake.

For as long as there has been a culture in the West, Western culture has felt a need to justify literature. The dignified function for an activity that by all standards at all comparable to the ones we apply to other things we value, is frivolous—a need to find a function for literature that has the practical weight of the other things that matter to us, things like food, shelter, love, gods, children, and law. People say lots of things to justify literature. We go through high school and sometimes life parroting them and hearing them parroted, but none of them explains why we go to the movies or why some Shakespeare plays (*Hamlet* and *Henry IV, Part 1* for instance) still make money in the theater and others (*Timon of Athens* and *King John*, for instance) do not.

Why do we value literature? And why do we value one work more or less than another? Why do we rate the Shakespeare plays we value so much higher than most other literature, and why do we value some of the most valued plays—*Hamlet*, for instance—more highly than other much-admired plays—for instance, *Henry IV, Part 1*?

It should be evident from the foregoing paragraphs that I want this essay to do something it is unlikely to be capable of doing: I want it to revolutionize the study of literature in classrooms and everywhere else.

Literary study rests on several seldom-examined assumptions. Ideally, I would like you all to examine and reject them, but I will be satisfied if you will see that they are only assumptions—albeit ones you may well choose to retain in place. The assumptions are these: (1) the assumption that any academic observation on a work or one of its elements must be auxiliary to an interpretation, an assertion that the work or element means something it has not previously been seen to mean; (2) the assumption that, if an observation does not lead to an interpretation, it is not worth making; (3) the assumption that analysis can and should change its readers' experience of the work analyzed, make it work better, or at least otherwise, than it has previously worked; and (4) the assumption that what the criticism reveals about the work should henceforth be active in our conscious experience of the work in question. (One more assumption could be added to this list, the assumption among students and some naive professional critics that any element in a work that cannot be seen to result from purposeful authorial intent can be dismissed as if it did not exist. That assumption, however, is so easily dismissed that I left it off the list. Anyone who finds it convenient to ignore literary effects that cannot be believed to be purposeful need only be reminded that although the Grand Canyon of the Colorado and its display of patterned color cannot, except perhaps among fanatically religious people, be reasonably thought to have resulted from authorial purpose, the Grand Canyon does exist and is beautiful.)

I will spend the rest of this essay talking about substantively incidental patterns in *Henry IV, Part 1* and *Hamlet*, patterns in elements that are at once different from one another and similar, simultaneously different and similar, as the sounds of a word are to those of words it rhymes with. They are patterns that do not usually call any attention to themselves and do not ordinarily become part of the conscious experience of sane audience members (except perhaps members who have been very recently and thoroughly primed by an ingenious critic).

My purpose is to suggest that such patterns are of the essence of their plays—in fact, that they give a play its essence, its being, its identity as one thing rather than an amalgam of elements more intensely themselves than they are parts of a whole. The patterns, superimposed on one another, overlay a play and net it together so it feels like a coherent whole, a thing rather than a collection.

I want now to point out some patterns in *Henry IV, Part 1* and some in *Hamlet*. I will start, not quite arbitrarily, with some of the patterns and kinds of patterns in which the second scene of *Henry IV, Part 1* participates.

Act 1, scene 2 recommends itself as a site for demonstration. It is particularly rich in the number and variety of different kinds of overlapping systems of coherence. Moreover, choosing it is less than arbitrary because, as in several later scenes (most notably 2.4, where Falstaff casually contradicts his original lies with new ones as he multiplies the numbers of his adversaries at Gad's Hill), coherence and incoherence are topics of overt concern to the characters in the scene.

The topic appears at its largest in Falstaff's inconsistency when he follows up his mock-solemn vow to reform ("I must give over this life, and I will give it over") by replying to Prince Hal's "Where shall we take a purse tomorrow?" with "Zounds, where thou wilt, lad. I'll make one" (1.2.101–106). The topic of coherence and incoherence figures earlier in the scene when Falstaff initiates the following exchange in response to some burlesque philosophizing by Hal on crime and punishment:

> FALSTAFF   By the Lord, thou sayst true, lad. And is not my hostess of the tavern a most sweet wench?
> PRINCE HAL   As the honey of Hybla, my old lad of the castle. And is not a buff jerkin a most sweet robe of durance?
> FALSTAFF   How now, how now, mad wag? What, in thy quips and thy quiddities? What a plague have I to do with a buff jerkin?
> PRINCE HAL   Why, what a pox have I to do with my hostess of the tavern?
>
> (1.2.42–51)

On a much smaller scale, Hal and Falstaff play athletically on the concept of coherence in the following passage where what is incoherent in the usual and obvious system for determining coherence is coherent in some other one:

> FALSTAFF   'Sblood, I am as melancholy as a gib cat or a lugged bear.
> PRINCE HAL   Or an old lion, or a lover's lute.
> FALSTAFF   Yea, or the drone of a Lincolnshire bagpipe.
>
> (1.2.78–81)

The key word here is "lion." The "lugged bear" is a fit enough companion to the "gib cat"; both are animals liable to melancholy, albeit very different kinds (tomcats are proverbial for their loud exhibitions of love melancholy, and a captive bear, dragged by the ears to the stake, would be more simply misattuned to its situation). A lion, however, is like and unlike a gib cat (both are felines; a lion is big and dangerous; a domestic cat is not). On the other hand, lions and bears are of different families, but both are big and dangerous. And in another dimension, the sounds of "old lion" introduce a phonic coherence by which "lover's lute" and the "drone of a Lincolnshire bagpipe" fasten to the substantively foreign topics they follow—topics that remain foreign, even though the popular notion that stringed instruments are strung with the gut of cats draws the lute toward the orbit of the gib cat and even though there is a likeness between the wail of lovesick tomcat and the noise of a bagpipe.

I will be talking throughout this essay about systems of relationship as perfectly irrelevant to understanding what is happening in *Henry IV, Part 1* and *Hamlet* as the overlapping systems of relationship that connect the disconnected elements in the exchange about melancholy. The idea of attending to nonsubstantive patterns may seem foreign to you. It is not. We are all familiar with the idea of rhythm (and with the comparable idea of rhyme, an idea I have already likened to the physics of the patterning that concerns me here). What we describe when we talk about rhythm in verse or prose is a recurring constant that gives an extra coherence to inherently disparate elements strung together in sentences. What I will be talking about from here on are rhythms of repeated topics, labels for topics, situations, and relation-ships—rhythms that like the ones that counter the topical sprawl in the passage over-lain by the various relationships among "gib cat," "lugged bear," "old lion," "lover's lute," and "Lincolnshire bagpipe," say no more than the purely phonic rhythms we are used to recognizing and recognizing as vehicles of form, not substance.

I will start with a rich situational likeness between 1.2 of *Henry IV, Part 1* and 1.3. I start there because the likeness can be pleasing to a mind that perceives it and can tempt that mind to follies of benign fabrication. The second half of 1.3 is a structural echo of the scene that precedes it, a scene with which it ostentatiously contrasts. At line 166 of 1.2, its central figure, Falstaff, leaves the stage. Thereupon the remaining characters, Hal and Poins, plot against him. Falstaff's supposed accomplices in a theft will turn on him and steal what he has stolen. At line 126 of 1.3, its central figure, the king, leaves the stage. Thereupon the scene's other principals, the Percys, King Henry's accomplices in usurping the crown of Richard II, plot to steal it from their former confederate.

If one were to point out that unostentatious parallel to students, they would be likely to try to "make something" of it by saying, for instance, that the rhymelike relation between the scenes causes us to make comparisons between their participants (a comparison the previously unobserved parallel has obviously not caused us to make). The assertion of such logically plausible untruths is, however, the way of the classroom and the way of the literary world in general, a world where "to analyze" and "to interpret" are routinely treated as if they were synonyms. It is high time that all parties acknowledged some self-evident facts—for instance, the fact that the parallel pointed out here between the second and third scenes of *Henry IV, Part 1* has not, as far as I know, pushed itself into the consciousness of theater audiences or of readers, a fact that testifies that the parallel does not generate the observations a critic can plausibly say it does.

How was it for your mind when you read my exposition of the neat echo one set of thieves provides for the other? Did my description of the parallel tell you something that had always figured in your perception of the play? And if so, have you assumed the parallel, so obvious to you, to be equally obvious to the mass of other people, so obvious that you would see no point in showing it to students? (Remember that what one bothers to reveal to others is, by definition, something one takes to be, or likely to be, unknown to them.) No one who answered no to either of my last two questions has any business pretending that consciousness of the parallel is or should be part of our experience of *Henry IV, Part 1* much less pretending that the parallel provokes us to thought or informs us of something.

As I said before, I do suggest that although they do not inform us, such phenomena as the parallel between 1.2 and 1.3 of *Henry IV, Part 1* do inform *the play*, do give form to it, help hold its separable parts together and make their union "realer" than it would otherwise be. The parallel, I suggest, gives the scenes an extra dimension of relationship, a humble dimension comparable to the dimension rhyme gives to "sat" and "hat."

With that reminder, I will now go back to describing and discussing patterns of simultaneous likeness and difference in *Henry IV, Part 1* and *Hamlet*.

What is true of scenes that "rhyme" as 1.2 and 1.3 do (and as the three departure scenes that comprise Act 3 do) is also true of characters. The most obvious parallel between contrasting characters is the one between Prince Hal and the other "young Harry," Hotspur, a pairing of simultaneously like and unlike figures that Shakespeare went to great lengths to achieve (as the introduction of some texts will delight to tell you, the historical Hotspur [born 1364] was not only not the same age as Hal [born 1387] but older than Hal's father [born 1367]). Less obvious but probably more efficient in their contributions to the play's feel of organic oneness are the casual likenesses among Falstaff, Worcester, and Glendower (the very differently accomplished liars who act as surrogate fathers: Falstaff to Hal, Worcester to Hotspur, and Glendower to Mortimer) and the even more casual likeness between Falstaff and Hotspur, the two most obviously different characters in the play.

Falstaff and Hotspur are both mocked for uncontrolled volubility. Worcester comments on his inability to interrupt Hotspur. He has striven vainly to stem the stream of Hotspur's invective against the king and responds sarcastically to Hotspur's "Good uncle, tell your tale. I have done": "Nay, if you have not, to it again. / We will stay your leisure" (1.3.265–267). And Prince Hal is similarly mock-courteous in 2.4 when Falstaff winds himself calling Hal names:

FALSTAFF 'Sblood, you starveling, you elfskin, you dried neat's tongue, you bull's pizzle, you stockfish! O, for breath to utter what is like thee! You tailor's yard, you sheath, you bowcase, you vile standing tuck—
PRINCE HAL Well, breathe awhile, and then to it again. . . .

(2.4.254–259)

There is incidental likeness too between Hotspur and Falstaff in their shared tendency to become overheated—Falstaff literally ("Falstaff sweats to death, / And lards the lean earth as he walks along," 2.2.114–115), Hotspur figuratively when he falls into rages. (Note, however, that Hotspur too is said to sweat. In the next scene after the one that ends with the lines about the sweating Falstaff in retreat, Shakespeare introduces a gratuitous reference to sweat. He has Hotspur's wife Kate describe her husband asleep, restlessly dreaming of battle and so "bestirred," she tells him, "that beads of sweat have stood upon thy brow.")

Actually, when one comes to think about it (as I again remind you one does not in the normal course of events), it is hard to find a character in *Henry IV, Part 1* who is not like or likened to the others. For an extreme example, remember that Hal makes plans for a play extempore in which Falstaff will play Kate Percy.

Having twice mentioned Kate, this is probably as good a point as any to call attention to a particularly complex example of repetitions that are also not repetitions. Consider the following four-piece sequence: (1) In 2.3.37–124, we hear a domestic conversation between Hotspur and Kate, a conversation from which Hotspur suddenly swerves to inquire about horses and one roan in particular (2.3.69–77) and back to which Kate calls him in a speech that she begins by calling him a "paraquito" (2.3.90). (2) In the next scene, Prince Hal comments to Poins about their just concluded practical joke on Francis the drawer and drifts from there into imagining a scene both like and unlike the one we just saw, a scene he says he and Falstaff will act out (the italics for "parrot" and "roan" are mine):

> That ever this fellow should have fewer words than a *parrot*, and yet the son of a woman! His industry is upstairs and downstairs, his eloquence the parcel of a reckoning. I am not yet of Percy's mind, the Hotspur of the north, he that kills me some six or seven dozen of Scots at a breakfast, washes his hands, and says to his wife "Fie upon this quiet life! I want work." "O my sweet Harry," says she, "how many hast thou killed today?" "Give my *roan* horse a drench," says he, and answers "Some fourteen," an hour after. "A trifle, a trifle." I prithee, call in Falstaff. I'll play Percy, and that damned brawn shall play Dame Mortimer his wife.
>
> (2.4.101–114)

(3) Hal and Falstaff do indeed improvise a play (2.4.387–499); it is not the promised exchange between Hotspur and Kate but the scene between Hal and the king that Falstaff predicts for the next day, the scene, he tells Hal, in which "thou wilt be horribly chid" (2.4.384). (4) Finally—completing a pattern that runs "real" event, imagined burlesque of that event, staged burlesque of a real event of the future, real event—in 3.2 we watch and hear the actual interview Hal and Falstaff had anticipated in their tavern playlet of the previous evening.

The play also goes in for incidental linear links between sharply distinguished scenes and sharply distinguished parts of scenes, links whereby an element at the beginning of a new action repeats an element from the conclusion of its predecessor. Consider 1.2 again. The last speech of that scene, Hal's solemn blank-verse soliloquy, contrasts ostentatiously with the scene of prose banter it concludes:

I know you all, and will a while uphold
The unyoked humor of your idleness.
Yet herein will I imitate the sun,
Who doth permit the base contagious clouds
To smother up his beauty from the world,
That, when he please again to be himself,
Being wanted, he may be more wondered at
By breaking through the foul and ugly mists
Of vapors that did seem to strangle him.
If all the year were playing holidays,
To sport would be as tedious as to work,
But when they seldom come, they wished-for come,
And nothing pleaseth but rare accidents.
So when this loose behavior I throw off
And pay the debt I never promisèd,
By how much better than my word I am,
By so much shall I falsify men's hopes;
And, like bright metal on a sullen ground,
My reformation, glitt'ring o'er my fault,
Shall show more goodly and attract more eyes
Than that which hath no foil to set it off.
I'll so offend to make offense a skill,
Redeeming time when men think least I will.
He exits.
(1.2.202–224)

On the other hand, Hal's solemn promise to imitate the sun comes at the end of a scene in which his first speech imagines "the blessed sun himself" as "a fair hot wench in flame-colored taffeta" (1.2.10–11) and Falstaff has insisted on Hal's identity as king's son. (Note, by the way, the link, between this scene and the one it follows, that "the blessed sun" makes as an echo of the king's lament that Northumberland should be the father of "so blest a son" as Hotspur, 1.1.79.) And Hal's serious promise to throw off his loose behavior echoes Falstaff's joking concern earlier in the scene for his own reputation and his soul ("I must give over this life, and I will give it over," 1.2.101–102).

Moreover, "I know you all" and Hal's characterization of his wastrel self as a mere disguise make yet another connection to the dialogue with which they so obviously contrast. They come less than a minute after Hal has worried that Poins's Gad's Hill plot will miscarry because Falstaff and their other colleagues in thievery will recognize them—and even less than that after Poins has both described their disguises for Gad's Hill and told Hal what he knows those colleagues to be:

PRINCE HAL Yea, but 'tis like that they will know us by our horses, by our habits, and by every other appointment to be ourselves.
POINS Tut, our horses they shall not see; I'll tie them in the wood. Our vizards we will change after we leave them. And, sirrah, I have cases of buckram for the nonce, to immask our noted outward garments.
PRINCE HAL Yea, but I doubt they will be too hard for us.
POINS Well, for two of them, I know them to be as true-bred cowards as ever turned back; and for the third, if he fight longer than he sees reason, I'll forswear arms.
(1.2.180–192)

As Hal's soliloquy contrasts with the rest of 1.2, so 1.3 (the court scene that follows) is insistently different from its private, informal predecessor. The king, who contrasts in different ways with Hal and Falstaff, has the first speech of 1.3, a public speech to his court at large and thus urgently dissimilar to the soliloquy it follows. But what does the king say? He says his recent behavior has been deceptive and vows henceforth to show himself for what he really is, in effect that he has been in disguise:

> My blood hath been too cold and temperate,
> Unapt to stir at these indignities,
> And you have found me, for accordingly
> You tread upon my patience. But be sure
> I will from henceforth rather be myself,
> Mighty and to be feared, than my condition. . . .
>
> (1.3.1–6)

For another example of linear linkage between a new scene and the one just ended, consider 3.2 and 3.3. The king concludes the earlier scene by urging haste on his troops; "advantage," he says, "feeds" the enemy "fat while men delay" (3.2.185). The stage thereupon clears, and what the king said metaphorically about an abstraction is echoed physically before us. The grotesquely obese Falstaff enters and begins 3.3 with a lament for a supposed loss of flesh:

> Bardolph, am I not fallen away vilely since this last action? Do I not bate? Do I not dwindle? Why, my skin hangs about me like an old lady's loose gown. I am withered like an old applejohn.
>
> (3.3.1–4)

To conclude this selective survey of incidental unifiers in *Henry IV, Part 1*, I will point to four topics that stud the play in something like the way repeated ornamental motifs do buildings or rooms. (Such concentrations of incidentals are often called image patterns, although the individual elements rarely evoke a picture.) The four are these: time (notably dates and gratuitously precise details of time of day and year); death by hanging; birds; and, above all, horses. As is usual in Shakespeare, these topics act to give nonlogical coherence to the play by a sort of alliteration of incidental substance. Like real alliteration, an alliteration of topics can communicate, either specifically or by establishing mood, but has its principal effect, homogenization, whether it has content or not. For instance, the ostler scene (2.1) seems—unless we postulate a Shakespearean fascination with commonplaces of criminal procedure—to be in the play only to drum its topics—time of day, horses, and hanging—in the audience's ears (2.1 is light on birds; its 103 lines of prose contain only three bird references, two to cocks and one to turkeys).

There is probably no need to demonstrate that the fabric of *Henry IV, Part 1* is shot through with references, often substantively gratuitous references, to the four topics I listed. I will settle for a token display of references to horses. All the way through the play, everybody talks about horses. If the instances of the word "horse" were equally distributed through Shakespeare's thirty-seven canonical plays, there would be about eight per play; *Henry IV, Part 1* has thirty-eight. Hotspur, whose nickname is itself from horsemanship, is regularly about to take horse, and talking to his wife in 2.3, his virility is charmingly indicated in a careful confusion of sexual and equestrian activity: "Come, wilt thou see me ride? / And when I am a-horseback I will swear / I love thee infinitely" (2.3.106–108). The chivalric nature of the Douglas, who "runs a-horseback up a hill perpendicular" (2.4.355–356), is also presented literally. On the other hand, the anti-heroic Falstaff is twice specifically frustrated in his efforts to get on horseback—first at Gad's Hill in 2.2 when he storms about demanding his horse like a burlesque Richard III, and again in 3.3 when he gets a command of foot, an infantry command, and wishes it had been of horse, a cavalry command (3.3.197–198).

What birds, hanging, time, and horses do for *Henry IV, Part 1*, such recurring topics as suicide, playacting, ears, following, speaking–not speaking, memory, and cosmetics do for *Hamlet*. Sometimes they are directly discussed. Sometimes they are, apparently accidentally, the chosen metaphors for saying this or that about something else. Sometimes an alliterating topic intrudes for no apparent substantive purpose and does nothing but pull together otherwise disparate matters. As an example in that last category, consider the casual electricity in the arcs of relationship between "union" (glossed in the text itself as a word for "pearl") and "Follow my mother" in the lines Hamlet speaks as he forces the king to drink what remains of the poisoned cup prepared for Hamlet and drunk by the queen:

> Drink off this potion. Is thy union here?
> Follow my mother.
>
> (5.2.357–358)

"Union" is no longer current as a word for "pearl" and was never common. For Shakespeare's original audiences, the usual senses of "union" were the ones familiar to later ages, ones relating to unification and oneness. Prepared by earlier references, however, any *Hamlet* audience effortlessly understands "union" here to say "pearl." Nonetheless, the immediately succeeding reference to the other partner in the marital union that generates so much of the play's action gives the lines a crazy extra unity, gives the physical juxtaposition of "Is thy union here?" and "Follow my mother" a crazy extra "rightness"—makes the union of the two phrases feel natural.

The fleeting harmony in discord that occurs in "Is thy union here? Follow my mother," is typical of the patterning of *Hamlet*. For example, that very pair of sentences echoes Hamlet's overt earlier play on the idea of the union of married couples:

> HAMLET . . . Farewell, dear mother.
> KING   Thy loving father, Hamlet.
> HAMLET My mother. Father and mother is man and wife,
>   Man and wife is one flesh, and so, my mother.
>
> (4.3.58–61)

Moreover, "Follow my mother" participates in a play-long tendency to introduce the idea of following. Sometimes it seems introduced gratuitously. For instance, in 2.2, when Hamlet inquires about the current popularity of the approaching troop of actors,

Shakespeare chooses to have him phrase the query this way: "Do they hold the same estimation they did when I was in the city? Are they so followed?" (2.2.357–358).

Something similar happens ten lines before the end of the play when Fortinbras phrases his assertion of sovereignty in terms that introduce the pervasive idea of memory into the play one last extra time: "I have some rights of memory in this kingdom, / Which now to claim my vantage doth invite me" (5.2.432–433). The punctuation given here is that of the First Folio and the First Quarto. The Second Quarto reads "rights, of memory." But no punctuation can do much to account for the introduction of memory into the speech. Although "rights of memory" makes perfectly good sense, the phrase is accidental to it. The particular context does not call for mention of memory. Mention of memory is more a topic of the play at large than of Fortinbras's sentence.

As the foregoing samples will by now have suggested, *Hamlet* exhibits the same range of patterning that *Henry IV, Part 1* does. Overlapping patterning in *Hamlet* is as dense in *Hamlet* as in *Henry IV, Part 1* and has the same sort of homogenizing effects. For instance, the relationships among the incidentals of 1.2 of *Hamlet* and 1.3 are comparable to the relationships between 1.2 and 1.3 of *Henry IV, Part 1*. *Hamlet* 1.3, concerned with domestic matters in Polonius's family, contrasts sharply with the court scene it follows and echoes it. Both scenes focus for a time on filial obedience (Hamlet agrees to forgo his return to Wittenberg: "I shall in all my best obey you, madam," 1.2.124; Ophelia agrees to break with Hamlet: "I shall obey, my lord," 1.3.145). And both scenes offer large helpings of wisdom measured out to innocents by people more experienced than they in the ways of the world (the queen and king to Hamlet on mortality and the decorum of mourning, 1.2.70–75, 90–110; Laertes and Polonius to Ophelia about the casual sexual mores of royalty, 1.3.6–48, 98–144; and Polonius's "few precepts" to Laertes, 64–86).

And for an example of a linear link between urgently distinct sections of Hamlet, consider the link made by "cannon" and "canon" in 1.2. The lines quoted immediately below are the last four of the speech on which the king exits the scene and the first four of Hamlet's first soliloquy. They overlay a distinct break between two sections of the scene. The King concludes his exit speech:

> No jocund health that Denmark drinks today
> But the great cannon to the clouds shall tell,
> And the King's rouse the heaven shall bruit again,
> Respeaking earthly thunder. Come away.
> *Flourish. All but Hamlet exit.*
> HAMLET   O, that this too, too sullied flesh would melt,
> Thaw, and resolve itself into a dew,
> Or that the Everlasting had not fixed
> His canon 'gainst self-slaughter!
>
> (1.2.129–136)

The echo of artillery from line 130 in the word "canon" meaning "law" six lines later is enough by itself to deny the completeness of the division between the soliloquy and the public conversation that precedes it. As it is, however, before the term "self-slaughter" reduces what comes before it to a straightforward assertion about divine law, the verb "to fix against" and the sound of "canon" in "fixed his canon 'gainst" have gone a good way toward introducing the idea of gun emplacement into the speech. Moreover, by virtue of its reference to slaughter, the term "self-slaughter"—the very term that removes artillery as a topic of the speech—also tucks the idea of carnage back into the sentence from which it simultaneously removes it. Indeed, when the phrase "fixed his canon 'gainst self-slaughter" comes to rest, "canon," the most warlike sounding word in its clause, is, aside from the incidental pronoun "his," the only one that has no ideational affinity left for weaponry and violent death.

The kind of pull toward union that the "cannon"-"canon" lines effect in 1.2 occurs over a greater gulf when 1.4, the scene where Hamlet and Horatio hear the king taking his rouse, echoes 1.2. If the Q2 stage direction—"*A flourish of trumpets and two pieces goes of[f]*"—is to be trusted and if as is probable the "pieces" specified are cannon, then we hear at about line 7 of 1.4 what the king promised in 1.2. Shortly afterwards, in line 52, in context of ideas of bursting and of projectiles, Hamlet refers to his father's "canonized bones."

Here, in no particular order, are more examples of unifying pattern in *Hamlet.*

When 1.5 finishes after Hamlet's announced intent to dissemble and the next scene, 2.1, opens with Polonius's detailed instructions for dissembling by Reynaldo, the likeness is quietly affirmed in the repetition of the elements of Hamlet's "put on" (meaning "adopt" in "put an antic disposition on," 1.5.192) in Polonius's charge to Reynaldo to "put on" Laertes "what forgeries" Reynaldo pleases (2.1.21–22, where "put on" means "attribute to").

The so-called closet scene, the exchange between Hamlet and the queen in 3.4, is the second of Hamlet's two intense interviews with women. It echoes the first, the so-called nunnery scene, the part of 3.1 where Hamlet rails and rages at Ophelia (3.1.96–162). Even when a director ignores the likeness between the two and does not underscore it by blocking the later scene as a visual echo of the first, it will be one anyway. In the nunnery scene, Hamlet repeatedly bids Ophelia farewell and repeatedly resumes his tirade; he does the same thing with Gertrude in the closet scene.

An unobtrusive pattern in intrusive walkers overlays the first scene of Hamlet. Barnardo is one as the scene begins; the Ghost is another at line 47 and again at line 138; finally, at line 181, Horatio tells us that "the morn in russet mantle clad / Walks o'er the dew of yon high eastward hill" (181–182).

Rosencrantz and Guildenstern, themselves a rhyming pair, are the second of two pairs of inseparable outsiders in the play. They echo Cornelius and Voltemond, the Danish ambassadors to Norway. (Note that Voltemond is entirely extra in 1.2 and that Cornelius is likewise in 2.3, the second of their two scenes.)

The "hot-cold-sultry" exchange between Hamlet and Osric in 5.2 echoes the "camel-weasel-whale" passage in which Hamlet earlier mocked another politically pliant fool:

HAMLET   . . . Put your bonnet to his right use: 'tis for the head.
OSRIC   I thank your lordship; it is very hot.
HAMLET   No, believe me, 'tis very cold; the wind is northerly.
OSRIC   It is indifferent cold, my lord, indeed.
HAMLET   But yet methinks it is very sultry and hot for my complexion.
OSRIC   Exceedingly, my lord; it is very sultry. . . .

(5.2.105–113)

HAMLET   Do you see yonder cloud that's almost in shape of a camel?
POLONIUS   By th' Mass, and 'tis like a camel indeed.
HAMLET   Methinks it is like a weasel.
POLONIUS   It is backed like a weasel.
HAMLET   Or like a whale.
POLONIUS   Very like a whale.

(3.2.406–412)

One very quiet, very efficient unifying network in *Hamlet* is that composed of variations on the idea of "setting people up" to be searched into. Both the nunnery scene and the closet scene result from plots to spy on Hamlet. So do his first scenes with Rosencrantz and Guildenstern. Polonius's schemes to spy on Laertes in Paris participate in the pattern too. The largest element in the pattern is, of course, "The Murder of Gonzago," performed for the specific purpose of catching the conscience of the king.

Before I finish sampling the patterning in *Hamlet*, I want to say that, as it was in *Henry IV, Part 1*, the matter of pertinence and impertinence, coherence and incoherence, is of concern to the characters themselves in *Hamlet*. For one among many examples of such concern, consider the following sequence, one improbably triggered by Polonius's advertisement for the players ("The best actors in the world, either for tragedy, comedy, history, pastoral, pastoral-comical . . . ," 2.2.420–421):

HAMLET   O Jephthah, judge of Israel, what a treasure hadst thou!
POLONIUS   What a treasure had he, my lord?
HAMLET   Why,
One fair daughter, and no more,
The which he lovèd passing well.
POLONIUS, (*aside*)   Still on my daughter.
HAMLET   Am I not i' th' right, old Jephthah?
POLONIUS   If you call me "Jephthah," my lord: I have a daughter that I love passing well.
HAMLET   Nay, that follows not.
POLONIUS   What follows then, my lord?
HAMLET   Why,
As by lot, God wot. . . .

(2.2.427–440)

Here, as in the gib-cat passage in *Henry IV, Part 1*, the lines insist on the multiplicity of systems of coherence. What Hamlet says *does* follow is "As by lot, God wot," which is impertinent to the issue of the justice or injustice of calling Polonius Jephthah but which has the undeniable pertinence it *does* have in an unexpected set of terms; it is the next line of the ballad Hamlet has quoted. Moreover, it pertains in yet a third system, a phonic system, established by Hamlet's charge of impertinence: "As by lot, God wot" rhymes with "Nay, that follows not."

Rather than prolong my list of examples from *Hamlet,* I want to turn now to a question I asked earlier. Why is a truly great play like *Henry IV, Part 1* not ranked with *Hamlet* among the very greatest of Shakespeare's greatest plays? I have been pushing the idea that substantively negligible patterns, patterns ordinarily (and thus properly) unobserved by our conscious minds, are a (if not *the*) source of the greatness of *Henry IV, Part 1* and *Hamlet.* As the relative lengths of the parts of this essay devoted to patterns in *Henry IV, Part 1* and in *Hamlet* suggest, the patterning in *Henry IV, Part 1* is so intense that it is fun to describe it to others—more intense and lots more interesting than the patterning in *Hamlet.* Common sense suggests that I would conclude that (as, if you think about it, it cannot really be) the consensus on the relative greatness of *Henry IV, Part 1* and *Hamlet* is wrongheaded and that people ought to value or pretend to value the two at least equally.

Common sense is wrong again.

The patterning in *Hamlet* is just as heavy as the patterning in *Henry IV, Part 1,* but it does not weigh as heavily on the play. By saying that the patterns in *Henry IV, Part 1* weigh comparatively heavily, I mean that though they do not force themselves on our consciousnesses, they make the play feel organized, organized as opposed to organic. What I'm suggesting is that compared to *Hamlet, Henry IV, Part 1* is like a room that has not only been carefully decorated but feels as if it has been carefully decorated. On the other hand, *Hamlet* (like *Macbeth, The Winter's Tale, Twelfth Night,* and a couple of other Shakespearean superstars) is comparable to a carefully decorated room in which a complex of symmetries and contrasts feel inevitable, as inevitable as the markings of a sparrow or the colors of a field of grain.

As compared with *Hamlet, Henry IV, Part 1* feels "managed." Its patterns of simultaneously like and unlike elements are much *neater* than *Hamlet's.* Consider the three liars who act as father substitutes in *Henry IV, Part 1.* The parallel between Falstaff and Worcester is strong enough to press it almost to consciousness. The extra "rightness" Glendower brings to the play as foster father to Mortimer is so recessive as probably to go unnoticed even by an analyst in triumphant command of the parallel between Falstaff and Worcester. The recessiveness of its least member makes the pattern in foster fathers unusually subtle for *Henry IV, Part 1.*

But just compare it with the pattern in avenging sons in *Hamlet.* The parallel between Hamlet and Laertes is ostentatious, almost as ostentatious as the one between Prince Hal and Hotspur in *Henry IV, Part 1* and more so than the one between Falstaff and Worcester. As with Falstaff, Worcester, and Glendower, one can notice the parallel between Hamlet and Laertes without noticing that Fortinbras is an avenging son too. And if Fortinbras's presence in the pattern is recessive, that of Pyrrhus (who joined the Greek siege of Troy only in response to the death of his father, Achilles) is unlikely ever to call even an ardent classicist's attention to itself. I submit that such shadows of likeness are the chief means by which *Hamlet's* identity comes to feel inevitable where that of *Henry IV, Part 1* feels like the product of a craftsman.

Of the likenesses I pointed out between unlike things in *Henry IV, Part 1*, the subtlest is probably that between "the blessed son" in 1.2 and "so blest a son" in 1.1. As far as I can see, links that subtle are rare in *Henry IV, Part 1*. They are not rare in *Hamlet*, where, wanting the kind of punning glitter available in "sun" and "son," they are even subtler, even further from calling attention to themselves as effects of literary carpentry. For examples, consider these, all pointed out to me in a personal letter from Professor James O'Rourke: "tenders of his affection" (1.3.108–109) reappears transformed in 3.1.176 as "his affections do not that way tend"; "angels and ministers of grace" (1.4.43) reemerges in 5.1 as "minist'ring angel" in "I tell thee, churlish priest, / A minist'ring angel shall my sister be / When thou liest howling" (250–252); and "the dead waste and middle of the night" (1.2.208) returns reshaped in 2.2.250–254, the lines in which Hamlet and Guildenstern joke laboriously about Fortune:

> HAMLET   Then you live about her waist, or in the middle of her favors?
> GUILDENSTERN   Faith, her privates we.
> HAMLET   In the secret parts of Fortune? O, most true! She is a strumpet.

Both *Henry IV, Part 1* and *Hamlet* are rich in patterns generated by likenesses in unlike things. A vital distinction between the two plays is that *Hamlet*'s patterns of likeness often introduce an extra element of difference. Consider again the pattern in "setups" for surreptitious investigation. It is at once perfect and imperfect. In all but one of the instances I listed, the spying is direct; Reynaldo, however, is to get knowledge of Laertes's lifestyle by coaxing it from third parties. And think again about the pattern in avenging sons. It coexists with a pattern in dangerous nephews (Fortinbras, Lucianus the murderer in "The Murder of Gonzago," and Hamlet himself). Hamlet and Fortinbras participate in both patterns; Laertes, Pyrrhus, and Lucianus do not. Consider too the simultaneous order and disorder inherent in the fact that the ostentatious similarity between the murder of Gonzago and the murder of the senior Hamlet is slightly and casually scrambled when the murderer in the play within the play (the character parallel with Claudius in *Hamlet* proper) turns out not to be the victim's brother but what Hamlet is to Claudius—a threatening nephew to the king.

The foregoing speculations on the reasons why *Henry IV, Part 1* is not generally valued as highly as *Hamlet* constitute a casual excursion into aesthetic theorizing and may be written off as authorial self-indulgence. But what about the rest of the essay? What good might it be to teachers set upon introducing students to a Shakespeare play?

A lot, I hope.

My guess is that at least 90 percent of what is said in classrooms, scholarly articles, and books about Shakespeare plays (and for that matter, literary works in general) could be said about their stories or the sorts of situations in which we see their characters. All the way through school and college I was bothered by the gulf between my experience of a given Shakespeare play and what teachers and scholarly introductions implied it should be or would have been had I been fixated on one or another philosophic concern or historical phenomenon.

If, as essay topics and classroom discussions implied, the function of *Hamlet* in the societies that have loved it so long was to figure out whether he was or was not "actually" mad, how did its puzzles and speculation on them relate to the value society puts on it? If, as essay topics and classroom discussions implied, *Hamlet* was good because it told the story it took us hours to dig out of the archaic diction from which its indirectly informative sentences are composed, why was *Hamlet* more valued than a plot summary? And if *Henry IV, Part 1* was of value for such lessons and secular doctrines as can be plucked up from it, could they not be just as justly picked out in the summary? And if the "real" play was the solemn stranger described in the introduction to the text, why not throw out the play and keep the interpretation?

If, as essay topics and classroom discussions implied, the value of *Henry IV, Part 1* was as a site for discussion of Elizabethan ideas of kingship or loyalty to friends or whatever, why did we bother with the play? Why not directly stimulate discussion of those topics? No wonder students often behave as if society's motive in requiring them to read *Hamlet* is to test their docility and willingness to go gracefully through motions. People piously told me they valued the beauty of Shakespeare plays, but they talked about the ideas in them, ideas easily available elsewhere—and probably in textbooks the school already owned. And if, as essay topics and classroom discussions implied, Shakespeare was good because he showed us this or that about the human condition, why value his plays over movies downtown that demonstrated and investigated the same well-known truths and problems?

The big virtue of looking at the sort of phenomena I have looked at here is that in doing so one looks at stuff that however wanting in ideational glamour, is there, is of the play and not of its story or of the ideas it deals out in passing. To look at the unimportant (the literally unimportant, the nonimporting) organizations that cohabit with the story enacted is to look at the play itself, is to tell the truth (however boring to young minds that want to solve the real problems of the real world).

Whatever the kind of criticism demonstrated and recommended here may lack, it is a valuable alternative to the wanton creativity ordinarily practiced and encouraged by academics at all levels, an honorable alternative to a criticism that uses Shakespeare's plays as occasions to talk about other things. As long as teachers persist in presenting Shakespeare's plays as mines for ideational materials abundant elsewhere and not as the jewels they are—and that all genuinely popular art is—students will continue to emerge as they do now from high schools, colleges, and graduate literature programs convinced that the study of literature is the practice of saying the kinds of things they are used to hearing said and has nothing whatever to do with the realities of literary experience as they know it to be.

PART TWO

Teaching Shakespeare Through Performance

·

MICHAEL TOLAYDO

EDITOR

"The Play's the Thing"

ROSEMARY MURPHY WALSH
FOLGER SHAKESPEARE LIBRARY

Many teachers, students, and yes, actors and directors are afraid of Shakespeare. During a weekly meeting of the theater faculty at our local high school for the performing arts, five professional directors turned down the opportunity to direct students in Shakespeare scenes at the Folger Library's annual student festival. They all believed that the plays were inaccessible to students, that the words were too difficult and old-fashioned. Since I was low on the faculty totem pole, the assignment fell to me.

It was a grand opportunity. Since then I have taught Shakespeare at the university, high school, and middle school levels and to teachers at the Teaching Shakespeare Institute.

In a classroom setting, it is vital at the very beginning to grab students' attention and enthusiasm. A great way to do this, and to initiate students to the idea of moving around in performance, is to engage in a series of warmups. Actors get ready to work by relaxing and moving, vocalizing and concentrating; the same process readies students to work with Shakespeare.

There are two advantages of this kind of warmup: Your students will be acting before they have had time to think about it, and they will be familiar with the process of improvisation, a useful tool in the study of Shakespeare. Other exercises for warming up may be found in *Improvisation for the Theater,* by Viola Spolin (Northwestern University Press).

At the Teaching Shakespeare Institute, I usually start with a "rolling improv." The class counts off by ones and twos and lines up in two teams on opposite sides of the room. You clear the front of the classroom and in the center of this "stage" place a chair in case students would like to use it in their improv.

Each student will perform twice. The first actor from one team starts on stage. The first actor from the other team enters and *initiates the improvisation* with a statement or a question. Imagination should run rampant. For example:

"So, Mrs. Jackson, how would you like your hair cut today?"
"Mommy, Paul just ate a snail!"
"Lee, I'm tired of your late nights."
"Bless me, Father, for I have sinned."
"Woof, woof." (Student is a dog.)

The onstage actor responds, and the two actors carry on with the improv. The students have two objectives: they must *continue* speaking for twenty seconds, and they must *stop* after twenty seconds. The teacher, acting as timekeeper, will say "Rotate" every twenty seconds. At the word "Rotate," the student who began onstage exits, leaving the student who entered and initiated the first improv. The second student from the opposite team enters, speaks a first line, and begins the second improv. At "Rotate," the student who began one improv becomes the "accomplice" in the next.

Each student, then, both initiates a scene and responds to a scene. When everyone has taken a turn, to great final applause, the teacher can remind students that they are all actors since each has now acted on stage twice.

Another improvisational warmup, "Car," focuses students' concentration and expands their sense of dramatic possibility. In the cleared space in your classroom, arrange four numbered chairs like this, leaving room for person X to stand:

$$2 \qquad 1$$

$$3 \qquad 4$$

$$X$$

Number 4 is the driver; 3 is front-seat passenger or shotgun; 2 and 1 are in the backseat. X is a hitchhiker. Place students in the numbered seats and ask the rest of the class to line up on one side of the room.

The people are in the car driving to Florida—or Seattle, Austin, or the Wisconsin Dells—for a vacation. All of them share an attribute or a condition. To start off the exercise, the teacher assigns this attribute to the first car. For example, everyone has a cold, or everyone is whining, or everyone has poison ivy, or everyone is angry. While concentrating on the attribute, the passengers must talk about their trip. They talk for thirty seconds.

One at a time, the remaining members of the class enter the improv as hitchhiker X, who stops the car and asks for a ride while *displaying but not telling* a new attribute for the rest of the passengers to adopt. A hitchhiker starting off with *"Bonjour mes amis . . ."* will send all the occupants of the car to French accents. "I-I'm f-f-freezing. M-may I have a r-ride?" means that the passengers must be chilled too.

After ten seconds, the hitchhiker takes passenger 1's place, and everyone shifts up one seat. The driver exits, and the new carload continues to talk about the drive using the hitchhiker's attribute. After thirty seconds, a new hitchhiker comes along; the driving trip, and the improv, keep rolling. All students participate in five improvisations—one they originate and four others in which they creatively follow and augment another's lead.

Improvisation of contemporary situations works beautifully in tandem with a scene from a Shakespeare play. Ask students, for example, to focus on the dialogue between Lady Percy and Hotspur in Act 2, scene 3 of *Henry IV, Part 1*. Ask them to read, identify problem words, paraphrase, and identify the objectives, or what a specific character wants at a specific moment.

Now set up a contemporary premise to mirror the action of the scene. The most important part of setting up this kind of improvisation is that the modern characters' objectives must match those of the Shakespeare characters. Lay out the situation and let the students take over:

Mike has a big upcoming event on his mind, and it has made him distracted. Cynthia is upset because he hasn't been paying attention to her. She lists at least five times when he's ignored her. She's worried and hurt. A friend enters to tell Mike that it's time to leave for the event. Mike and Cynthia start to tease each other with insults and endearments. By the end of the improvisation, their relationship must be resolved. Who is selfish? Do they care for each other? Why doesn't he place her first in his thoughts? Or does he?

In the improvisation, students should be allowed to be as creative as they like as long as they stay within the framework. Some good scenes in *Hamlet* to explore through contemporary improvisation are:

1.1.22–190. Horatio, Marcellus, Barnardo, Ghost
1.2.165–281. Horatio, Marcellus, Hamlet, Barnardo
2.1.84–134. Ophelia, Polonius
3.1.96–162. Hamlet, Ophelia

Many different kinds of students respond positively to working with Shakespeare in ways that actors do. They make many wonderful discoveries and develop a familiarity with plot and character. When students move through warmups and situation improvisations back to performing the scene in Shakespeare's own language, their new levels of knowledge and perception will be evident to them and to you too.

Ambulatory Shakespeare; or, The Question Is the Answer

MICHAEL TOLAYDO
ST. MARY'S COLLEGE OF MARYLAND

As a working teacher, I believe that an initial approach to the plays can best be achieved through the performance of an immediately comprehensible scene. This approach generates and puts into play the tools and skills necessary to examine those more difficult and complex portions of the play, while it supplies students with confidence in their own good ideas and opinions. A "performed" scene provides the class with direct experiences and insights into a play that can be used by the teacher in a variety of ways. The discoveries made during performance sessions will connect and add information and generally resonate throughout further study of the play.

Two different methods for involving students in the process of performance are outlined here. The first focuses on *Henry IV, Part 1*, the second on *Hamlet*, though each technique can be used with any play.

Both of these methods involve many questions. Textual questions are asked not to solicit definitive answers but to propose several interpretive possibilities and choices. These interpretations may be challenged later as students come to grips with more of the play. This is fine, an important part of the process. What is important here is that students are accumulating a bank of knowledge about the scene and about Shakespeare's use of language.

Henry IV, Part 1

This is a slightly streamlined version of a basic scene performance exercise detailed in *Shakespeare Set Free: Teaching* Romeo and Juliet, Macbeth, *and* A Midsummer Night's Dream, that actively places students squarely in the middle of Shakespeare's language.

When I speak of performance, I am not speaking about creating a scene for stage performance, nor am I suggesting that this work involves acting skills. I am rooted in the notion that in getting up on their feet and *doing* a scene in the classroom, students will discover that this exercise is a learning experience all by itself. By beginning to study a play in this way, and not necessarily beginning with the first scene of the play, you can open up the play and provide the basis for further active exploration of plot, character, structure, language, genre, or What You Will.

Without question, some of Shakespeare's language is not easy; however, not all of it is difficult. Each play contains much dialogue that is easily comprehensible to virtually all age groups. By beginning in the classroom with an approachable scene, we can learn, through performance, to take on more complex areas of study and make them more absorbing for teachers and students alike. This approach will work with students of any age, elementary school through graduate seminar. Since each class is different and only you know the strengths, weaknesses, and needs of your students, there are sections in the following exercise you may wish to expand, adapt, skip, change, and rearrange. This introductory session may take two class periods; it is a worthwhile investment. During further study of the play students can use these tools to analyze other complex scenes.

I begin to teach every new play by arriving in the class—well before any assignments or books are distributed—with photocopies of a group scene. Group scenes, those with five or more characters, involve more students, and they are usually easy to understand because they are full of exposition. Every play you teach contains at least one and usually several scenes you can use in the same way. You will naturally notice that we do not have to begin the study of a play by starting with Act 1, scene 1. In *Hamlet,* for example, the entrance of the court before the play within the play (3.2) works extremely well. Act 2, scene 2, of *Henry IV, Part 1* is a perfect choice because it is an active group scene that depends upon a lot of imagination to be realized.

Copy this scene in large type by means of your computer or on an enlarging photocopier. Make sure that all the notes and the glossary are omitted from the copied pages. You may find this particular scene a little long for your use; however, you can easily cut it to make it shorter, or after the first enactment of the scene assign its completion as a homework exercise.

I make sure that there are copies of the scene for the whole class. As I hand them out, I ask that no one looks at them until my signal, well aware that some of my students will want to see what is on the page.

I do not ask for volunteers but select my readers. I do not necessarily select my actor-type students or confident readers to read only the good parts. Since any scene you select will contain parts of varying complexity and length—in this scene, Bardolph and Peto have only one line apiece—your students with reading difficulties can leap into the action immediately. Nor do I ask males to read only the male roles and females to read only female parts. We will be reading this scene several times, and we want to find out what the scene is about, not who can play a particular part well. I am not casting a play but involving students in the text and its meanings and, I hope, breaking down a few stereotypical assumptions along the way.

In this scene, because the parts of the Prince and Falstaff are long, I select a different Prince and a different Falstaff for each page, labeling them Prince and Falstaff 1, 2, 3, and 4. Each reader of the Prince and Falstaff reads his or her part only for the page assigned. If the speech continues over to the next page, the next Prince or Falstaff takes over immediately, midspeech.

I inform my readers that they should not worry about correct pronunciation but do the best they can and pronounce unfamiliar words the way they think they should sound. There are no Elizabethans around to tell us how words were pronounced, and it really does not matter very much; eventually we will collectively come to a pronunciation we feel is right for our scene. Readers should try to read for sense and not worry about acting the parts. If they want to act, that's fine, but it's not important in this process. Lastly, readers need to read loud enough so that the rest of the class can hear. I want all students to acquire a bank of words they will eventually feel at home with.

After they have read through the scene, I praise the readers, then select fourteen more readers and ask them to read the scene again. This second reading is not to get a "better" reading but to encourage further familiarity with the text. While the readers read, I ask the rest of the class to listen and to note what differences and new information they observe in the scene.

Discussion begins with a few questions. I emphasize that for the purposes of this discussion, the answers to the questions must be contained within the scene and its possibilities, not through a knowledge of the rest of the play or through fantasy. The photocopied scene is our entire play. *Students must find lines and ideas in the dialogue to support their views.*

In the initial discussion, I ask questions like this:

1. Who are these guys? (Possible answers: a gang; a band of robbers.)

2. How do you know? (Find the lines in the text that support your argument.)

3. What is going on here? What are these guys up to? How do you know? (Any answer is acceptable as long as it can be supported from the text. Possible answers: The robbers are going to hold up some travelers. The travelers are carrying money that belongs to the king. It says so right here. Also, the Prince is going to rob his friend.)

4. Do these guys know each other well? Have they robbed before? Are they comrades, or are they getting together for the first time to carry out this robbery? Look for clues in the dialogue that support your opinion.

Since the class will *direct and enact* this scene, the students must decide—for the purposes of this in-class enactment—whether the characters in the scene are old or new friends, since old friends relate differently than new acquaintances. Ask for a hand vote; majority rules.

Your students may discover during this or a later reading that Poins's "O, 'tis our setter. I know his voice" informs us that they know enough to have an informant or an inside man for the robbery.

Your students may not pick up on this information until performance. They may not discover it at all. What matters is that they are given the opportunity to decide for themselves from what they have discovered. The questions I ask are only to prompt further possibilities and discoveries. I may let them play the scene as new friends and then ask "Has anyone figured out what Poins means when he says, 'O, 'tis our setter. I know his voice'?" A student may say, "The gang know each other and are professionals." Another may counter, "This is still their first robbery as a group. They just know enough about robberies to have someone on the inside." These answers prompt further questions you may or may not wish to address. This methodology, however, requires the students continually to dig into the scene.

5. Who's the boss of this group? How do you know? Who would like to be the boss of this group? How do you know? Is there more than one boss? (Possible answers: The Prince is the boss of the group; A Prince is more important. Falstaff is the boss; he seems to lead the robbery, as in "Strike! Down with them! Cut the villains' throats! . . . Down with them! Fleece them!") I hope that someone brings up what Falstaff means by "masters." Is Falstaff urging his men, friends, or leaders on? If no one is sure or we cannot come to a decision, we put the question aside to be answered later.

Sometimes I assign a student to write on the blackboard or on paper all answers generated in discussion. These answers need to be supported directly or circumstantially from the text of this scene.

Then reassign parts and ask the students to read the scene through again. This time I ask students to make notes of what new information they discover and to circle any word or phrase they don't understand.

After this reading, we begin another round of discussion:

1. What kind of gang or group is this with a Prince as part of it? Does he seem to be a real Prince, or is that his name? (Your students will find the lines that indicate that he is the Prince of England.) What do you think about his robbing Falstaff? How does Ned Poins fit into this mix? Why does Falstaff give up so easily when the Prince and Poins rob them? Is the robbery of the travelers dangerous? What time of day is it? Is there any poetry in the scene? How do we know that Falstaff is fat and that the Prince is thin? Is Falstaff a bully? a loudmouth? an egomaniac? a good fighter? a leader? Are there any horses in the scene? (Possible answers: A real Prince who takes part in a robbery can't be a good Prince. The Prince is cool. Ned Poins seems to be the Prince's man. It's night because they can't see each other. The Prince keeps calling Falstaff fat, so maybe he is. It's a dangerous, deadly fight. It's funny; no one gets hurt. There are horses. There are no horses because Shakespeare knew he would have trouble putting real animals on the stage; so he has Poins say, "I have removed Falstaff's horse . . . ," and First Traveler says, "The boy shall lead our horses down the hill.")

2. Ask for comments about anything else going on in this scene.

3. Ask what words and phrases the students have circled. (Frequent answers: "frets," "gummed velvet," "levers," "What a plague mean you to colt me thus?" "ostler," "I'll peach for this," "setter," "vizards," "exchequer," "gorbellied," "grandjurors," "Sir John Paunch.")

I may lead students to some answers, but not more than a few. Many of these meanings will be provided a context by other members of the class. For the answers to questions their peers can't answer, direct students to a good text like the New Folger edition, the *Oxford English Dictionary*, or C. T. Onions's *A Shakespeare Glossary*.

You may wish to read the scene one more time with another set of readers or with previous readers speaking different roles. Ask a few more questions. Ask *them* to ask questions. I usually include a fast read-through involving each class member. We form a circle. One student begins to read Poins's first line. As soon as the reader comes to a question mark, a period, a colon, a semicolon, or an exclamation point—commas do not count—she stops reading, and the next person in the circle picks it up. We want this reading to be smooth and even, and to make sense.

The students are now ready to put the scene on its feet. I select a new cast to act out the parts. This can be anyone who hasn't yet had a turn or anyone who wants to. *The remainder of the class will direct the scene. No one is uninvolved.* The operating principle here is that there are many different workable ways to stage this scene, not one correct way. Before actual performance work, we need to consider these questions:

1. Where does this scene take place? What time of day is it? (Frequent student answers: "in the country," "in the town," "in London," "at night," "at dawn.")

The cast and directors need to check the text to make sure the location "fits." If someone suggests London, make sure he searches the dialogue to discover why this scene probably doesn't take place there. Once a location has been agreed upon, what does it look like? What period is it in? Elizabethan? Modern? If Elizabethan, what does the place look like? Using chairs and desks and anything else in the room, create the space you decide upon.

2. Who should come on stage from where? With whom? Why? Does the text give you a clue? Remember that the *text* is only the dialogue; most often the stage directions are the creation of editors. More specific questions to think about and vary: Is the Prince out of sight and if so, where? Does he reveal himself, or can we see him listening to Falstaff's speech about him? Do we see him and Poins hiding during the first robbery? Why yes? Why no? Since both are possible, which choice works best for this group?

3. Who's the most important person in the scene? Who *thinks* he's the most important person in the scene? How do you act it out to show this?

4. How does the cast enact the decisions made earlier—about the boss, whether these guys have met before this meeting?

After getting advice from the directors, the cast acts out the scene once. After this first run-through, cast and directors discuss what worked, what changes they would make in the next enactment. The same cast, or a newly selected one, plays the scene again incorporating suggested changes.

Ask for comments on the process of getting a scene on its feet. Is it as complicated as they would have thought? Why? Why not? Point out the advantages of working this with a group, incorporating many creative viewpoints and many minds working on the same questions.

The students—without the aid of notes, translation, or "helpful" explanatory material from the teacher—have come to understand what's happening in a scene from a Shakespeare play by working through the process of getting the scene from the page into performance. Though I have included dozens of questions, it is not necessary to go into such detail in the classroom. What is important is to establish that there are many possibilities and that during this process of discovering them, students are learning Shakespeare.

HENRY IV
Part 1

ACT 2, SCENE 2

Enter Prince, Poins, [Bardolph,] and Peto.

POINS   Come, shelter, shelter! I have removed Falstaff's horse, and he frets like a gummed velvet.
PRINCE   Stand close.   [*Poins, Bardolph, and Peto exit.*]

Enter Falstaff.

FALSTAFF   Poins! Poins, and be hanged! Poins!
PRINCE   Peace, you fat-kidneyed rascal. What a brawling dost thou keep!
FALSTAFF   Where's Poins, Hal?
PRINCE   He is walked up to the top of the hill. I'll go seek him.

[*Prince exits.*]

FALSTAFF   I am accursed to rob in that thief's company. The rascal hath removed my horse and tied him I know not where. If I travel but four foot by the square further afoot, I shall break my wind. Well, I doubt not but to die a fair death for all this, if I 'scape hanging for killing that rogue. I have forsworn his company hourly any time this two-and-twenty years, and yet I am bewitched with the rogue's company. If the rascal have not given me medicines to make me love him, I'll be hanged. It could not be else: I have drunk medicines.—Poins! Hal! A plague upon you both.—Bardolph! Peto!—I'll starve ere I'll rob a foot further. An 'twere not as good a deed as drink to turn true man and to leave these rogues, I am the veriest varlet that ever chewed with a tooth. Eight yards of uneven ground is threescore and ten miles afoot with me, and the stony-hearted villains know it well enough. A plague upon it when thieves cannot be true one to another! (*They whistle, within.*) Whew! A plague upon you all!

[*Enter the Prince, Poins, Peto, and Bardolph.*]

Give me my horse, you rogues. Give me my horse and be hanged!

PRINCE   Peace, you fat guts! Lie down, lay thine ear close to the ground, and list if thou canst hear the tread of travelers.

FALSTAFF   Have you any levers to lift me up again being down? 'Sblood, I'll not bear my own flesh so far afoot again for all the coin in thy father's Exchequer. What a plague mean you to colt me thus?

PRINCE   Thou liest. Thou art not colted; thou art uncolted.

FALSTAFF   I prithee, good Prince Hal, help me to my horse, good king's son.

PRINCE   Out, you rogue! Shall I be your ostler?

FALSTAFF   Hang thyself in thine own heir-apparent garters! If I be ta'en, I'll peach for this. An I have not ballads made on you all and sung to filthy tunes, let a cup of sack be my poison—when a jest is so forward, and afoot too! I hate it.

Enter Gadshill.

GADSHILL   Stand.

FALSTAFF   So I do, against my will.

POINS   O, 'tis our setter. I know his voice.

[BARDOLPH]   What news?

[GADSHILL]   Case you, case you. On with your vizards. There's money of the King's coming down the hill. 'Tis going to the King's Exchequer.

FALSTAFF   You lie, you rogue. 'Tis going to the King's Tavern.

GADSHILL   There's enough to make us all.

FALSTAFF   To be hanged.

PRINCE   Sirs, you four shall front them in the narrow lane. Ned Poins and I will walk lower. If they 'scape from your encounter, then they light on us.

PETO   How many be there of them?

GADSHILL   Some eight or ten.

FALSTAFF   Zounds, will they not rob us?

PRINCE   What, a coward, Sir John Paunch?

FALSTAFF   Indeed, I am not John of Gaunt, your grandfather, but yet no coward, Hal.

PRINCE   Well, we leave that to the proof.

POINS   Sirrah Jack, thy horse stands behind the hedge. When thou need'st him, there thou shalt find him. Farewell and stand fast.

FALSTAFF   Now cannot I strike him, if I should be hanged.

PRINCE, [aside to Poins]   Ned, where are our disguises?

POINS, [aside to Prince]   Here, hard by. Stand close.

[The Prince and Poins exit.]

FALSTAFF   Now, my masters, happy man be his dole, say I. Every man to his business.

[They step aside.]

Enter the Travelers.

FIRST TRAVELER   Come, neighbor, the boy shall lead our horses down the hill. We'll walk afoot awhile and ease our legs.

THIEVES, [advancing]   Stand!

TRAVELERS   Jesus bless us!

FALSTAFF   Strike! Down with them! Cut the villains' throats! Ah, whoreson caterpillars, bacon-fed knaves, they hate us youth. Down with them! Fleece them!

TRAVELERS   O, we are undone, both we and ours forever!

FALSTAFF   Hang, you gorbellied knaves! Are you undone? No, you fat chuffs. I would your store were here. On, bacons, on! What, you knaves, young men must live. You are grandjurors, are you? We'll jure you, faith.

Here they rob them and bind them. They all exit.

Enter the Prince and Poins, disguised.

PRINCE   The thieves have bound the true men. Now
could thou and I rob the thieves and go merrily to
London, it would be argument for a week, laughter
for a month, and a good jest forever.
POINS   Stand close, I hear them coming.

[*They step aside.*]

Enter the Thieves again.

FALSTAFF   Come, my masters, let us share, and then to
horse before day. An the Prince and Poins be not
two arrant cowards, there's no equity stirring.
There's no more valor in that Poins than in a wild
duck.

As they are sharing, the Prince and Poins set upon them.
PRINCE   Your money!
POINS   Villains!

*They all run away, and Falstaff, after a blow or two,
runs away too, leaving the booty behind them.*
PRINCE
Got with much ease. Now merrily to horse.
The thieves are all scattered, and possessed with fear
So strongly that they dare not meet each other.
Each takes his fellow for an officer.
Away, good Ned. Falstaff sweats to death,
And lards the lean earth as he walks along.
Were't not for laughing, I should pity him.
POINS   How the fat rogue roared!

They exit.

Hamlet

After students have become familiar with this process of working with text, you may want to approach a scene in another way in order to introduce them to other possibilities. The first part of this exercise takes place in the classroom. The second part has proven a useful and instructive homework assignment, requiring your students to carefully read, analyze, discuss, and present through performance a clarified point of view.

Distribute photocopies of an excerpted section of Act 3, scene 2, of *Hamlet*. I often use this excerpt for classwork even when I am teaching a different play because it illustrates the homework assignment perfectly.

HAMLET
Excerpt from ACT 3, SCENE 2

The trumpets sounds. Dumb show follows.

Enter a King and a Queen ⟨very lovingly,⟩ the Queen embracing him and he her. ⟨She kneels and makes show of protestation unto him.⟩ He takes her up and declines his head upon her neck. He lies him down upon a bank of flowers. She, seeing him asleep, leaves him. Anon ⟨comes⟩ in another man, takes off his crown, kisses it, pours poison in the sleeper's ears, and leaves him. The Queen returns, finds the King dead, makes passionate action. The poisoner with some three or four come in again, seem to condole with her. The dead body is carried away. The poisoner woos the Queen with gifts. She seems harsh awhile but in the end accepts ⟨his⟩ love.

[*Players exit.*]

I select seven or eight people to work the scene in class. A READER reads the text; performers enact the KING, the QUEEN, the POISONER (Lucianus); and three or four others play the poisoner's ATTENDANTS who carry the body off. We clear a space in the classroom, and I ask the performers to listen and *mime* the actions as the reader describes them. I ask the reader to read slowly and to allow the performers to complete their actions before she moves on. I ask the class to watch and to see if the performers suit their actions to the words.

Usually this first scene will be done too quickly and with a lack of detail. After the laughter dies down, we discuss the scene's possibilities. I solicit comments and questions about the performance of the text. Then I ask questions, perhaps some of these: Were the King and Queen acting "very lovingly" when they entered? How do we *do* "very lovingly"? What does "show of protestation" mean? Did the poisoner kiss the crown? Did he put it back on the king's head? Or did he put it on the ground? Or did the crown disappear after it was taken off the king's head? Or did the poisoner take it with him? What does "makes passionate action" mean? How do we do "passionate action" in mime? What does "condole" mean? Was "the dead body carried away" or dragged by the attendants? Do we carry it respectfully? How quickly was the queen wooed? How do we *do* "she seems harsh awhile but in the end she accepts his love"? Did the reader give the performers enough time to complete their actions? Did the performers listen carefully to the reader? These questions may help students focus on what they might have missed in the initial performance.

I then divide the class into performing companies, giving each company ten to fifteen minutes to work on the scene. They will present the same scene to the rest of the class. I ask that they pay attention to the details, working out by *doing* how they wish to express these details. Answering some of the following questions for themselves may help groups focus their interpretations: Is your scene more like a dance? Would extremely exaggerated movement work better? Is it more contemporary and realistic? Is it a serious presentation, or should it be comic? Should your scene be underscored with music? Are there sound effects? Does the reader read in a flat voice, or should she use her voice expressively? These suggestions (and the more creative ones your students think up) are excellent ways to approach the style of the presentation. The important thing is to try to tell the story with detailed movement and actions in a fluid and consistent manner. It is *very* important that each group actively work on the scene rather than just sitting around talking about it.

After the rehearsal period, each group presents its version to the rest of the class. Ask about the benefits of seeing the same text performed in so many different ways. If there is time, I will ask each group to recast roles and present the scene again, improving on their last presentation, or in a different style if they'd like. One of the important things we've learned and demonstrated is how style and specific movement and gesture can create an exciting visual text.

For the homework assignment, I form different groups. I provide each group with photocopies of a scene excerpt from the play we are studying. For the exercise to be successful, it is important to select and excerpt dialogue that has considerable action. Each group will create from the dialogue a narrative text to be performed. Each group can work on the same scene excerpt, or different groups can work on separate excerpts, sometimes from different acts. Excerpts from a single scene, performed in sequence, makes for a terrific class. I remind my students to use one another as resources and a good text like the New Folger edition, the *Oxford English Dictionary*, or C. T. Onions's *A Shakespeare Glossary* to look up phrases and words they don't understand.

Here is an example of how student discussions might proceed on their way to an intrinsic interpretation using as a homework assignment the first scene of *Hamlet*. The scene begins with these seven lines:

BARNARDO Who's there?
FRANCISCO Nay, answer me. Stand and unfold yourself.
BARNARDO Long live the King!
FRANCISCO Barnardo.
BARNARDO He.
FRANCISCO You come most carefully upon your hour.
BARNARDO 'Tis now struck twelve. Get thee to bed, Francisco.

Something is wrong here. Usually it is the standing guard who challenges a new arrival. In this case, the challenge comes from Barnardo, who is relieving Francisco on the watch. Perhaps they cannot see each other, or Francisco has fallen asleep or is not in his place. However, as we learn later in the play, Denmark is in a state of readiness for war. For the man on guard to be surprised does not bode well. Barnardo's "Long live the King" seems like a password or an identification code. Francisco further states, "You come most carefully upon your hour." The word "carefully" in this context implies a variety of choices and meanings. Barnardo seems nervous. He informs us that it is midnight (what happens at midnight?) and he implies that he wants Francisco to leave: "Get thee to bed, Francisco." Usually if someone is a little apprehensive, he would want company.

In the next section of lines, Francisco foreshadows a sense of dread with his "And I am sick at heart," which prompts Barnardo's "Have you had quiet guard?" Francisco informs us that nothing has happened and once again hints that he'd like to leave: "Well, good night." Barnardo immediately asks Francisco to make sure that Horatio and Marcellus, who should be on their way, "make haste." Hearing them, Francisco acts correctly, this time with a challenge: "Stand! Who's there?" No soldier, Horatio replies, "Friends to this ground," and Marcellus, a soldier, adds, "And liegemen to the Dane," which bears a similarity to Barnardo's "Long live the King." Before Francisco leaves, Marcellus asks, "Who hath relieved you?" This tells us two things. Marcellus cannot see Barnardo, and Marcellus knows that Barnardo is supposed to have relieved Francisco by this time and needs to check. He reinforces his need to know with his "honest soldier."

We learn later in the scene that Francisco has not seen the Ghost, that Marcellus and Barnardo have, and that it would not speak to them. The apprehension and tension in the scene now made clear.

The resulting descriptive narrative of one group might read like this:

Hamlet
Act 1, scene 1

The bell strikes twelve. A man is discovered on stage asleep.

Enter Barnardo a sentinel trying to be as quiet as possible. The sleeping figure lets out a snore. Barnardo slamming the base of his pike onto the floor immediately gets into an attack position. The sleeping man awakes, jumps up and with the same action presents himself to Barnardo in an identical pose. The two men recognize each other. Barnardo salutes and points to the bells. Barnardo tries to get Francisco to leave. Francisco takes his time implying that he has had a bad night. Hearing a noise, Francisco suddenly wheels around, slams his pike onto the floor, and faces in a new direction with his pike at the ready. Enter Horatio and Marcellus. They salute. Francisco returns their salutes. As he is about to leave, Marcellus takes him aside and whispers in his ear. Francisco nods and points to Barnardo. Francisco exits. Marcellus, Horatio, and Barnardo, looking around, huddle together in group.

Naturally this is only one of many possible versions. In a modern interpretation, for example, Barnardo would point to his watch instead of the bells. You can quickly build a collection of excerpted scenes of your own by asking your students to give you permission to use their narrations for other classes.

In assigning a scene to be performed in this way, you have asked your students to analyze a scene on their own. Their creative efforts will demand scholarly, literary, and theatrical techniques involving an active collaborative relationship with the playwright and his language.

PART THREE

In the Classroom

.

N<small>ANCY</small> G<small>OODWIN</small>
E<small>DITOR</small>

In "The Celtic Element in Literature," W. B. Yeats talks about the rituals of the ancient Celts, who waved their hands and murmured and danced "until they felt their souls overtopping the moon," implying boldly that it is possible for humans to combine language and movement for the expansion of personal energy. This sort of expansion is what I imagine will happen to your students as they move through the Shakespeare units in this section.

How will they expand? Will their emotions intensify? Will they see the scenes more clearly? Will their minds analyze and synthesize elements more often? Will they bond more completely with the characters? Will they see the dramatic situations from multiple points of view? All of this and more, for the central approach our editing team uses is whole-brained and intense. I think of it as *informed performance.* Our chief method is acting. Movement with language. Get the students on their feet, give them a script of a Shakespeare scene, run the lines through their brains and mouths and bodies several times, let them move and interact in the manner that the words suggest, force them to work out for themselves what the lines say, and then, when they are full of Shakespeare's language and movement, ask them questions and let them make decisions with the authority of experienced actors.

But the method doesn't stop there, for our purpose is not to help students know more about acting but to help them know more about Shakespeare. We ask student actors to use their experienced eyes to look more closely at Shakespeare's language: to compare a speech with a companion passage, to read a speech in a quarto or folio edition, to trace images, to consult the *Oxford English Dictionary* about the denotation of a particular word at the time Shakespeare penned it. As *Shakespeare Set Free: Teaching* Hamlet *and* Henry IV, Part 1 fuses scholarship and acting, so do the teaching units.

It was not a hasty fusion. For four years we planned and tested and culled and balanced activities to inform and energize your students. We designed the units to be taught back to back. Besides thematic ties, there are teaching ties. The log assignments, acting skills, and language activities begun in *Hamlet* carry over to *Henry IV, Part 1.* For the teachers and students who take on both units, the rewards are "express and admirable." However, time is precious in a classroom, so many of you will be able to schedule only one. Therefore, we also designed the units to stand on their own. It is true that for the *Henry* unit we imagined some sort of previous Shakespeare experience, but that is not required. Either unit could be a "palpable hit" with students who are inexperienced with, or even hostile to, Shakespeare.

So here it is. A way to teach Shakespeare through informed performance. This work is yours with all our best wishes. Move through it with tumult. Expand. Overtop, if not the moon, your expectations of what teaching Shakespeare in the classroom can be.

Nancy Goodwin
Clinton High School
Clinton, Oklahoma

Hamlet

•

Patricia Thisted
EDITOR

Dear Colleagues,

In the text of the New Folger edition of *Hamlet* you will find 421 question marks. The play begins with Barnardo asking, "Who's there?," and the word *question* appears fifteen times in the script. Whenever a play asks as many questions as *Hamlet* does, we can be sure that audiences, readers, actors, directors, and scholars will expend considerable effort to find answers.

As teachers, we often have the tendency to answer these questions for our students by explaining and interpreting the text. We tell them what the play "is supposed to mean." This unit is designed to provide students with an opportunity to discover their own answers to the questions asked in *Hamlet*. By finding ways for students to make personal connections with *Hamlet*, we stop being translators, and students take over the role of teacher themselves.

When Diane Mertens and I first worked on this unit at the Folger Library, we realized that we had very different teaching situations and very different teaching styles. Diane teaches in a coeducational college-prep Catholic school in Madison, Wisconsin, and deals with honors and advanced-placement students. I teach in a small rural community on the eastern plains of Colorado where longhorn cattle graze not far from my classroom window; my school has neither honors nor advanced-placement English classes. What our students do have in common is a willingness to work hard on difficult material and a recognition of the need to risk in order to succeed. Through three years we implemented our ideas, modified, added and eliminated material, argued over methods, and generally kept open a dialogue from which this unit has resulted. The strategies have been tested and retested with students in vastly different but real classroom situations.

Our experiences with these students have convinced us that the single most efficient tool for unlocking Shakespeare's language is performance. Students who would otherwise approach *Hamlet* with fear and boredom can be "hooked" into the play from the beginning if they are actively involved in decisions about the ways to approach and enact the text.

As you use the daily plans, you will notice that we have included a variety of activities, many more than can realistically fit into a class period. One reason for this is to provide a sampling of the activities that have been successful in our classrooms.

Second, because of students' diverse learning styles, different activities will be variously successful with different students. Some will benefit from the physicalizing of soliloquies; others will learn more from their daily logs. Feel free to pick and choose; you know what will be effective with your students. When we've given directions, these are only guidelines. You must be the judge of what will work and how much to assign. Feel free to eliminate lines, speeches, even scenes. Directors do it all the time. The most revolutionary and liberating thing that we have learned from our association with the Folger is that students needn't read every word of a play. They'll get it quite nicely anyway.

The one element that you cannot eliminate is performance. We perceive performance as vertical textual analysis. Actors must pay close attention to the text to make the characters and the plot come to life for the audience. In the same way, students must use the text to make choices about the way they will perform. You will find them arguing about words and lines, discussing interpretations of how to enact a scene. In short, they will have become active learners, not just people sitting at desks.

Be willing to take a risk. The approach we are advocating is indeed risky. As teacher, you will no longer be in charge of what your students learn. As they take on responsibility for what they learn, they will gradually take charge themselves.

Because students will be learning differently and will choose to learn different things—not fewer, just different—we encourage you to resist the urge to evaluate their learning with traditional quizzes and tests. We evaluate logs (usually on the thoroughness of the responses), dramatic reading, acting company performance and prompt books, essays or shorter writing assignments. We also have students choose lines that they'd like to "own" through memorizing them.

Students say that their journey through *Hamlet* has indeed been difficult but that they feel a wonderful sense of accomplishment at the end. They have experienced a Shakespearean play meaningfully and feel confident that they can handle another in the future.

Good luck as you embark on your journey through this unit. I believe that, like our students, you will feel a new sense of accomplishment as you help students make their own connections with *Hamlet*.

Pat Thisted

Pat Thisted
Ellicott Junior-Senior High School
Ellicott, Colorado

UNIT CALENDAR FOR
Hamlet

1	2	3	4	5
LESSON 1 Logs	LESSON 2 Acting 1.1 Text: 1.1.1–80	LESSON 2 Acting 1.1 *(cont.)* Text: 1.1.1–80	LESSON 3 Hamlet vs. Claudius Text: 1.2	LESSON 4 Hamlet's Mental State Text: 1.2.133–64
6	**7**	**8**	**9**	**10**
LESSON 5 The Second Family Text: 1.3	LESSON 6 The Ghost in Performance Text: 1.5	LESSON 7 Spies and Informants Text: 2.1	LESSON 8 A Closer Look at Language Text: 2.2.187–574	LESSON 9 The "O, what a rogue" Soliloquy Text: 2.2.576–634
11	**12**	**13**	**14**	**15**
LESSON 10 Voicing the Argument Text: 3.1.64–98	LESSON 11 The Nunnery Scene Text: 3.1.99–175	LESSON 12 The Nunnery Scene on Video Text: 3.1.99–175	LESSON 13 Acting "The Mousetrap" Text: 3.2.98–321	LESSON 14 "The Mousetrap" on Video Text: 3.2.98–321
16	**17**	**18**	**19**	**20**
LESSON 15 Physicalized Speech Presentations Text: 3.2.419–32; 3.3.40–101	LESSON 16 The Closet Scene Text: 3.4	LESSON 17 Character Committees Text: 4.1–4.7	LESSON 17 Character Committees *(cont.)* Text: 4.1–4.7	LESSON 18 The Mad Scene Text: 4.5
21	**22**	**23**	**24**	**25**
LESSON 19 The Gravediggers Scene Text: 5.1	LESSON 20 The Last Gasp Text: 5.2	LESSON 21 Questions	LESSON 22 Making a Scene: *Hamlet* Festival in Rehearsal	LESSON 22 Festival Rehearsal *(cont.)*
26	**27**	**28**		
LESSON 22 Festival Rehearsal *(cont.)*	LESSON 22 Festival Rehearsal *(cont.)*	LESSON 22 Festival Performances		

LESSON 1 "The Ratifier and Props of Every Word"

Logs

WHAT'S ON FOR TODAY AND WHY

In the course of this unit, our goal is for students to

- develop an appreciation of Shakespeare's language
- use performance as a way to understand Shakespeare's language
- understand that the text of *Hamlet* is a script containing textual and subtextual signals
- learn and use several close-reading techniques
- recognize universal themes found in *Hamlet*.

To help students reach all these goals, we ask them to keep reading logs. We have used the word "log" rather than "journal" or "notebook" since a log is a record of a journey. Ideally, students enter their comments on action, character, and language after reading a scene rather than writing several entries at once. The logs thus become the record of each student's journey through the play.

If students are conscientious about keeping the logs daily, they will take very little time. Often our students include class notes in their logs, thus keeping a truly complete record of their journeys through *Hamlet*.

Having students write in logs and teachers evaluate the writing may seem an arduous task, one easily eliminated from the long list of possible assignments. However, our experience has been that logs are where students come to grips with the play on their own terms and teachers learn what students really think.

We tell students to be absolutely honest in their logs, to write what they're thinking and feeling about the play at any given time. For us, one of the most helpful components of the log assignment sheet is item 3, "Questions." Sometimes the very act of posing a question helps the student to answer it for himself, and we have found those answers tucked within the entries.

So we begin the *Hamlet* unit with logs and questions.

WHAT TO DO

1. Establish the Log

Tell students that they are about to begin a study of *Hamlet* and that a central part of this study will be to keep a log. Talk to students about the log. Establish its importance from day one and set firm expectations for keeping the log throughout the unit.

Distribute Handout 1: The Log. Talk through it. Answer questions.

Emphasize that logs are an *ongoing assignment*. Tell students to make a log entry after every reading assignment, even if there is other homework and even if you don't remind them.

2. Model Entries

If you like, read one or two entries other students have written. On Handout 1, there are several—all unedited, all from "regular" senior English classes at Ellicott Junior-Senior High School in Ellicott, Colorado.

3. Write

For their first log entry, ask students to write questions about *Hamlet*, about Shakespeare, about the unit.

4. Respond

Invite students to read entries aloud. See if they can answer one another's questions. Use this golden moment to answer questions about Shakespeare and show your enthusiasm for *Hamlet*. There won't be many times in life when another human will ask you "Where did Shakespeare learn to write?" or "What's the big deal about *Hamlet?*"

HOW DID IT GO?

As you read the logs, you will find clues about an important question for any unit: What do students want to know?

ॐ

HANDOUT 1

THE LOG

While reading the play, you will keep a log (that is, a record) of your journey through it. Log entries will consist of such things as scene summaries; comments on the action, characters, language, themes, and so forth; and your personal reactions to those elements of the play.

Record all log entries in a notebook.

You are in charge of your own personal log. You will decide what to write and in what form, but there are three rules:

1. Clearly label each entry with the act and scene number.
2. Write after every reading assignment.
3. Over the course of the play, respond to a variety of the components so that by the end you will have considered each component several times.

Write in your own voice. Interact with the play. Grades will be based on the thoroughness of your responses.

Entries: For each scene, do a minimun of *three* of the following:

1. Summarize the action of the scene.

2. Comment in one sentence on what you think is the significance of this scene. What would the play be like without it?

3. Ask questions about the scene. Has anything in the scene caused you confusion? Ask one of the characters in the scene a question—or ask me a question.

   Example:

   2.1—Questions: Polonius—what's your problem? Reynaldo—are you going to spread the bad word about Laertes? I hope you don't. Ophelia—how strongly do you feel about Hamlet? you'd better avoid him totally before something terrible happens! Hey, Hamlet—what are your feelings toward Ophelia? Do you care about her? (Kenda White)

4. Quote lines from the scene that you enjoyed and comment on them.

   Example:

   1.1—Horatio says "Most like. It harrows me with fear and wonder." This line really explains to us what all three of the guards are feeling when they see this ghost. They are all frightened by it, yet they wonder why it came to them and why it is dressed the way it is. It really sets the mood for the whole scene because it lets us know that they are anxious. The first few lines in this scene really shocked me because we didn't know anything about these characters yet they were all so nervous and jumpy. Plus they were very suspicious and cautious of everything. (Daniel Grooms)

5. Describe your reactions to a character, action, or idea you confronted in the scene.

Example:

1.2—King Claudius seems like a flake to me. He seems to know what he's talking about but to me it's like it's rehearsed or something. I can understand him trying to be friends with Hamlet, but it seems to me that he is just doing it to make himself look good. I don't think he means anything of what he said to Hamlet. (Julia Abernathy)

6. Talk about the relationships characters have to one another, quoting specific words or phrases to give evidence for your opinion.

Example:

4.1—I'm not sure if Gertrude is honest to Claudius or Hamlet. I can't decide if she's trying to BS Claudius or if she has betrayed Hamlet. I felt really confused about just who was on whose side. I want Gertrude to just be covering for Hamlet, telling Claudius what he thinks he already knows, not that Hamlet is in complete control. But then again Hamlet told his mother not to go to Claudius and she did, so Gertrude doesn't seem so great to me. (Dani Doty)

7. Pretend you are an actor playing one of the characters in the scene. Get inside that character's mind. Tell how the character feels about herself, about other characters, about the situation of the scene.

Example:

1.2—I feel sorry for Hamlet! He comes home to find out that his mother is married to his uncle and his father is dead. Then to find out that his buds are seeing his father's ghost! He's really getting confused and messed in the head. No wonder he wishes it was legal to commit suicide. This poor kid must have some problems, big time! I think he's getting curious as to why this all is happening at once. I think he's getting a whiff of a dead rat! (J.A.)

LESSON 2 "The Whisper Goes So"

Acting 1.1

ॐ

PLAY SECTION COVERED IN THIS LESSON

1.1.1–80 The guards and Horatio see the ghost of the dead King Hamlet.

LINES: Barnardo, 27; Francisco, 9; Marcellus, 21; Horatio, 26

ॐ

WHAT'S ON FOR TODAY AND WHY

Saying the words and acting Act 1, scene 1, lines 1–80 (1.1.1–80) gives students immediate knowledge of the people, situations, and wordplay in *Hamlet*. So we will begin with acting. We will use the methods of Michael Tolaydo and Rosemary Walsh, so a review of their articles in Part Two of this volume would be the perfect start.

To help create the mood, if you like, bring costumes and props for students to use. Since 1.1 is a night scene, turn off the lights. A few cloaks and swords will do wonders.

Because establishing the actors' approach is so important, we will allow two days for this lesson.

WHAT TO DO

1. Read Around

Distribute photocopies of 1.1.1–80 ("Who's there?" to "This bodes some strange eruption to our state") with stage directions and notes removed. Have students sit in a circle; then ask them to read the scene round-robin, stopping at each period, question mark, and exclamation point.

While reading, ask students to circle unfamiliar words. Then have the class look up and discuss the meanings, making sure students have a sense of the scene.

Then have students reread the scene round-robin, changing readers each time the character changes, paraphrasing each line from Elizabethan into their own words, perhaps into modern slang.

2. Questions

Ask the following questions about 1.1.1–80, making sure all answers come by referring to the text. Here are some suggestions:

- Who are these people? Where are they, and what are they doing?
- What information does Shakespeare provide about the physical setting?
- What atmosphere/mood is created by this setting?
- What do the physical aspects of the setting suggest about the characters' behavior?
- What does the opening question "Who's there?" imply about Barnardo and about the situation?
- Does anything in the conversation between Barnardo and Francisco reinforce these implications?
- What additional information do we gain about Barnardo and Francisco from their conversation?
- Shakespeare wrote into the body of the play many signals and directions. What do the commands and questions in lines 1–20 suggest about staging this scene?
- What inferences can be drawn about Horatio's character? about his relationship to the guards?

3. Deciding How to Play the Ghost

Examine the entrance of the Ghost. What does the Ghost do once it is on stage? How does the Ghost's appearance affect the other characters? the audience? (You should avoid prematurely informing students of your knowledge of the description of the Ghost by Horatio and Marcellus in 1.4. Allow the students to form their own initial impressions and to change them later as they get more information from the text.)

4. Setting the Scene

What is the mood of this scene? What does the set look like? Where would you put the entrances and the exits? Who should be positioned where? What do the actors need for props?

5. Acting the Scene

Ask for volunteers to get the scene on its feet. The rest of the students will act as directors. Frequently stop the actors to ask the directors for help. How should actors move, stand, sit? What actions are suggested by the lines? What actions can be added, especially by actors who aren't speaking?

Have the students try the scene several ways. Change actors frequently so each student gets a chance to perform.

6. Homework

Ask students to read 1.1 and 1.2 and write in their logs, following the format established in Handout 1.

HOW DID IT GO?

Ask students to do an oral evaluation of the scene. Ask: Which of the student-directed choices worked and why? What were the apparent purposes of the opening scene? What predictions can the students make about future events based on the opening lines of scene 1?

Did students get involved in the text? Did they object to classmates' suggestions and argue about the right way to stage the scene? If so, they are listening to Shakespeare's language and learning about the people in *Hamlet*.

LESSON 3 "Weighing Delight and Dole"

Hamlet vs. Claudius

PLAY SECTIONS COVERED IN THIS LESSON

1.2.1–39 In his opening speech, Claudius takes command of the action.

LINES: Claudius, 39

1.2.66–96 Claudius tells Hamlet to cast off his black clothes and heavy mourning.

LINES: Claudius, 9; Queen, 8; Hamlet, 14

1.2.133–164 Hamlet's "O, that this too, too sullied flesh" soliloquy.

LINES: Hamlet, 32

WHAT'S ON FOR TODAY AND WHY

Exploring subtext is an actor's way of getting inside a character and deciding what the character might be thinking as he speaks a certain group of words. Word choice and choice of idiom or metaphor can *suggest* a speaker's attitudes or motives. For example, I might say to you, "Oh my, you got your hair cut last night!" Since "Oh my" in our part of the twentieth century usually expresses mild dismay, the sentence implies distaste for the haircut. Thus, I might be thinking, "What a terrible hair style. It makes her look like a sheep dog."

In this lesson, we will ask students to speculate on what a character is thinking as she speaks. To lead them to make informed judgments, we will ask them to look closely at the words the characters use and how they use them. Instead of continually using the teacher as interpreter ("This means . . . ") and as chorus ("This is really very funny"), we will help students draw their own conclusions based on careful reading.

WHAT TO DO

1. Important Questions from the Log Assignment

In their reading assignment after Lesson 2, students encountered a number of problems that affect *Hamlet*, any one of which could take a class period to discuss. Although we can't give them a great deal of time, let the students bring up the issues most on their minds. Ask: In reading scenes 1 and 2, did you come across situations or comments that could cause problems for Hamlet? Students usually mention Claudius's drinking, his taunting of Hamlet with barbs like "unmanly grief," his letting Laertes go back to school but not Hamlet; Hamlet's foolhardiness in following the Ghost against the advice of his companions.

2. Getting the Politics Right

Since students could be unclear about the political situation between Denmark and Norway, discuss this with them, asking students to look to the text for references to the tension (men on guard, for example).

3. Close Reading of Claudius's Opening Speech

Examine Claudius's initial speech to show how language reveals character.

- *Use of royal "we":* In Shakespeare's time, when kings or queens represented their countries and talked about public issues, they used the royal "we"; when dealing with private matters, they used "I." When a monarch switches from first-person plural to first-person singular, this is a textual clue that signals a change in situation or tone. Why does Claudius continue to use the royal "we" when addressing Hamlet, whom he calls his "son"?
- *Antithesis:* Look for antithesis, the balancing of two contrasting ideas, words, phrases, or sentences in parallel grammatical form: "An auspicious and a drooping eye," "with mirth in funeral and with dirge in marriage," and so forth. What feelings do these juxtapositions evoke?
- *Choice of words:* Why does Claudius remember old Hamlet with "wisest sorrow" rather than "deep sorrow"? Why does he say it "befitted" them to bear their "hearts in grief"? The class might brainstorm different synonyms for these words and compare the effectiveness of their word choices to the words in the text.
- *Order of ideas he presents:* Although Hamlet's mourning is of major concern to Claudius, why does he justify his marriage to Gertrude, deal with Norway's impending invasion, and respond to Laertes's petition before he addresses Hamlet?

4. Looking for the Underlying Thoughts of Hamlet and Claudius

Examine the exchange between Claudius and Hamlet in 1.2.66–96 ("But now, my cousin Hamlet and my son" to "To do obsequious sorrow") with an emphasis on understanding the subtext of each character in this scene.

Ask: When Claudius says, "But now, my cousin Hamlet and my son," what does he really want? What is he thinking? Why might he choose a public place to greet Hamlet?

Ask: When Hamlet says, "'Seems,' madam? Nay, it is. I know not 'seems,'" what does he really mean? What is he thinking about his mother? Why does Hamlet use puns (like the pun on "kind," which can mean "affectionate" or "natural and lawful" in line 67, and the pun on "common," which can mean both "universal occurrence" and "vulgar" in line 76) and riddles (like his reply in line 69, "Not so, my lord. I am too much in the sun," to Claudius's question "How is it that the clouds still hang on you?") when he speaks to Gertrude and Claudius?

5. Homework

Ask students to read aloud Hamlet's soliloquy "O, that this too, too sullied flesh" (1.2.133–164) several times and paraphrase it in their logs. Then ask them to note signals in the language that give clues to Hamlet's innermost thoughts—for example, choice of words, construction of phrases, sequence of thought. Does he hide behind puns as he does with Claudius? What does the antithesis reveal?

HOW DID IT GO?

If you refused to guide their reactions to Claudius and Hamlet and if students began to grapple with the language of the scene, the lesson was terrific. At this point, we don't expect our students to comprehend Claudius and Hamlet in all their complexity. This is difficult stuff, and it will take a while. As long as they're making the effort, trust the system.

LESSON 4 "It Cannot Come to Good"

Hamlet's Mental State

❧ _____

PLAY SECTION COVERED IN THIS LESSON

1.2.133–164 Hamlet soliloquizes on his mother's hasty remarriage.

LINES: Hamlet, 32

❧ _____

WHAT'S ON FOR TODAY AND WHY

The "sullied flesh" soliloquy is rich with words that produce pictures in the mind. Because these pictures flash by so quickly, we can help students enjoy a stronger visual effect by slowing down and focusing on the images. To make them tangible, we will ask students to illustrate them with physical objects. For this lesson, you will need bags of props—any odd junk will do. Also, you will need art pads or blank paper and magic markers so that if students want to use a prop that is not in the bag, they can quickly sketch it.

For an excellent example of this technique, see the videotape *Teaching Shakespeare: New Approaches from the Folger Library*, available from Vineyard Video Productions, Elias Lane, West Tisbury, Massachusetts 02575. Here a student physicalizes Sonnet 130, "My mistress' eyes are nothing like the sun," with a Walkman, sunglasses, mirror, and rouge.

This lesson will include the first in a series of performances that are scattered throughout this unit. Students will act with script in hand. Because it is essential for students to do the assignment well, we will give them Handout 2: Preparing Scenes for Performance and lead them through it so they will hear in concrete terms what we expect them to do to prepare.

Here is a preview of the scenes we will perform in class. You can assign them all now or as they come up.

- **1.5.1–98** ("Wither wilt thou lead me?" to "Adieu, adieu, adieu. Remember me"). Claiming that he is the spirit of Hamlet's father, the Ghost asks Hamlet to avenge the murder of King Hamlet.
  LINES: Hamlet, 12; Ghost, 86

- **2.2.187–237** ("How does my good Lord Hamlet?" to "These tedious old fools"). Polonius tries to draw out Hamlet on the subject of Ophelia.
LINES: Polonius, 24; Hamlet, 27

- **2.2.240–338** ("My honored lord" to "man delights not me"). Hamlet meets Rosencrantz and Guildenstern, whom he exposes as spies from Claudius.
LINES: Guildenstern, 11; Rosencrantz, 17; Hamlet, 72

- **3.2.96–317** ("They are coming to the play," to "Come, the recorders!"). Hamlet uses rude remarks to stir up the audience. The players perform a play about a king murdered by poison in the ear.
LINES: Player King, 44; Player Queen, 31; Prologue, 3; Hamlet, 64; Queen, 3; King, 7; Rosencrantz, 2; Lucianus, 7; Polonius, 7; Horatio, 4; Ophelia, 19

- **5.1** Hamlet finds the gravediggers comical until he learns that the grave is Ophelia's.
LINES: Gravedigger, 110; Other, 18; Hamlet, 134; Horatio, 12; King, 10; Queen, 12; Laertes, 18; Doctor, 14

- **5.2.239–449** (from "Come, Hamlet, come and take this hand from me" to "Go, bid the soldiers shoot"). The final fight.
LINES: King, 27; Hamlet, 75; Laertes, 35; Osric, 8; Queen, 7; Horatio, 32; Fortinbras, 19; Ambassador, 6

To evaluate students, use class comments, a short checklist of your own devising, or the classy evaluation form in Lesson 3 of the *Henry IV, Part 1* teaching plans.

WHAT TO DO

1. Reviewing Homework

Ask students to get out their soliloquy paraphrase and subtext work. Even though we know there are no definitive answers, ask: What is really bothering Hamlet?

2. Planning the Physical

Divide students into groups of three to five and send them off with a sack of props, a drawing pad, a bag of magic markers, their logs, and these instructions:

- Read the soliloquy aloud twice.
- Combine the best of the paraphrases in your logs to piece out what Hamlet is saying.
- Physicalize the soliloquy with props, drawings, or students posing as statues. That is, select physical objects to hold up while certain words or phrases are read. For example, as the narrator reads "sullied flesh,"

another student might hold up a bandaged arm. For "melt, thaw, and resolve itself into a dew," students might hold up a series of quick drawings—an ice cream cone starting to drip, an ice cream cone dripping profusely, an ice cream cone reduced to a puddle. Or a student could mime a melting ice cube.

3. Physicalizing the Soliloquy

Have students present their performances. Talk about why students used the props they did. Again, ask the unanswerable: What is really bothering Hamlet?

4. Introduction to Scene Performance

Explain how the class will use the actor's approach to Shakespeare. Pass out Handout 2: Preparing Scenes for Performance. Review it thoroughly. Solidify expectations. Encourage students who are preparing scenes to get together outside class for rehearsal.

Assign some students to prepare 1.5.1–98 to be presented during the lesson after next. Since the part of the Ghost is large, suggest a "revolving door" technique; that is, four students can stand back to back and alternate choral reading with individual reading as they slowly turn to face the audience. For costumes, the Ghosts might wear cardboard armor or military caps. Tell students if and how you will evaluate the scene.

HOW DID IT GO?

If students came up with concrete images for various words in the soliloquy, you're right on. If students who usually feel overwhelmed by the language got involved, even better. If all students helped one another to "see" more pictures in the soliloquy, the lesson was perfect.

ﻉﻼ

HANDOUT 2

PREPARING SCENES FOR PERFORMANCE

Follow the steps listed below. Your goal is to communicate the written text, to "flesh out" the character you will perform. Focus on tone of voice, stress and inflection, effective use of pauses, and, if you like, movement.

1. Read your part *aloud* several times.

2. Check the definitions of words you don't know.

3. Answer the following questions about your character to help you with your interpretation. Write the answers to these questions in your log.

   - What does your character want in the chosen scene?
   - What does the character do to get it?
   - What obstacles stand in his or her way?
   - How does your character really feel about what is happening in the scene? How can you tell?
   - What do other characters say about your character in the scene?
   - What does the character's language reveal about his or her personality? Think about the meaning behind his or her words. Write down a few phrases he says that might demonstrate something about his or her personality or are characteristic of his or her mode of expression.
   - How has this scene added to your knowledge of the character?

4. Look at relationships among characters in the scene.

5. Use both the text and your own creativity to help you find a suitable prop or costume that represents your character.

6. Arrange a rehearsal with other students in your scene before you perform.

ﻉﻼ

5

"The Effect of This Good Lesson Keep"

The Second Family—Meet Laertes, Ophelia, and Polonius

&

PLAY SECTION COVERED IN THIS LESSON

1.3 Before he leaves for France, Laertes gives advice to his sister, then listens to advice from his father.

LINES: Laertes, 54; Ophelia, 21; Polonius, 70

&

WHAT'S ON FOR TODAY AND WHY

Students will relate a situation in the play to their own experiences by doing a contemporary improvisation. Additionally, they will explore relationships in Polonius's family and compare these to the relationships in the royal family. They will explore language devices as ways of analyzing character.

Read "The Play's the Thing" by Rosemary Walsh on page 49 in Part Two of this book. Then, if you've received the Warner Brothers video *Mel Gibson Goes Back to School with* Hamlet, preview it to see a good example of contemporary improvisation. In one part, Gibson has groups of students act out Horatio telling Hamlet about the Ghost, and in another scene we see Polonius questioning Ophelia about what Laertes said. This is in the segment that deals with language. If your school has not received a copy, find one and make a copy of it, since copying has been authorized. Watching the scene will help you understand how to direct students in contemporary improvisation. If you want to show your students this video, do it, but do it *after* they've created their own improvisations. Students relate well to the informal way Gibson deals with the text.

WHAT TO DO

1. Improvisations

Divide students into groups of three. Give them ten to fifteen minutes to prepare a contemporary improvisation of 1.3. Ask students to paraphrase the language of the script in colloquial speech and make up a parallel situation in which the words make sense; perform it as if it were happening today.

Circulate. Observe. Choose one or two groups to perform for the class.

2. Family Relationships

Using 1.3 as a basis for their answers, ask students to describe the family relationships: Laertes and Ophelia, Polonius and Laertes, Polonius and Ophelia. What does each of these people want? How do they treat each other? How is this family similar to or different from the Claudius/Gertrude/Hamlet family? the Old Hamlet/Gertrude/Hamlet family?

3. Polonius's Language Clues

With students, carefully examine the language of Polonius's "Give thy thoughts no tongue" speech by focusing on his language:

- Look at "but" constructions—"Be thou familiar, but by no means vulgar," for example. What is their effect?
- What can we infer about Polonius from his choice of words? What do Polonius's words reveal about his beliefs, philosophy, and values?

4. Homework

Ask students to read 1.4 and 1.5 and write in logs.

HOW DID IT GO?

If each student participated in a contemporary improvisation and could see the relationship of his improvisation to the Polonius/Ophelia/Laertes scene, things are going great. Don't give in to the temptation of telling the students that Polonius is an old fool. Just ask the questions and let them do the work. By referring to the text for the answers, they'll figure it out for themselves—some more quickly than others.

LESSON 6 "I Could a Tale Unfold"

The Ghost in Performance

&

PLAY SECTIONS COVERED IN THIS LESSON

1.5.1–98 Claiming that he is the spirit of Hamlet's father, the Ghost asks Hamlet to avenge the murder of King Hamlet.

LINES: Hamlet, 12; Ghost, 86

1.5.99–212 Hamlet swears Horatio and Marcellus to secrecy, then vows to put on an "antic disposition."

LINES: Hamlet, 89; Ghost, 4; Horatio, 15; Marcellus, 8

&

WHAT'S ON FOR TODAY AND WHY

Students will perform the first of the assigned scenes. The performance will show that students have been wrestling with the language and making appropriate decisions about character, props, diction, and costumes.

Additionally, students will closely examine Hamlet's language after his visit from the Ghost.

WHAT TO DO

1. Performing the Ghost Scene

Ask students to perform 1.5.1–98 and to explain their rationale for choosing props and costumes.

Discuss with actors and audience the acting choices students made and other interpretations, always referring to the text for verification.

2. Unfolding the Tale

Ask students watching the scene to list on the board the information revealed by the Ghost and to talk about its significance.

3. Whither Wilt Thou Lead Me?

Ask students to look at 1.5.99–212. Examine Hamlet's language after he sees the Ghost and during his conversation with Horatio and Marcellus. What assumptions can we make about Hamlet's state of mind from the words he uses and the way he speaks to his companions at this point in the play? Speculate on why Hamlet decides to put on an "antic disposition."

4. Homework

Ask students to read 2.1 and 2.2.1–186 ("Welcome, dear Rosencrantz" to "O, give me leave") and write in logs.

Have two groups prepare scenes:

- Group 1—2.2.187–237, Hamlet's encounter with Polonius
- Group 2—2.2.240–338, Hamlet's meeting with Rosencrantz and Guildenstern

HOW DID IT GO?

If students got involved in the discussion following the performance and risked at least one idea (even if it was off the mark) about Hamlet's language after the appearance of the Ghost, they're learning the strategy you're teaching.

Collect logs any time now for a first evaluation. Student's questions will tell you a great deal about how they are interacting with the text. Base grades on the thoroughness of their responses.

LESSON **7** "Gaming, My Lord"

Spies and Informants

❧ _____

PLAY SECTIONS COVERED IN THIS LESSON

2.1.1–83 Polonius sends Reynaldo to Paris to spy on Laertes.

LINES: Polonius, 69; Reynaldo, 14

2.1.84–134 Ophelia reports to her father that Hamlet, in a disturbed state, visited her.

LINES: Polonius, 23; Ophelia, 28

❧ _____

WHAT'S ON FOR TODAY AND WHY

Further close study of language allows students to recognize character traits. Today we will use pantomime to convey the thoughts in 2.1.84–134. This passage is so rich with concrete images that it is easy to do and great fun.

WHAT TO DO

1. Determining Polonius's Values

Have students read aloud 2.1.1–83. Ask them to find and circle words and phrases that reveal Polonius's values. Then ask what they conclude about Polonius's character. Have them list several character traits they have inferred from Polonius's words and behavior in the scene, and suggest lines from the scene that support this conclusion.

2. Playing the Newly Mad Hamlet

Pantomime what isn't seen in 2.1.84–134. ("My lord, as I was sewing in my closet" to "And to the last bended their light on me"). Divide students into groups of three and have many scenes running simultaneously, or run one scene for the whole class.

Have one student read the lines while the other two mime the prescribed actions, including adjustments to clothing. When, for example, the text calls for Hamlet to enter with "his doublet all unbraced, / No hat upon his head, his stockings fouled, / Ungartered, and down-gyvèd to his ankle," the student playing Hamlet might roll up one pant leg, make his socks look funny, unbutton his shirt, or whatever the student directors think the scene demands.

3. Discussion

Ask: What is Hamlet up to in this scene? Why is he treating Ophelia this way? Why Ophelia, of all people? Does Hamlet love Ophelia? If not, how does he show this? If yes, what possible reasons could he have for putting on this show for her?

Ask: What about Ophelia—does she love Hamlet? What is her reaction to his behavior? Try to pinpoint her feelings for him.

4. Homework

Ask students to read 2.2.187–338 ("How does my good Lord Hamlet?" to "Why did you laugh then, when I said man delights not me?") and write in logs.

Remind the two performance groups that they are up tomorrow.

HOW DID IT GO?

If students are starting to examine the text of the play for the answers to their questions about character, you have made an important breakthrough.

LESSON 8 "Words, Words, Words"

A Closer Look at Language

&

PLAY SECTIONS COVERED IN THIS LESSON

2.2.187–237 Polonius tries to draw out Hamlet about Ophelia.

LINES: Polonius, 24; Hamlet, 27

2.2.240–338 Hamlet meets Rosencrantz and Guildenstern, whom he exposes as spies from Claudius.

LINES: Guildenstern, 11; Rosencrantz, 17; Hamlet, 72

2.2.445–574 Hamlet entices the players to do a small scene.

LINES: Hamlet, 71; First Player, 49; Polonius, 6; Rosencrantz, 1; Guildenstern, 0

&

WHAT'S ON FOR TODAY AND WHY

Students will demonstrate their ability to understand the text by performing it, and they will use mime to visualize the action described in the First Player's speeches (2.2.445–560). Then we will give students the language and experience to analyze text by demonstrating how Shakespeare uses three classical language tricks: double entendre, pun, and classical allusion. Excellent background work for teachers and students alike would be to read "Shakespeare's Hamlet" and "Reading Shakespeare's Language," pages xiii–xxiii in the New Folger edition of *Hamlet*, where Barbara Mowat and Paul Werstine explain clearly and simply the basics of Shakespeare's wordplay in *Hamlet*.

WHAT TO DO

1. Hamlet Attacks Polonius

Ask students who prepared 2.2.187–237 to perform it. Afterward, discuss acting choices the students made. Ask: If you were doing a movie version of this scene, what would the set look like? Where in Elsinore would you place it? What furniture, props, costumes, music, and special effects would you use?

2. Hamlet Attacks Rosencrantz and Guildenstern

Next watch the students who prepared 2.2.240–338. As with the previous scene, question them about setting, props, costumes, acting choices.

3. Exploring the Language in these Scenes

As a class, explore

- *the use of double entendre:* Double entendre is the trick whereby authors set up words or phrases so that they have two meanings—a clean one and a bawdy one. Ask students to search for double entendres in 2.2.187–237. Possible finds: *conceive, conception.*

  Next look at 2.2.240–254. There is a series of double entendres in the exchange between Hamlet and Rosencrantz and Guildenstern, who claim to live about the waist of Lady Fortune: *favors, privates, secret parts.*

  Ask: Why might Hamlet be using these words? Does he mean to be bawdy?

- *the use of pun:* Like double entendres, puns have two levels of meaning; however, it is not required that one of the levels of meaning have a sexual connotation. Ask students to search 2.2.187–237 for puns. Example: "What's the matter?"

4. Letting Students Loose with Language

Look at 2.2.295–338 ("Were you not sent for" to "man delights not me"). Ask students to notice *all* language tricks Shakespeare uses in this passage. Open up all possibilities. Let students have the joy of discovery. They may not know Greek and Latin terms, but they will find much: metaphors, similes, alliteration, anastrophe (reversals), parallel construction, and more.

Ask: Is there any place in these scenes when Hamlet stops playing with Polonius or Rosencrantz and Guildenstern and talks straight from the heart? If so, what happens to the language tricks?

5. What's Hecuba?

Focus on 2.2.445–574. Explain that Shakespeare, like other authors, often refers to people and situations in classical Greek and Roman literature. Ask students to find some *classical allusions* in this passage. The New Folger edition notes help to identify classical standbys like Ilium, Cyclops, Mars. Then ask one student to read the passage while three others mime the actions of Pyrrhus, Priam, and Hecuba, or summarize the tale and show a video version of this scene. The students can see the emotion the player creates and Hamlet's response to the performance.

Discuss possible reasons for Hamlet's interest in the relationships in this trio and how their relationships mirror and do not mirror the plot of *Hamlet*.

HOW DID IT GO?

These scenes are often very difficult for students. The use of double entendre and puns is fairly straightforward, but students might need several more directed questions to help them arrive at their own conclusions about what's going on between Hamlet and Polonius and between Hamlet and his friends Rosencrantz and Guildenstern. Certainly Aeneas' tale of Priam's slaughter is a puzzle. If they're making honest attempts to deal with the text, they're doing fine. By this time, several will be putting it all together.

LESSON **9** **"The Motive and the Cue for Passion"**

The "O, What a Rogue" Soliloquy

ঌ
_____

PLAY SECTION COVERED IN THIS LESSON

2.2.576–634 In the "O, what a rogue" soliloquy, Hamlet berates himself, then develops a plan of action.

LINES: Hamlet, 59

ঌ
_____

WHAT'S ON FOR TODAY AND WHY

Students often find Hamlet's longer soliloquies difficult to understand because of the density of their language. Today we want to pierce that density with sharp questions so that students can see Hamlet's internal conflicts more clearly and feel them more strongly.

Specifically, we will work with the "O, what a rogue" soliloquy and challenge students to think about why Hamlet berates himself so. For homework, we will ask students to contemplate the "To be or not to be" soliloquy. Read ahead to the next lesson. If you decide you want to use the prepared script of this soliloquy, copy Handout 3 and have it ready for today's homework.

Today we will do the first of a series of comparative video workshops. To prepare, read "'I Have Had a Most Rare Vision': Teaching Shakespeare with Video" by Michael LoMonico on page 217. Collect two or three *Hamlet* videotapes:

• The 1948 Laurence Olivier film won Academy Awards for best picture and best actor. It begins with Olivier's infamous line about *Hamlet* being about a "man who couldn't make up his mind." Rosencrantz and Guildenstern are gone, and there are many cuts and changes. Olivier, who said that he was influenced by Dr. Ernest Jones's essay "Hamlet and Oedipus," gives us a Freudian interpretation of the play. Gertrude is played by Eileen Herlie, who was 28; Olivier was 41. Others in the cast include Basil Sydney as Claudius, Jean Simmons as Ophelia, and Stanley Holloway as a Gravedigger. This version is inexpensive and available from The Writing Company (1-800-421-4246).

- The 1969 film directed by Tony Richardson stars Nicol Williamson as Hamlet and Anthony Hopkins as Claudius. It catches the rebellious spirit of the late 1960s and features the pop singer Marianne Faithfull as Ophelia. If you look carefully, you may see Anjelica Houston as one of the court ladies. It is available from The Writing Company (1-800-421-4246).

- The 1970 Hallmark Hall of Fame television production, which stars Richard Chamberlain as Hamlet and Michael Redgrave as Polonius, is not yet available on video but can be rented on 16-millimeter. Directed by Peter Wood and adapted by John Barton, this version features John Gielgud as the Ghost. It is available for rental from Films Inc. (1-800-323-4222).

- The 1980 BBC version, directed by Rodney Bennet, stars Derek Jacobi as Hamlet, Claire Bloom as Gertrude, and Patrick Stewart as Claudius. As for being true to Shakespeare's script, this is the most complete version of the play on this list. It is available from The Writing Company (1-800-421-4246).

- The 1990 New York Shakespeare Festival production, directed by Kevin Kline, has been shown on PBS occasionally but is not available for sale. Kline plays Hamlet, and Diane Venora plays Ophelia.

- The 1990 *Hamlet* directed by Franco Zeffirelli stars Mel Gibson as Hamlet, Glenn Close as Gertrude, Alan Bates as Claudius, and Helena Bonham-Carter as Ophelia. It is available from The Writing Company on videotape or laser disk.

Cue the tapes up to the "O, what a rogue" soliloquy.

WHAT TO DO

1. Phrase and Paraphrase

Have students sit in a circle and read the speech round-robin, each student reading only to a semicolon, period, question mark, or exclamation point. While reading, students can note unfamiliar words. Then discuss meanings, making sure students have a sense of the speech. If there are troublesome lines, paraphrase them.

2. Piercing Questions

Give students a list of to-the-point questions and ask them to wrestle with them:

- It is obvious to the audience or reader that Hamlet is alone onstage. What else, then, could he mean when he begins, "Now I am alone"?
- Why is the Prince calling himself a "rogue" and a "peasant slave"?

- Hamlet compares himself to the player. What does this comparison reveal about Hamlet's self-perception?
- Throughout *Hamlet*, much violence is done to ears. How does Hamlet's "cleave the general ear" relate to other "ear" references? Shakespeare uses the word *ear* twenty-seven times in this play. Do any of these resonate with you?
- Hamlet uses a lot of theatrical terminology in his speech. Find some examples ("cue," "stage," "play"). Why might Hamlet be thinking in theatrical terms?
- Find lines or phrases that explain why Hamlet thinks himself a coward. Do you think he is a coward, or is he acting cautiously by looking for external evidence to prove Claudius's guilt?

A sample of student responses to these questions:

"The questions are a big help. I felt pretty good about the soliloquy before, but answering the questions made me think about it more, and now I understand it better."

"Hamlet feels like garbage, feels like a whore, trapped."

"He's always acting, almost in a play of his own."

"He's asking himself 'who are my friends?' because he can't trust anyone."

"He's finally got everyone away from him. He wants to be alone because of what he has to do."

"He feels like a coward because maybe he's used to 'fixing stuff,' and now he has to take time to figure out what's what."

3. More Questions

Ask: What piercing questions do you have? Invite students to probe aggressively. Turn to other students for the answers.

4. Viewing the Soliloquy

Show two or more videotapes of this speech and compare the actors' interpretations of the soliloquy. Mel Gibson's will please the teenage audience, but Laurence Olivier's is masterful, and perhaps the best of all is Kevin Kline's.

After viewing, ask: What does a visual element add to our understanding of the speech? Does it help to see an actor deliver the soliloquy? How? How does the setting affect your understanding of the soliloquy? What do the tonal elements add? How does being able to hear the words add to your understanding? How does the actor's use of stress, inflection, and pauses affect your understanding of the soliloquy?

5. Homework

Now that students are becoming more adept at soliloquies, ask them to read aloud several times "To be or not to be" (3.1.64–96). Tell them not to worry too much about what every detail means but to get a general idea of Hamlet's thoughts.

HOW DID IT GO?

If the class was noisy and students were actively involved with the text, the lesson went well. If they left the room curious about the questions they raised, what could be better?

LESSON 10   "To Be or Not to Be"

Voicing the Argument

❧

PLAY SECTION COVERED IN THIS LESSON

3.1.64–96 Hamlet debates the question of death.

LINES: Hamlet, 33

❧

WHAT'S ON FOR TODAY AND WHY

To demonstrate that Hamlet's major soliloquies are debates, arguments, discussions and/or discoveries "between self," students will look for the inner argument and script this most famous soliloquy as a debate, which they will perform as a choral reading. In this way, students will hear all sides of Hamlet's serious contemplation of death.

Students can create their own debate script in class, but if you prefer, you can ask them to do it as homework, or you can give them the prepared script, Handout 3: The "To Be" Debate, and have two students rehearse it as homework. If you're really daring, try the "To be" choral reading composed by Nancy Goodwin's students in Clinton, Oklahoma (page 221).

Whichever tactic you take, you will need to locate a tape recorder and a large space for this activity.

WHAT TO DO

1. Convert the Soliloquy to an Argument

Ask students to work in groups and convert the "To be" soliloquy to a script of two voices debating. Remind them that the purpose of dividing the speech is to show the different sides of an inner debate. Choose one script for the class to use for choral reading. Ask the other students to mark their scripts accordingly.

2. Reading with Two Voices

Select two students with contrasting voices and ask them to stand, face each other, and read the selected "To be" script.

3. Practicing with Two Groups of Voices

Divide the class into two groups, putting each group as far away from the other as possible. A commons area or cafeteria would be ideal. If no large space is available, a classroom will work—just warn your neighbors. Each group practices reading one part of the script used in step 2, above. The goals here are to use pitch, tone, inflection, and stress to emphasize the meaning of the words and lines and to read in unison as if each of the two groups were one voice.

4. Reading with Two Groups of Voices

When the groups finish practicing, have them face each other and read their parts loudly and angrily to the other group. While this is going on, you could stand in the middle of the two groups with a tape recorder and record their reading.

5. Hearing the Choral Reading

Reconvene the class and play the tape so that students can hear their performance.

6. Discussing the Soliloquy

Explore the antitheses (see Lesson 3) in the soliloquy and discuss how antithesis demonstrates Hamlet's state of mind. Ask students to say as clearly as possible just what Hamlet's inner argument is and whether he resolves it.

Discuss whether the separation of "voices" helped student understanding of the soliloquy.

7. Homework

Ask students to read 3.1 and write in logs.

Assign the third scene for performance: 3.2.96–317 ("They are coming to the play. I must be idle" to "Come, the recorders!"), to be performed in Lesson 13. The Player King, who has a larger speaking part than other characters in this passage, might be played in the same revolving-door manner as the Ghost in 1.5, using two or more readers.

HOW DID IT GO? The class discussion will let you know to what degree the students understand the complexities of Hamlet's struggle with suicide.

&

HANDOUT 3

THE "TO BE" DEBATE

Reader 1: To be or not to be—that is the question:

Reader 2: Whether 'tis nobler in the mind to suffer
The slings and arrows of outrageous fortune,

Reader 1: Or to take arms against a sea of troubles
And, by opposing, end them.

Reader 2: To die, to sleep—
No more—and by a sleep to say we end
The heartache and the thousand natural shocks
That flesh is heir to—

Reader 1: 'Tis a consummation
Devoutly to be wished.

Reader 2: To die, to sleep—
To sleep, perchance to dream. Ay, there's the rub,
For in that sleep of death what dreams may come,
When we have shuffled off this mortal coil,
Must give us pause.

Reader 1: There's the respect
That makes calamity of so long life.

Reader 2: For who would bear the whips and scorns of time,

Reader 1: Th' oppressor's wrong,

Reader 2: The proud man's contumely,

Reader 1: The pangs of despised love,

Reader 2: The law's delay,

Reader 1: The insolence of office,

Reader 2: And the spurns
       That patient merit of th' unworthy takes,
       When he himself might his quietus make
       With a bare bodkin?

Reader 1: Who would fardels bear,
       To grunt and sweat under a weary life,

Reader 2: But that the dread of something after death,

Reader 1: The undiscovered country from whose bourn
       No traveler returns,

Reader 2: Puzzles the will
       And makes us rather bear those ills we have

Reader 1: Than fly to others that we know not of?

Readers 1 and 2: Thus conscience does make cowards of us all,
       And thus the native hue of resolution
       Is sicklied o'er with the pale cast of thought,
       And enterprises of great pitch and moment
       With this regard their currents turn awry
       And lose the name of action.

LESSON **11** **"Ha, Ha, Are You Honest?"**

The Nunnery Scene

❧

PLAY SECTION COVERED IN THIS LESSON

3.1.99–175 With Polonius and Claudius hiding so that they can overhear the meeting, Ophelia approaches Hamlet, who turns on her, denies having loved her, attacks womanhood, and tells her to get to a nunnery.

LINES: Ophelia, 35; Hamlet, 42

❧

WHAT'S ON FOR TODAY AND WHY

To deepen their understanding of subtext and motivation, students will do the "nunnery" scene (3.1.99–175) several times, using different subtexts and objectives. By *objective* we mean what a character wants in a particular scene, his goal. For example, at the beginning of 3.1, we might say that Claudius's objective is to find out exactly what Hamlet is up to, whether his "confusion" is real or feigned. Acting on this objective, Claudius first questions Rosencrantz and Guildenstern. Then he and Polonius prepare to spy on the meeting between Hamlet and Ophelia. By varying the objective and therefore the subtext for Hamlet in this scene, students will explore several interpretations, looking at the text for clues to performance.

To encourage students to use their scripts, copy this scene so they can write notes in the margins. The homework instructions for this lesson are longer than usual, so save a good piece of time at the end of class or have the performance assignment written out so you can give each actor a copy.

WHAT TO DO

1. Establishing Three Objectives

Divide the class into three groups to direct and perform three interpretations of the nunnery scene:

· Hamlet knows from the beginning of the scene that Polonius and Claudius are watching him.
· Hamlet does not know until later in the scene that he is being watched. The group decides when, based on the script.
· Hamlet never knows that he is being watched.

For each interpretation, ask: What is Hamlet's objective? What specific gestures, inflections, movements, or pauses could an actor use to show this objective? How does this objective affect the subtext? Work this out fully for each situation, looking carefully at the script.

2. Rehearsing with Objectives in Mind

Send the groups off for further analysis and rehearsal. Allow ten to fifteen minutes. Groups must be able to point to evidence in the text to support acting choices they make.

3. Performance

Have each group perform its interpretation of the scene and discuss textual clues used to support the interpretation. Have the class discuss the three possibilities and how each affects the interpretation of Hamlet's character.

4. Homework

Ask students to write in their logs which version of the nunnery scene they prefer and why. Or have students prepare this topic as a one-page paper and evaluate it as you do student essays.

Also ask students to read 3.2 and follow the procedure for writing in their logs.

HOW DID IT GO?

Class discussion at the end of the performances will give you immediate feedback about whether students understand the concept of objective, and their performances will reveal whether they can tie objectives to character behavior and speech. Usually, by this point in the play, things are coming together nicely for most students. They see the characters as complex humans, and although they may not know how it will end, they can predict how these people will affect one another throughout the play.

LESSON 12 "Get Thee to a Nunnery"

The Nunnery Scene on Video

ð

PLAY SECTION COVERED IN THIS LESSON

3.1.99–175 With Polonius and Claudius hiding so that they can overhear the meeting, Ophelia approaches Hamlet, who turns on her, denies having loved her, attacks womanhood, and tells her to get to a nunnery.

LINES: Ophelia, 35; Hamlet, 42

ð

WHAT'S ON FOR TODAY AND WHY

The stage history of the nunnery scene is notable for its diversity. Directors have set it in rooms public and private, paced the tempo fast and slow, made Hamlet violent and tender. One question all directors have to settle: Is Ophelia chaste? The Gibson movie version, for example, presents Ophelia as an innocent young girl. On the other hand, Jeanne Roberts tells us that in one of the sources for *Hamlet* Ophelia is pregnant by Hamlet, an element full of possibilities for a director. The 1993 London stage production with Kenneth Branagh in the lead presented a sexually experienced Ophelia; the nunnery scene was set in her bedroom with Claudius and Polonius hiding in a large wardrobe and Hamlet seducing Ophelia as the scene unfolds.

We have just seen student-directed productions and considered multiple interpretations. To bring the complexities of the nunnery scene into sharper focus, we will compare and contrast two video excerpts. Choose two productions and cue them up to 2.1.97 ("Soft you now, / The fair Ophelia").

WHAT TO DO

1. Nunnery Scene 1

View the first version of the scene. Give students a few minutes to make notes on what they saw. Suppress discussion for the moment.

2. Nunnery Scene 2

Repeat the procedure for the second production.

3. Compare and Contrast

Discuss the two scenes. Make conclusions about the directors' concepts and techniques. Ask students to use the nunnery scene as evidence of Hamlet and Ophelia's romance. How did it start? How long has it gone on? What does Ophelia like about Hamlet? What does Hamlet like about Ophelia? How do they see each other? What do they do together? How much sexual attraction is there between them? What do they fight about? How does Ophelia see their future? How does Hamlet see their future? What aspects of acting, directing, and video technique lead students to these opinions?

4. Homework

Ask students to write in their logs which version of the scene, student or professional, they prefer and to tell why.

Remind the group of their performance of 3.2.96–317 tomorrow.

HOW DID IT GO?

Students generally love to write about the production they like and to explain why they like it. After all of your careful work, students should be using many specific textual references to support their observations and inferences. If your students seem stumped, ask some directed questions to stir up their thoughts and responses.

LESSON **13** "Miching Mallecho"

Acting "The Mousetrap"

🐁 _____

PLAY SECTIONS COVERED IN THIS LESSON

3.2.96–144 Hamlet uses rude remarks to stir up the audience before the play.

LINES: Hamlet, 31; King, 3; Polonius, 5; Ophelia, 7; Rosencrantz, 2; Queen, 1; Horatio, 0

3.2.145–317 The players perform a play about a king murdered by poison in the ear. Claudius is disturbed and leaves.

LINES: Player King, 44 (and dumb show); Player Queen, 31 (and dumb show); Prologue, 3; Hamlet, 33; Ophelia, 12; Queen, 2; King, 4; Lucianus, 7; Polonius, 2; Horatio, 4; Rosencrantz, 0

🐁 _____

WHAT'S ON FOR TODAY AND WHY

The scene performed today is jarring. We see Hamlet harassing Ophelia with nasty cracks, taunting his mother with jibes about her hasty marriage, and manipulating the play to catch the murderer Claudius. The play within the play is a distillation of Hamlet's suspicions, but the scene before the play is also disturbing. Almost every character in the play is present—and hostile.

Do not let this performance go flat. Encourage the extremes of behavior implied in the text.

On page 61 in Part Two of this book, Michael Tolaydo details a terrific exercise involving the dumbshow. It can be a marvelous addition to this lesson.

WHAT TO DO

1. The Performing Mousetrap

Students perform 3.2.96–317.

2. Discussion

Discuss the acting choices students made and alternative interpretations, always referring to the text for verification. Ask: What rude remarks does Hamlet say to Ophelia? How rude are they? Does he insult anyone else? How? At this point in the play, what is driving Hamlet? How much of a risk is he taking with the play experiment? What are the results? Who verifies them? What important information does Hamlet have in his grasp at the end of the scene? To whom can he report this? Is there anybody who could straighten out the situation? What are his options?

Ask: How did the student actors playing Claudius and Gertrude react to the "dumb show"? Why did they make the decisions to act in this manner? What did the student actor playing Claudius do on his line "Give me some light! Away"? Does the "mousetrap" scene prove the Ghost is honest?

3. The Dumb Show

Talk about what happens in the "dumb show" and possible reasons Shakespeare included it in the play.

4. The Player King's Speech

Have students summarize the Player King's speech. This can easily be summed up by focusing on two lines: "But what we do determine oft we break" and "That even our loves should with our fortunes change." Ask:

- What might Hamlet hope to accomplish by the Player King's and Player Queen's speeches?
- Earlier Hamlet asked the Player to "study a speech of some dozen or sixteen lines" that he would write and insert in the play. What possible evidence of Hamlet's inserted lines is there in the "mousetrap" scene?

5. Homework

Each student will prepare a physicalized version of a soliloquy. Divide the class into thirds: one third will work with 3.2.419–432 ("'Tis now the very witching time of night"); another third will take Claudius's speech 3.3.40–76 ("O, my offense is rank"); the final third will do Hamlet's speech 3.3.77–101 ("Now might I do it pat").

To review the instructions for physicalizing a speech, see Lesson 4. Students will share their physicalized passage in Lesson 16.

HOW DID IT GO?

The performance and students' responses will let you know how much of this scene students understand. Post-performance discussion questions will generate further student interaction with the characters, the scene, and Hamlet's actions. Students catch right on to this; it's not at all subtle.

LESSON **14** **"Be Not Too Tame Neither"**

"The Mousetrap" on Video

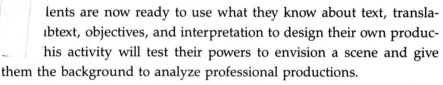

PLAY SECTIONS COVERED IN THIS LESSON

3.2.96–144 Hamlet uses rude remarks to stir up the audience before the play.

̣et, 31; King, 3; Polonius, 5; Ophelia, 7; Rosencrantz, 2; Queen, 1;

The players perform a play about a king murdered by poison in the ̣s is disturbed and leaves.

̣er King, 44 (and dumb show); Player Queen, 31 (and dumb show); ̣; Hamlet, 33; Ophelia, 12; Queen, 2; King, 4; Lucianus, 7; Polonius, 2; ̣Rosencrantz, 0

̣lents are now ready to use what they know about text, transla- ̣btext, objectives, and interpretation to design their own produc- ̣his activity will test their powers to envision a scene and give them the background to analyze professional productions.

For the second part of today's lesson, locate two videotapes and cue them up to 3.2.96–317. The videos starring Derek Jacobi and Mel Gibson are good choices, but any on the list from Lesson 9 would be enjoyable. The Jacobi production script is close to the Folio text; Zefirelli has moved speeches around or cut them totally.

WHAT TO DO

1. Our Mousetrap Production

Invite students to plan in detail a film production of 3.2.96–317, the mousetrap scene. They can have any professional actors they want and an unlimited budget, but not unlimited time: only one fifteen-minute planning session, so use it well. Methodically work through the scene:

- Cast the parts.
- Briefly describe the set. Arrange classroom furniture to approximate the set or have a student draw it on the board.
- Take Hamlet first. What is his body type? What style of movement does he have? Is he jumpy or smooth or lethargic? Does he change at

any point? Does he move around the whole space, or does he stay in a smaller area? What about his facial expressions? tone of voice? Find three or four of his most important lines and figure out how he says them and his facial expressions as he says them.

· Do the same sort of work for Ophelia, then Claudius, then Gertrude.
· How will you do the players? What style of actors are they? What props, tricks, costumes, will they use? Where will they stage the play?
· What will you do with Horatio? Where can you put him so the audience can see him observing the King?

2. Mousetrap Scene—Version 1

View the first version of the mousetrap scene. Write about it. Allow quiet interaction, but don't let discussion rage until students have seen both scenes and written about them.

3. Mousetrap Scene—Version 2

Go through the same steps for the second production. Suppress discussion until students are finished writing.

4. Comparison

Now let the comments spew forth.

5. Essay

Assign an essay based on the productions. Allow at least a week for the students to complete this assignment. Many will want to see the scenes again, so put the tapes on reserve in the media center or check them out to students overnight. *Topic:* Choose the production of the mousetrap scene you like best. Discuss the interpretation the acting company is trying to convey. Then discuss the acting in this interpretation. Include such things as Hamlet's behavior toward Ophelia, the staging of the play within a play, Claudius's and Gertrude's reactions, the movement in the scene.

6. Homework

Ask students to read 3.3 and 3.4 and write in their logs.

HOW DID IT GO?   To evaluate this lesson, ask yourself:

· Did students build a credible scene using Shakespeare's words and their imaginations?
· Did students pay close attention to the video scenes?
· How sophisticated were they in analyzing the videos?

LESSON **15** "I Will Speak Daggers"

Physicalized Speech Presentations

ੴ_____

PLAY SECTIONS COVERED IN THIS LESSON

3.2.419–432 Hamlet prepares for an interview with his mother.

LINES: Hamlet, 14

3.3.40–76 Claudius tries to pray, but his offense is too rank.

LINES: King, 37

3.3.77–101 Hamlet finds the moment to kill Claudius but won't do it because Claudius is praying.

LINES: Hamlet, 25

ੴ

WHAT'S ON FOR TODAY AND WHY

Visualizing the implications of words and the images they evoke helps students understand character and theme. With their physicalized speeches, students will examine and convey to other students Shakespeare's images.

Beginning with Act 4, we will take a new tack on *Hamlet*, moving from a plot and word approach to a character approach. Students will adopt characters, analyze them, write surrogate journal entries for them in their logs, and discuss them in character committees. Although students will summarize the plot of each scene in their logs, we will not spend class time testing their comprehension; therefore, log reading becomes even more important. To launch students on this new course, make copies of Handout 4: Character Committees.

WHAT TO DO

1. Group Meetings

Group students according to which speech they prepared as homework for Lesson 13. Allow students 10–15 minutes to combine their efforts for one presentation. If necessary, they can add introductions to set up the scenes or epilogues to explain.

2. Presentations

Have groups present their physicalized speeches. Don't let group members sit down until they have made plain to everyone what goes on in their speech.

3. What These Passages Contribute to Character

Discuss character actions and motivation based on the three speeches. What has happened to the action of the play because of these three speeches?

4. Character Committees

Pass out Handout 4: Character Committees. Explain to students that for Act 4 they will approach *Hamlet* from the viewpoint of a particular character. Assign each student a character: Gertrude, Claudius, Ophelia, or Laertes. Tell them to read Act 4 and to summarize each scene in their logs as usual, but instead of doing the other log questions, to use the questions from Handout 4, making entries only for the scenes where their character appears. This assignment is due two lessons from today.

HOW DID IT GO?

Student presentations will reveal in tangible terms whether students can recognize Shakespeare's images. Their discussion will reveal whether they are connecting the images in patterns.

🙪

HANDOUT 4

CHARACTER COMMITTEES

As you read Act 4, focus on the character you are assigned (Gertrude, Claudius, Ophelia, or Laertes) and respond to the questions listed below in your log. Lesson after next, you will meet with other students who studied the same character to prepare a ten-minute presentation on your character that you'll present the next day. This presentation should be informative and insightful. You may use any format that appeals to your group as long as your presentation includes the information asked for in the following questions. As usual, any conclusions you draw must be supported with textual references. Remember that the answers to the questions will provide you only with the raw data for your presentation. Your job as a group is to assemble the data into an interesting and informative presentation.

Character Questions:

1. What new information did you learn about your character in Act 4 that would help an actor or actress understand him or her better?

2. In each scene where your character appears, what is his or her motivation and objective? In other words, what does he or she really want? (Sometimes this will be difficult or impossible to determine.)

3. How does your character feel about the events in Act 4? about Hamlet?

4. What do other characters say about your character and how do they react to him or her? How does your character feel about other characters?

5. How does your character affect the events of each scene in which he or she appears? How is he or she affected by the events of each scene in which he or she appears?

6. How is your character important to this act? In other words, do you learn something new about the plot through him or her? Do you gain any insights about Hamlet by comparing/contrasting him to your character?

7. What questions are raised by your character's words and/or behavior in this act?

8. What questions that you've previously had are answered by your character's words and/or behavior in this act?

🙪

LESSON 16 "An Act That Blurs the Grace"

The Closet Scene

🙠

PLAY SECTION COVERED IN THIS LESSON

3.4 Polonius hides behind the arras once too often. Hamlet confronts his mother in a violent scene.

LINES: Polonius, 9; Hamlet, 178; Gertrude, 47; Ghost, 6

🙠

WHAT'S ON FOR TODAY AND WHY

If there is one scene in *Hamlet* that audiences understand innately, it is Hamlet's fight with his mother. You can introduce it any way you like. Improvise it, ask questions about fights students have had with parents, speak from the dais about Sigmund Freud—but students are going to understand this scene. So show it. Choose the video production you like best and show it.

WHAT TO DO

1. Previewing 3.4

Remind students that several days ago they read 3.4. Tell them to turn to it. Ask: What is going on? What state is Hamlet in? Gertrude? Polonius? Then ask a couple of questions about staging: How would you present the ghost? How violent would you make Hamlet? An intriguing question: What would you use for the arras Polonius hides behind? In some productions it is heavy, like tapestry. Sometimes it is rich, like velvet. A 1989 London production starring Daniel Day Lewis used a sheer white curtain that was by special effect drenched with blood when Hamlet's sword struck Polonius through it.

2. Viewing 3.4

See, then discuss, the scene. Most productions take the violence and/or Oedipal relationship between Hamlet and his mother further than students imagine.

HOW DID IT GO?

How *can* it go? After this scene, students are in deeper than they ever thought.

LESSON 17 "We Shall Express Our Duty in His Eye"

Character Committees

❧ _____

PLAY SECTIONS COVERED IN THIS LESSON

4.1 Gertrude tells the King about Polonius's death.

LINES: King, 34; Queen, 12; Rosencrantz, 0; Guildenstern, 0

4.2 Hamlet refuses to tell where Polonius's body is.

LINES: Hamlet, 21; Gentleman, 1; Rosencrantz, 8; Guildenstern, 1

4.3 Claudius sends Hamlet to England.

LINES: King, 46; Rosencrantz, 4; Hamlet, 27

4.4 Hamlet encounters Fortinbras.

LINES: Fortinbras, 8; Captain, 12; Hamlet, 47; Rosencrantz, 1

4.5 The appearance of the mad Ophelia is disturbing to Laertes, the King, and Gertrude.

LINES: Queen, 16; Gentleman, 15; Horatio, 3; Ophelia, 75; King, 71; Messenger, 11; Laertes, 50; Others, 2

4.6 Horatio receives a letter from Hamlet.

LINES: Horatio, 27; Gentleman, 2; Sailor, 5

4.7 Claudius and Laertes plot to kill Hamlet in a duel.

LINES: King, 146; Laertes, 47; Messenger, 6; Queen, 22

❧ _____

WHAT'S ON FOR TODAY AND WHY

In *Hamlet,* so much attention is focused on the title character that students often neglect to consider the function of other important characters. Character committee work forces students to pay closer attention to the lines and language of a particular character and to see ways to compare and contrast that character to Hamlet. Additionally, group work elicits a more varied and extensive set of responses.

So that students will have the time they need to work through all the material they have collected in their logs, we will allow two days for this lesson.

1. Day 1: Committee Meetings

Based on the characters assigned for Act 4, have students meet in four groups. Students spend one day going over the responses to their questions and deciding on a way to present this information to the class.

2. Day 2: Presentations

Let groups present their findings. These may vary. Example: For their presentation of Claudius, two students each wore a crown and enveloped themselves in one cape. One represented what their group perceived as the evil side of Claudius, his "hidden thoughts," as they put it; the other represented his public image.

Groups can make videotaped presentations if they choose.

3. Homework

Ask students to read 5.1 and write in their logs.

Students are used to working in groups by this time and generally have a wonderful time with this assignment. If your students need more structure than this assignment provides, set up a schedule that creates specific jobs and responsibilities for the day of discussion and for the presentation.

Many events important to the plot occur in Act 4, but we have elected not to deal with them directly. If the character committee reports failed to cover items you think students need to know—for example, that Hamlet is on his way back to Denmark—hold a catch-up session.

LESSON 18 "Alas, Sweet Lady, What Imports This Song?"

The Mad Scene

❧ _____

PLAY SECTION COVERED IN THIS LESSON

4.5 The appearance of the mad Ophelia is disturbing to Laertes, the King, and Gertrude.

LINES: Queen, 16; Gentleman, 15; Horatio, 3; Ophelia, 75; King, 71; Messenger, 11; Laertes, 50; Others, 2

❧ _____

WHAT'S ON FOR TODAY AND WHY

Act 4 has seven scenes. We reviewed all of them in Lesson 17, but there is one we should stop and view. Today students will see several famous mad Ophelias. Choose your videos and have them cued up.

WHAT TO DO

1. Analysis

Using the character reports from Act 4 as the basis for your discussion, talk about Ophelia's madness. Ask: Do you think it is real or feigned? Can you find possible causes in the text? How would you play 4.5? What could you do in the way of props, costume, set, or line delivery to show what you think Ophelia's state of mind is?

2. Video

Show two productions of this scene. As with the mousetrap and nunnery scenes, ask students to take notes after they see each production and to respond verbally after seeing both.

HOW DID IT GO?

This is a favorite scene for students to view. Some will want to play the mad Ophelia in the end-of-unit acting assignment.

LESSON 19 "Equivocation Will Undo Us"

The Gravediggers Scene

❧

PLAY SECTION COVERED IN THIS LESSON

5.1 Hamlet finds the gravediggers comical until he learns that the grave is Ophelia's.

LINES: Gravedigger, 100; Other, 18; Hamlet, 134; Horatio, 12; King, 10; Queen, 12; Laertes, 18; Doctor, 14

❧

WHAT'S ON FOR TODAY AND WHY

As the play is drawing to a close, Shakespeare starts to tie various strands together. The humor and the violence of this scene are difficult for students to visualize unless they use the basic tool of acting to help them.

WHAT TO DO

1. Cut the Scene

Put the students in groups and give them photocopies of 5.1. Working with pencils, ask them to cut about half of the gravediggers' lines from 5.1.1–180. Ask them to leave in the information essential to the plot but to take out the jokes they don't get. Ask one group to read its cut scene aloud.

2. Act the Scene

Using the same techniques employed in Lesson 1, perform 5.1. Try different kinds of movement. If possible, move to a larger area like a commons; find a stretcher for Ophelia and a skull for Yorick. Use simple costumes and dowels for swords. There are eight speaking parts in this scene, but involve all class members in the performance by switching actors or using multiple Hamlets and Laertes.

3. Discuss the Scene

Ask:

• How do the gravediggers' and Hamlet's comments on death relate to themes found in the play?

- How old is Hamlet? Why do you think Shakespeare revealed Hamlet's age near the end of the play?
- What is the touchy matter concerning Ophelia's death and burial?

4. Homework

Ask students to read 5.2 and write in their logs.

HOW DID IT GO?

At this point, it will be easy to see what's going on. As always, student involvement is the key, but by this time in the play, students should be comfortable enough with Shakespeare's language to catch much of the graveyard humor and show interest in the clouded nature of Ophelia's death.

LESSON 20 "Good Night, Sweet Prince"

The Last Gasp

❧ _____

PLAY SECTION COVERED IN THIS LESSON

5.2 Hamlet and Laertes duel. Hamlet, Laertes, the Queen, and the King die.

LINES: Hamlet, 237; Horatio, 57; Osric, 52; Lord, 8; King, 27; Laertes, 35; Queen, 7; Fortinbras, 19; Ambassador, 6

❧ _____

WHAT'S ON FOR TODAY AND WHY

The final scene of Hamlet brings so many threads together that it is often difficult for even advanced readers to follow the rapid action. If you have followed the suggestions in this unit, students will have an excellent grounding in the performance approach to Shakespeare, so to speed things up a bit, we suggest that you allow students to watch one of the videos of this final scene. The Jacobi production is the truest to the text; the Gibson production adds a delightful humor to Hamlet's character. If you are lucky enough to have a live production in your area, by all means choose that alternative. Watch the final scene, tie together loose ends, and move to the final discussion.

WHAT TO DO

1. View 5.2

Ask students to watch any taped or live production of 5.2, taking notes on the acting and movement.

2. Discuss

Discuss the acting and directing choices. By this time, students should be proficient at generating their own questions and observations about the ways actors and directors interpret the written text, but if necessary, prompt them:

· Follow the poison. Who has it, where is it, who drinks it, and what are its effects?

· How important is it for the actors to perfect the swordplay?

· What is Claudius's reaction to Gertrude's death? On what lines does he show this reaction?

- How important is Fortinbras? Some directors, like Zefirelli, leave him out entirely.
- How important is Horatio? How can a director convey this?

3. Homework

First, have students write in their logs two or three questions about the play that haven't been answered for them. These will be the basis of tomorrow's discussion. These questions should go beyond the who, what, when, and where of plot that can be answered by checking the text but should deal with the *why* of the play.

Additionally, ask students to look carefully through their logs and character committee notes to extract information they will use in a final assignment.

HOW DID IT GO?   Your students have explored Hamlet the character and *Hamlet* the play. They have struggled with the text to find their own answers to their own questions. They probably haven't found all the answers, but education is a continuing journey.

LESSON 21 "Is 't Not Possible to Understand in Another Tongue?"

The Question—We've Come Full Circle

WHAT'S ON FOR TODAY AND WHY

With play in hand—and head and heart—we will move to a final question-and-answer session, always extremely popular and satisfying for students. They like having the last word, especially the last question.

While some questions are answered in the text, many remain forever unanswered. As a form of closure, a question-and-answer session allows students to explore the play's questions that remain unanswered for them.

It also serves as the foundation for a writing assignment about the character students followed in Act 4. This can be a fully developed out-of-class paper, or you could convert this assignment to an in-class essay. Length, due date, and paper specifications are up to you.

WHAT TO DO

1. Questions

Move the desks into a circle or sit around a table, seminar-style. Round-robin fashion, ask each student to pose a question that remains unanswered for him or her. For example, what still puzzles them about Hamlet, about other characters? What questions would they ask a character? the playwright?

List the questions on the board or on an overhead, or ask a member of the class to act as a recorder.

2. Answers

Present these questions as topics for group exploration and discussion. The teacher should serve as referee, allowing students to suggest answers.

3. Hypotheses

If you have elected to do the out-of-class paper, ask students to write down a preliminary hypothesis about one of the characters in *Hamlet*, a hypothesis they will fully explore in a paper.

If you like, ask students to read their hypotheses to the rest of the class. Invite other students to add their insights.

4. Character Paper

Tell students to refine or revise their hypotheses based on class discussion and write a paper about one of the characters in *Hamlet*.

To help them collect evidence and solidify thoughts to support their hypothesis, give them Handout 5: Character Papers and ask them to complete it for homework.

HOW DID IT GO?   The caliber of questions, peer responses, and general atmosphere in the room will tell you whether students are winding up their study of *Hamlet* wanting to know more, are enthusiastic about Shakespeare, and will seek out Shakespearean productions to view in the future.

ક

HANDOUT 5

CHARACTER PAPERS

Write an analysis of the character you followed through Act 4 of *Hamlet*.

Step 1: Scene Notation

After you and other members of your character committee have compared notes and the conclusions you've reached, you should have a pretty good grasp of your character throughout Act 4. Now go back in the play and note each scene in which your character has previously appeared.

Step 2: Thinking and Answering Questions

· What was your first reaction to your character? What led you to this reaction?
· What information did you learn in succeeding scenes?
· How did the character affect Hamlet? How was the character affected by Hamlet?
· What is the character's strongest personal quality?
· What happens to your character in Act 5?
· In the course of the play, did your character change?

Step 3: Focused Prewriting

· Write three words you think best describe your character.
· Choose one of these words and write a paragraph explaining why this word fits your character.
· Look for a quote in the play that illustrates this quality.

Step 4: First Draft

With this paragraph as a basis, start the first draft of your character paper. Be sure to include at least the following points:

· a description of the character
· an explanation of the character's significance in the play
· your opinion about the character's changes during the play and the importance of the changes
· a comparison of your character to Hamlet

Step 5: Revision

Consult with a peer, or read your own paper with an eye for revision.

Step 6: Final Copy

Prepare your manuscript and submit on _____.

ક

LESSON 22 "Therefore This Project Should Have a Back"

Making a Scene: *Hamlet* Festival

The emphasis of this unit has been on performance. Devote the final week to polished scenes from the play. Students are eager to put to use what they have learned and to show off what they know. This is productive. This is fun. This is time well spent. Almost unanimously, students indicate that performance is the single most helpful tool in understanding Shakespeare.

WHAT TO DO

1. Day 1: Forming Acting Companies

Divide the class into groups small enough for everyone to have a meaningful role in the production of a scene. A group of four to five people is about right, though groups three to six can also work well. Everyone should be on stage at least some of the time, and everyone should say at least one line.

2. Day 1: Choosing Scenes

Give students Handout 6: *Hamlet* Scenes for Acting Companies. If you like, let groups negotiate with you about doing scenes not on the list.

3. Day 1: Reviewing Directions

Distribute Handout 7: Acting Company Directions. Make sure each student knows what you expect.

Tell them how you will evaluate the scenes. We suggest that students contract for a grade. This is the scale we use:

C: a well-rehearsed scene, incorporating clear movements, that demonstrates an understanding of the characters and the action and has a clear plan guiding the direction of the scene

B: a well-rehearsed scene, incorporating clear movements, that demonstrates an understanding of the characters and the action and has a clear plan guiding the direction of the scene; the use of costumes and props to enhance the scene; and a simple set

A: a well-rehearsed scene, incorporating clear movements, that demonstrates an understanding of the characters and the action and has a clear plan guiding the direction of the scene; the use of costumes and props to enhance the scene; a simple set; a concerted effort to memorize lines. (Within the confines of a week to plan and prepare this performance, total memorization is difficult. Students can hold prompt cards, but they should have most of their lines under control.)

4. Days 1–4: Rehearsal

Provide time and space for rehearsal. Act as a floating consultant to the acting groups but let this be their production.

5. Day 5: *Hamlet* Festival

Set aside at least one full class period for the festival. Hold it in the classroom or move it to an auditorium or a commons area and perhaps invite other classes. Ideally, this audience would be tuned in to Shakespeare and would appreciate the efforts of your class. Consider videotaping the performances. Students love seeing themselves later. If you like, ask a student to design a playbill.

HOW DID IT GO?

Students have spent the week in serious interaction with a great piece of classical drama—and all under their own steam. What could be better?

There are many possible evaluations for the unit as a whole—student assessments of various components, freewriting about the *Hamlet* experience, comprehension surveys, peer evaluations of collaborative projects, viewing the scenes on videotape, and more. But one question tells you whether you won the day: Do students look on *Hamlet* as theirs? If the answer is yes, sit down and put your feet up. You did it.

ॐ

HANDOUT 6

HAMLET SCENES FOR ACTING COMPANIES

Many scenes in *Hamlet* make for great performances. Here is a list of some that students especially enjoy. If your company prefers a scene that isn't on the list, negotiate with your teacher.

1.5.1–98 Claiming that he is the spirit of Hamlet's father, the Ghost asks Hamlet to avenge the murder of King Hamlet.
LINES: Hamlet, 12; Ghost, 86

2.2.187–237 Polonius tries to draw out Hamlet about Ophelia.
LINES: Polonius, 24; Hamlet, 27

3.1.99–175 With Polonius and Claudius hiding so that they can overhear the meeting, Ophelia approaches Hamlet, who turns on her, denies having loved her, attacks womanhood, and tells her to get to a nunnery.
LINES: Ophelia, 35; Hamlet, 42

3.2.96–144 Hamlet uses rude remarks to stir up the audience before the play.
LINES: Hamlet, 31; King, 3; Polonius, 5; Ophelia, 7; Rosencrantz, 2; Queen, 1; Horatio, 0

3.2.145–317 The players perform a play about a king murdered by poison in the ear. Claudius is disturbed and leaves.
LINES: Player King, 44 (and dumb show); Player Queen, 31 (and dumb show); Prologue, 3; Hamlet, 33; Ophelia, 12; Queen, 2; King, 4; Lucianus, 7; Polonius, 2; Horatio, 4; Rosencrantz, 0

4.3 Claudius sends Hamlet to England.
LINES: King, 45; Rosencrantz, 4; Hamlet, 27

4.5.122–225 In her visit to the King and Queen, it is obvious that Ophelia has gone mad.
LINES: Laertes, 44; King, 25; Queen, 2; Ophelia, 30; Others, 2

5.1 Hamlet finds the gravediggers comical until he learns that the grave is Ophelia's.
LINES: Gravedigger, 100; Other, 18; Hamlet, 134; Horatio, 12; King, 10; Queen, 12; Laertes, 18; Doctor, 14

5.2.239–449 The final fight.
LINES: King, 27; Hamlet, 75; Laertes, 35; Osric, 8; Queen, 7; Horatio, 32; Fortinbras, 19; Ambassador, 6

ॐ

HANDOUT 7

ACTING COMPANY DIRECTIONS

Present a well-planned and prepared scene from *Hamlet*. Your scene should last 7–10 minutes; you may cut lines if your scene is too long.

Procedure:

1. Choose a name for your group—be creative.

2. Choose your scene from the list provided.

3. Follow the procedure we used the first day of our *Hamlet* unit:

   a. Read your scene round robin again and again until you feel you understand it well.
   b. Ask each other lots of questions about the lines, the characters, the action.

4. Get a concept. What is the main idea of this scene, and how will you convey it?

5. Talk about stage arrangement, costumes, music, special effects, or anything else that will help convey your concept of this scene.

6. Stage the scene. Make group decisions about where the scene takes place, what the scene looks like, where entrances are, who should be positioned where, what characters need for props, how characters arrive, what characters do, and so on.

7. Rehearse.

8. Perform.

Suggested time line:

Day 1. Choose and read the scene until you understand it; get a concept; talk about how to use costumes, props, music, or other effects to convey your concept.

Day 2. Cut (if necessary) and set the scene.

Day 3. Cast, set movement, and rehearse.

Day 4. Rehearse with costumes and props you've obtained outside class time.

Day 5. Festival performance!

Henry IV, Part 1

•

ANDREA ALSUP

EDITOR

A letter from one classroom teacher to another:

If history wasn't precisely as Shakespeare represents it in *Henry IV, Part 1* it should have been. The play is full of action and memorable characters. As I write this, my school room rings with Falstaff's laughter, Hotspur's rage, Kate's questions, Glendower's incantations, King Henry's chidings, Mistress Quickly's indignation, and Hal's observations. Its concerns are timeless: the transfer of power, the nature of honor, the question of courage, the strength of love.

Henry IV, Part 1 is a marvelous play to study with adolescents because it is about Prince Hal's rites of passage: he rebels against authority, chooses reprobates for friends, imitates heroes, assumes responsibility, and mourns lost childhood. I like to teach in thematic across-cultural and across-time arrangements. If you are at liberty to invent thematic units, *Henry IV, Part 1* is a good fit with works about the search for identity like *The Iliad, A Doll's House, Great Expectations, The Awakening, Death of a Salesman, Metamorphosis, Jane Eyre, The Wide Sargasso Sea,* or *Hamlet.* And in a nice shift from many of these, the protagonist survives.

In a more traditional Brit Lit or chronologically organized course, *Henry IV, Part 1* provides a nice transition from medieval to Elizabethan drama. It contains elements of a morality play, a comedy, a tragedy, and of course, an English chronicle. The fact that it is the second play in a tetralogy of history plays presents a few challenges. I have found that students need to know a little about the events of *Richard II* and how the succession of kings went in fourteenth-century England to understand the themes of robbery and rebellion in *Henry IV, Part 1.* Furthermore, to see Prince Hal fully mature to Henry V, students should look at key speeches in *Henry IV, Part 2* and *Henry V.*

Henry IV, Part 1 deserves to be acted because it is full of vivid characters in memorable places. As your students informally perform while reading their lines, they will understand Hal and Hotspur and Kate and Falstaff, even King Henry, because they will see themselves, their friends, their relatives, and their political leaders in these characters. The colleagues who collaborated on this teaching plan—Donna Denizé of Arlington, Virginia; Louisa Newlin and Mary Poole of Washington, D.C.; Skip Nicholson of Los Angeles; and I—have successfully taught this unit to high school sophomores, juniors, and seniors. One of my senior boys remarked to me that of "all the Shakespeare plays" he'd read in school, he'd understood this one best because he'd been most actively involved in the lessons for it.

The challenge for your students is to transform your classroom into a kind of rehearsal-in-progress, where all students will become actors (long speeches are divided or shared by students), where the corner by the bookcase is Henry's court, the one by the window is The Boar's Head, and the one with the pencil sharpener is the rebel camp. Once you have provided a little background and the structure for student acting groups, you are pretty much off the hook. No more line-by-line translating for disinterested nappers. Your job is to help students find answers (always more than one answer!) to questions about dramatically interpreting Shakespeare's language, to photocopy handouts, and to shuffle props. The real work is theirs, and joyful work it is.

It takes about twenty-five days to complete the lessons in this unit using this in-class performance format. If you then allow your class to form acting companies, to choose and rehearse and memorize the scenes they'd like to present for one another or for another class, you will need to allow another four or five class days for rehearsal. A festival of favorite scenes is a marvelous way to end the study of a Shakespeare play. I find the extra time well spent. Students often name the festival "best activity of the year" in their evaluations of my courses.

I hope your students and you find your study equally enjoyable.

Andrea Alsup
Hanover High School
Hanover, New Hampshire

UNIT CALENDAR FOR
Henry IV, Part 1

1 LESSON 1 What Happens in *Henry*	**2** LESSON 2 Text in Performance Text: 2.2.31–111	**3** LESSON 3 Actors in Rehearsal Text: 1.1; 1.2; 1.3.125–313	**4** LESSON 4 Performances, Act 1 Text: 1.1; 1.2; 1.3.125–313	**5** LESSON 4 Performances, Act 1 *(cont.)* Text: 1.1; 1.2; 1.3.125–313
6 LESSON 5 A Shaken Kingdom	**7** LESSON 6 The Blood on Henry's Hands	**8** LESSON 7 Setting Student Assignments Text: 2.3; 2.4.100–338; 2.4.339–569	**9** LESSON 8 Act 2 in Rehearsal Text: 2.3; 2.4.100–338; 2.4.339–569	**10** LESSON 9 Act 2 Onstage Text: 2.3; 2.4.100–338
11 LESSON 10 More Act 2 Onstage Text: 2.4.339–569	**12** LESSON 11 Workshop Day	**13** LESSON 12 Speech Explication	**14** LESSON 13 Rehearsing Act 3 Text: 3.1.1–197; 3.1.198–276; 3.2; 3.3	**15** LESSON 14 Act 3 in Performance Text: 3.1.1–197; 3.1.198–276; 3.2
16 LESSON 15 Over the Hump Text: 3.3	**17** LESSON 16 Calm Before the Battle Text: 4.1; 4.2; 4.3	**18** LESSON 17 Act 4 Onstage Text: 4.1; 4.2; 4.3	**19** LESSON 18 Writing Conferences	**20** LESSON 19 Battlefield Plans Text: 5.1; 5.2; 5.3; 5.4; 5.5
21 LESSON 20 Performing Act 5 Text: 5.1; 5.2	**22** LESSON 21 The Battle: An Epic Onstage Text: 5.3; 5.4	**23** LESSON 22 Project Workshop	**24** LESSON 23 Oral Projects; Essay Exam	**25** LESSON 24 Making A Scene: *Henry IV, Part 1* Festival in Rehearsal
26 LESSON 24 Festival Reheasal *(cont.)*	**27** LESSON 24 Festival Rehearsal *(cont.)*	**28** LESSON 24 Festival Rehearsal *(cont.)*	**29** LESSON 24 Festival Performances	**30+** Film: *Henry V*

LESSON 1 "Courage! To the Field"

What Happens in *Henry*

WHAT'S ON FOR TODAY AND WHY

The first day's primary activity summarizes the action of the entire play and establishes its settings. Often students fail to get an overview of the complete play when they are working in short time segments, so begin with the big picture.

To simplify what could be a confusing list of characters, divide students into three groups: the Courtiers, the Rebels, and the Pub Crawlers. These groups will perform in the summary today and in companies throughout the unit.

Prepare to lead students in two exercises designed to give them enough social, psychological, and political background to make the play their own: first, an illustrated character chart; second, a fifteen-minute *Henry*, an activity in which students act lines and the teacher narrates a summary.

Finally, get students to think about issues in the play by setting up log assignments.

WHAT TO DO

1. Casting Call

Give each student a copy of Handout 1: *Henry IV, Part 1*, which shows most of the people in the play grouped into Rebels, Courtiers, and Pub Crawlers. Talk about the characters. In particular, talk about Hal, his conflict with his father, his relationship with Falstaff and the rest of the Boar's Head revelers.

Tell students to keep this chart; in fact, they might use it as a bookmark as a handy reference.

2. The Whole Play

Designate areas in your classroom to serve as King Henry's court, the Boar's Head Tavern, and the rebel camp. Encourage students to make signs or props to distinguish these areas and to turn them into simple sets. Announce the group assignments and send students to their areas. Distribute Handout 2: Fifteen-Minute *Henry*. Explain that all the groups plus the narrator are going to do a summary of the play, that each group is to act out its designated speeches in the script.

Give groups a few minutes to practice delivery of their lines in unison or with action or whatever, as long as the presentation is dramatic and physically conspicuous.

If you want to make this hilarious fun, you can bring in bags of random items, such as colanders, scarves, wooden spoons, old bottles, umbrellas, to give to each group to aid their delivery of the lines. You needn't worry about the relevance of the items to the lines. Your students will find a connection—or not.

After a very brief rehearsal, read the *Henry IV* summary, pausing to cue the acting groups: "Court . . ." Have fun with "hamming" the script, but strive to convey the plot of the play.

3. The Whole Unit

Pass out Handout 3: Long-Term Assignments. Have a heart-to-heart talk about requirements for this unit—what students have to do, when they have to do it, and how good it has to be.

HOW DID IT GO?

At the end of the fifteen-minute *Henry*, ask students if they understand the general story. If they don't, do the exercise again.

HANDOUT 1

HENRY IV, PART 1

THE COURT

Earl of **Westmoreland**

Prince John of Lancaster
Hal's younger brother

Sir Walter **Blunt**

Sheriff, Lords, Attendants

THE BOAR'S HEAD TAVERN CREW

Hostess
Mistress Quickly

Bardolf

Peto

Falstaff

Poins

also Gadshill, Vintner, Drawers, Carriers, Travelers, and more

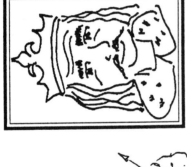

King Henry IV
Also called Bolingbroke . . .
Got the throne by deposing
the weak Richard II . . .
Successful soldier-king

Prince Hal
The heir apparent . . . son of
Henry IV . . . also called
Harry and later Henry V . . . .
His father is disappointed
because Hal runs with the
tavern crew rather than
assume his royal duties

THE REBELS
Some of these were formerly in the court.

Owen **Glendower**
Leader of the Welsh

Edmund **Mortimer**
Earl of March

Archibald, Earl of **Douglas**
Leader of the Scots

Richard Scroop Archbishop of **York**

Thomas Percy Earl of **Worcester**

Harry Percy, Earl of **Northumberland**
Hotspur's Dad

also Vernon, Soldiers, and others

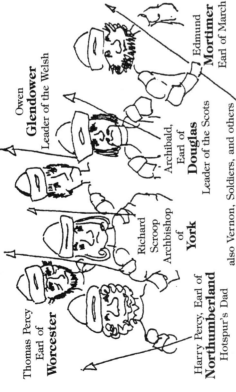

Harry Percy **Hotspur**
At first he fights for King
Henry IV; in fact, he's the
king's idea of a perfect
young man, but later he
leads the rebels

Lady Mortimer
daughter to Glendower
wife of Mortimer

Lady Percy
wife of Hotspur
sister of Mortimer

&

HANDOUT 2

FIFTEEN-MINUTE *HENRY*

This is a summary of *Henry IV, Part 1* for a narrator and three acting groups: the Court, the Pub Crawlers, and the Rebels. The narrator will read the lines in regular type. The three acting groups will read and act out their lines, which are set in bold.

Henry IV (Bolingbroke), having deposed the profligate but rightful King Richard II and caused his murder, seeks to atone:

COURT **I'll make a voyage to the Holy Land,**
     To wash this blood off from my guilty hand.
               King Henry, *Richard II,* 5.5.49–50 *(The Riverside Shakespeare)*

Learning that rebellion is raging along England's borders, Henry postpones his trip to Jerusalem. A rebel army led by the great Welsh warrior Glendower has defeated Henry's forces, but another uprising in Scotland has been put down by the brave young Harry (Hotspur) Percy. King Henry regretfully compares the valiant Hotspur to his son Henry, Prince of Wales (Hal), who is leading a life of "riot and dishonor":

COURT **O, that it could be proved**
     That some night-tripping fairy had exchanged
     In cradle-clothes our children where they lay,
     And called mine "Percy," his "Plantagenet"!
     Then would I have his Harry, and he mine.
               King Henry, *Henry IV, Part 1,* 1.1.85–89

While King Henry worries, Prince Hal carouses with his friends Poins, Peto, Bardolph, and the hugely fat knight Sir John Falstaff at the Boar's Head Tavern in Eastcheap. Falstaff, although twice Hal's age, accuses Hal of being a corrupter:

PUB CRAWLERS **Before I knew thee, Hal, I knew nothing, and now am I . . . little better than one of**
          the wicked.
               Falstaff, *Henry IV, Part 1,* 1.2.99–101

Poins suggests a robbery and deception of Falstaff, which Hal supports. When he is alone, however, Hal reveals that his wild behavior is a mask he will discard when it is time to assume responsibilities: "So when this loose behavior I throw off / And pay the debt I never promised, / By how much better than my word I am, / By so much shall I falsify men's hopes. . . ."

PUB CRAWLERS **I'll so offend to make offense a skill,**
          Redeeming time when men think least I will.
               Prince Hal, *Henry IV, Part 1,* 1.2.223–224

The King meets with Northumberland, Worcester, Sir Walter Blunt, and Hotspur, and demands that Hotspur deliver his prisoners. After the King leaves, Hotspur speaks his mind:

REBELS   **An if the devil come and roar for them,**
         I will not send them. I will after straight
         And tell him so. . . .
              Hotspur, *Henry IV, Part 1*, 1.3.127–129

But he doesn't. Instead, he and the others hatch a plot to join forces with Owen Glendower, Lord Mortimer, and the Archbishop of York, as Hotspur concludes:

REBELS   **Uncle, adieu. O, let the hours be short**
         Till fields and blows and groans applaud our sport.
              Hotspur, *Henry IV, Part 1*, 1.3.312–313

On the darkened highway near Gad's Hill, Falstaff and his accomplices rob some rich pilgrims. Hal and Poins, in disguise, rob Falstaff. Meanwhile, Hotspur reads a letter from a reluctant lord, is scolded by his wife Kate for neglecting her, and rides off to join the rebels. Back at the tavern, Hal accuses Falstaff of cowardice, and fat Jack defends himself with lies and exaggerations. When a summons to court arrives, Hal and Falstaff improvise a scene between King and Prince in which Jack, playing the wastrel son, pleads for his favorite knight:

FALSTAFF   **. . . for sweet Jack Falstaff, kind Jack Falstaff, true Jack Falstaff, valiant Jack Falstaff . . .**
           old Jack Falstaff, banish not him thy Harry's company, banish not him thy Harry's company.
           Banish plump Jack, and banish all the world.
HAL   **I do, I will.**
              Falstaff and Prince Hal, *Henry IV, Part 1*, 2.4.492–499

Mistress Quickly, the tavern's hostess, announces that the Sheriff has come, and Hal covers for Falstaff, who hides and falls asleep. Hal realizes that in the morning they must all go off to the wars. In Wales, the rebels meet to decide how to divide England into three shares after they win. Hotspur taunts Glendower about believing in magic and says of music:

REBELS   **I had rather be a kitten and cry "mew"**
         I had rather hear . . .
         Nothing so much as mincing poetry.
         'Tis like the forced gait of a shuffling nag.
              Hotspur, *Henry IV, Part 1*, 3.1.133–139

Yet Hotspur asks his wife to sing to him as Lady Mortimer has to her husband. The couples enjoy a peaceful interlude on the eve of war. Back at court, King Henry suggests that Hal might join the rebel forces against him, but the Prince assures his father that he will be loyal, redeeming his past sins on young Percy's head when they meet in battle:

COURT   **. . . I will wear a garment all of blood**
        And stain my favors in a bloody mask,
        Which, washed away, shall scour my shame with it.
              Prince Hal, *Henry IV, Part 1*, 3.2.140–142

Falstaff accuses Mistress Quickly of picking his pocket, but Hal exposes Jack as a fraud. To his further dismay, Falstaff has been given command of foot soldiers:

PUB CRAWLERS   **I would it had been of horse. Where shall I find one that can steal well? O, for a fine thief of the age of two-and-twenty. . . .**
Falstaff, *Henry IV, Part 1,* 3.3.198–200

In the rebel camp near Shrewsbury, Hotspur learns that his father is ill and will not send troops and that Glendower will be delayed by two weeks. Undeterred by reports of the "gallantly armed" Prince Hal at King Henry's side, Hotspur promises a warm welcome for the enemy:

REBELS   **They come like sacrifices in their trim,**
And to the fire-eyed maid of smoky war
All hot and bleeding will we offer them.
Hotspur, *Henry IV, Part 1,* 4.1.119–121

Near Coventry with his "charge of foot" soldiers, Falstaff meets Hal, who observes that the men are "pitiful rascals" indeed. Jack, who is much richer with the bribery money he has taken from the able-bodied men who are safe at home, is less concerned:

PUB CRAWLERS   **. . . good enough to toss; food for powder, food for powder. They'll fill a pit as well as better . . . mortal men, mortal men.**
Falstaff, *Henry IV, Part 1,* 4.2.66–68

At Shrewsbury, Hotspur insists on an immediate attack but sends the King a list of grievances, then promises to send Worcester as an emissary in the morning. As the sun begins to peer "bloodily" above the hills, Hal suggests a single-combat solution with Hotspur, whom he praises:

COURT   **I do not think a braver gentleman,**
More active-valiant, or more valiant-young,
More daring or more bold, is now alive . . .
Prince Hal, *Henry IV, Part 1,* 5.1.90–92

In the battle, Prince Hal saves his father from death then kills Hotspur in a brutal fight. Alas, he sees the still form of Falstaff on the ground:

COURT   **O, I should have a heavy miss of thee**
If I were much in love with vanity.
Prince Hal, *Henry IV, Part 1,* 5.4.107–108

But Falstaff has played the counterfeit. He ups and stabs the dead body of Hotspur, hoists it on his shoulders, and takes credit for killing him, which Hal allows, "if a lie may do thee grace." The day ends in a victory for the forces of King Henry IV.

ALL   **Rebellion in this land shall lose his sway.**
Henry IV, Part 1, 5.5.43

❧

HANDOUT 3

HENRY IV, PART 1: LONG-TERM ASSIGNMENTS

Dear student,

In the course of this unit, I hope you will come to understand Hal and Hotspur and Kate and Falstaff and Poins and Mistress Quickly and even King Henry as well as you understand your friends, your relatives, your classmates, and your political leaders. I expect each of you to:

- Present the play as 5 classroom performances, rigorously rehearsing the text beforehand
- Keep a writing log for short nightly assignments
- Take reading quizzes at the end of each act
- Do a close reading analysis of one assigned speech, to be presented to the class at the end of the reading
- Complete one writing project
- Complete one activity project
- Join with an acting company for a 15–30 minute memorized performance at the end of the play

For performing nightly assignments, you will receive instructions, reminders, and pep talks in class, but for the writing project and the activity project you are on your own. I have assembled a mix of possibilities. Consider your strengths and time constraints when you choose, and adhere to deadlines. If you have an idea of your own, negotiate with me. For individual help, confer with me outside of class. Use the projects to get to know the people of *Henry IV, Part 1*, and have fun.

Yours in Shakespeare,

Activity Projects

Your activity project is due on _____.

1. Write a script for a talking, living genealogy chart from Edward III through Henry VI, and enlist classmates to help you present it in full heraldic regalia.
2. Design a stage set—model or drawing—for a production of *Henry* you want to direct. Explain scene changes.
3. Design costumes—contemporary or period—for a production of *Henry.*
4. Research the performance history of *Henry IV, Part 1* and give an oral report with illustrations.
5. Become a character and show up for an interview—preferably in period costume.

6. Draw a comic book of one long or two short scenes.
7. Do character or theme collages with quotes.
8. Choose and record background music for one act of the play. Justify your choices with quotes.
9. Invent a diary for one of the major characters. Make it look as though it belonged to the character, and do at least five entries as if you were that person.
10. Paint a portrait of one of the major characters.
11. View *Chimes at Midnight* and write a review of it.

Writing Projects

Choose early. You'll want to take notes for documentation as you read. Your paper should have an arguable thesis—someone should be able to write an antithesis. Read, think, research, and produce a draft by _____. Be prepared to defend your thesis and show reasonable progress when you confer with your teacher on that date.

1. Compare *Henry IV, Part 1* with another piece of literature dealing with the theme of coming to maturity.
2. Discuss Hal's search for role models; how do his companions educate him about his country? How do the three worlds of the play—Court, Rebel, Tavern—converge in him?
3. Compare the rehearsal scene between Hal and Falstaff and the real meeting between Hal and his father.
4. Discuss the motifs of robbery and rebellion, or honor and courage, or wholeness (both individual and national) in each "world" of the play.
5. Trace a set of images as we did in class with *violence*. Do you notice certain images—like night or moon or food or fat—coming up time and time again? Follow up your notion of frequency by consulting the concordance or a computer program. Produce a list of citations—every time in *Henry IV, Part 1* that your word appears. Then find those passages and look for patterns. Are the images associated with certain people or places or events? Discuss the impact of your image on the play. To get you started thinking, here are the 15 most frequently used words in *Henry* (not counting prepositions, articles, and the like): arms, blood, brother, counterfeit, coward, devil, eye, face, faith, rear, great, hand, heart, heaven, honor.

FROM THE FOLGER SHAKESPEARE LIBRARY COLLECTION: LEWIS WALLER AS HENRY V IN A 1905 PRODUCTION.

6. Compare and contrast the first scene between Hotspur and Lady Percy with the scene in *Julius Caesar* in which Portia urges Brutus to come to bed. Then discuss the role of women in these scenes and in *Henry IV* as a whole.

7. Compare and contrast the patriarchal relationships in the play: Hal and King Henry; Hal and Falstaff; Hotspur and Northumberland; Glendower, Lady Mortimer and (son-in-law) Mortimer. What observations can you make about the relations of older and younger generations?

8. Creating a false persona seems an important step in the transformation of some rulers: Boling-broke's change to King Henry IV, Hal's change to Prince Henry, Malcom's adopting a persona to test Macduff's motives and loyalty in *Macbeth*, and others. Why is such a technique necessary? What does it accomplish?

9. Compare and contrast Hamlet's meeting with the Ghost to Hal's with his father.

10. Read the Richard Wilbur poem "Up, Jack" and the three critical comments on Falstaff and discuss their representations of Falstaff. Where do you stand?

FROM THE FOLGER
SHAKESPEARE LIBRARY
COLLECTION:
THE FRONTISPIECE TO
FRANCIS KIRKMAN'S
*THE WITS, OR SPORT UPON
SPORT* (1662). THE
EARLIEST PUBLISHED
ILLUSTRATION OF
FALSTAFF.

UP, JACK

Prince Harry turns from Percy's pouring sides
Full of the kind of death that honor makes
By pouring all the man into an act;
So simplified by battle, he mistakes

A hibernating Jack for dead Sir John.
"Poor pumpkin, I am cold since you are done,
For if you proved but yellow pulp within,
You were this nature's kindest earthly sun."

Exit the Prince; now Jack will rise again,
No larger now, nor spun of stuff more fine,
And only to his feet, and yet a god
To our short summer days and the world's wine.

Up, Jack! For Percy sinks in darker red,
And those who walk away are dying men.
Great Falstaff (*rising*) clears his thirsty throat,
And I'm content, and Hal is hale again.
        —Richard Wilbur, 1921–, American Poet

This is perhaps the most substantial comic character that ever was invented. . . . The secret of Falstaff's wit is for the most part a masterly presence of mind, an absolute self-possession, which nothing can disturb. His repartees are involuntary suggestions of his self-love; instinctive evasions of everything that threatens to interrupt the career of his triumphant jollity and self-complacency. His very size floats him out of all his difficulties in a sea of rich conceits; and he turns round on the pivot of his convenience, with every occasion and at a moment's warning.

—William Hazlitt, 1778–1830, Romantic Critic

He [Falstaff] is a man at once young and old, enterprising and fat, a dupe and a wit, harmless and wicked, weak in principle and resolute by constitution, cowardly in appearance and brave in reality, a knave without malice, a liar without deceit, and a knight, a gentleman, and a soldier without either dignity, decency, or honour.

—Charles Langbridge Morgan, 1894–1958, English Novelist and Critic

But Falstaff, unimitated, unimitable Falstaff, how shall I describe thee! thou compound of sense and vice; of sense which may be admired, but not esteemed; of vice that may be despised, but hardly detested. Falstaff is a character loaded with faults, and with those faults which naturally produce contempt. . . . It must be observed, that he is stained with no enormous or sanguinary crimes, so that his licentiousness is not so offensive but that it may be borne for his mirth. The moral to be drawn from this representation is, that no man is more dangerous than he that, with a will to corrupt, hath the power to please; and that neither wit nor honesty ought to think themselves safe with such a companion, when they see Henry seduced by Falstaff.

—Samuel Johnson, 1709–1784, British Essayist and Critic

FROM THE FOLGER SHAKESPEARE LIBRARY COLLECTION: INK AND WATERCOLOR SKETCH (CA. 1858) OF FALSTAFF BY GEORGE CRUIKSHANK.

LESSON **2** **"List If Thou Canst Hear"**

Text in Performance

ટ•

PLAY SECTION COVERED IN THIS LESSON

2.2.31–117 Falstaff, Peto, and Bardolph execute the robbery Poins planned; Poins and Hal then rob the robbers.

LINES: Prince Hal, 25; Falstaff, 37; Gadshill, 6; Poins, 8; Bardolph, 1; Peto, 1; Travelers, 6

ટ•

WHAT'S ON FOR TODAY AND WHY

Learning through the process of performance constitutes the focus of this unit. It necessitates a kind of close reading, the kind that actors do every time they interpret written words out loud and with action.

Students will read, in character and with forethought and preparation, most of the play, but they will not pull their chairs into a circle and read it cold. As with the *Hamlet* unit, they will make decisions about interpretation, pronounce the words as trippingly on the tongue as they are capable of, add movement and props to enhance those interpretations.

In Lesson 1, you divided the classroom into three areas—the court of Henry IV, the Boar's Head Tavern, and the rebel camp. Throughout the unit, student acting groups will present scenes in the three areas. As *Henry IV, Part 1* moves from area to area, so will the class. Actors in the court will present the scenes that occur there; the Pub Crawlers will present the Boar's Head and Gad's Hill scenes, and the Rebels will present the machinations of Hotspur, Glendower, and company. For the battle of Shrewsbury, which occurs at the end of the play, actors will use the center of the room.

The performance method carries this unit. Create enthusiasm for it. If students take their assigned parts seriously and rehearse them, the unit will succeed. If not, it will fall flat.

To demonstrate the performance method and to preview some of the characters in the play, today students will do a short scene from Act 2, scene 2 (2.2).

Afterward, if you like, let students have a look at 2.2 from the second quarto (Q2) of *Henry IV, Part 1*, printed in 1599, the earliest version in the Folger collection. (The earliest in existence is the first quarto, or Q1, printed in 1598.) Students might enjoy comparing the Q2 text to the one they are using.

WHAT TO DO

1. Read-through

As students did with the Ghost scene in *Hamlet* and as Michael Tolaydo describes in "Ambulatory Shakespeare," pass out the scripts and tell students to consider themselves an acting company with the job of doing this short scene (2.2.31–117). Quickly assign parts and do the initial read-through.

2. Piercing Questions

Ask questions like the ones Michael Tolaydo outlines, beginning on page 52.

Bring in, or ask students to bring in, hats and props and assign a distinctive trademark hat or prop for each character. Discuss the appropriateness of the trademark and establish that it will be used by this character throughout the unit.

Discuss words or phrases students don't understand. Paraphrase the rough spots.

3. On the Feet

Appoint directors and cast the scene. Make sure every student has a part either as actor or director. Get the scene (and the actors in it) on its feet. Bring to bear all their experience from previous Shakespeare units. Let them perform with scripts in hand, but expect students to communicate the scene to the audience.

4. Setting the Standard

Explain that students won't read all of *Henry IV, Part 1* but will read and perform the scenes that occur in their area. They will learn about the rest of the play by watching and listening to other acting groups. Set the standards for rehearsal and performance. Explain that student acting companies will have a major job in communicating their scenes to the rest of the class, that student audiences will have to do some sophisticated listening, and that all will have to prepare their scenes in advance and do the best job possible.

5. Student Acting Companies

Announce the first assignments:

- Courtiers—1.1
- Pub Crawlers—1.2
- Rebels—1.3.127—end

For homework, ask students to read their scene carefully and bring to class ideas for performing that scene.

6. Logs

As with *Hamlet*, students are to keep a log as they read and act *Henry*. See *Hamlet*, Lesson 1, for complete instructions. Start with this assignment: Reflect and write about how power changes hands—in the past, in the present, in totalitarian countries, in school, in families.

HOW DID IT GO?

Did students understand the performance method? Do they know it well enough to do it? How well did they sort out the characters? To what extent did they engage with the characters? How much of their acting and directing skills carried over from the previous study of a Shakespeare play? If you detect problems in any of these areas, start working on solutions. For example, do students need grades or rewards to get them on track? Do they need name tags or signs for the characters? Do whatever it takes to find the dark corners and light fires there.

The Hiſtorie

breake the pate on thee, I am a very villaine, come & be hangd, haſt no faith in thee?

Enter Gadſhill.

Gadſhill. Good morrow Carriers, what's a clocke?

Car. I thinke it be two a clocke.

Gad. I prethe lend me thy lanterne, to ſee my gelding in the ſtable.

1 Car. Nay by God ſoft, I know a tricke worth two of that I faith.

Gad. I pray thee lend me thine.

2 Car. I, when, canſt tell? lend me thy lanterne (quoth he) marry ile ſee thee hangd firſt.

Gad. Sirra Carrier, what time doe you meane to come to London?

2 Car. Time enough to goe to bed with a candle, I warrant thee. Come neighbour Mugs, wee'le call vp the Gentlemen, they will along with company, for they haue great charge.

Exeunt.

Enter Chamberlaine.

Gad. What ho: Chamberlaine.

Cham. At hand quoth picke-purſe.

Gad. That's euē as faire, as at hand quoth the Chamberlaine: for thou varieſt no more from picking of purſes, then giuing direction, doth from labouring: thou layeſt the plot how.

Cham. Good morrow maſter Gadſhill, it holds currant that I told you yeſternight, ther's a Franckelin in the wild of Kent, hath brought three hundred marks with him in gold, I heard him tell it to one of his company laſt night at ſupper, a kind of Auditor, one that hath abundance of charge too, God knowes what, they are vp already, and call for egges and butter, they will away preſently.

Gad. Sirra, if they meet not with Saint Nicholas clarks, ile giue thee this necke.

Cham. No, ile none of it, I pray thee keepe that for the hang-man, for I know thou worſhippeſt Saint Nicholas, as truely as a man of falſhood may.

Ga. What talkeſt thou to me of the hangman? if I hang, ile make a fat paire of gallowes: for if I hang, old ſir Iohn hangs with me, & thou knoweſt he is no ſtarueling: tut, there are other

Troians

of Henry the fourth.

Troians that thou dream'ſt not of, the which for ſport ſake are content to doe the profeſſion, ſome grace, that would (if matters ſhould be lookt into) for their owne credit ſake make all whole. I am ioyned with no footland rakers, no long-ſtaffe ſixepennie ſtrikers, none of theſe mad muſtachio purplehewd maltwormes, but with nobilitie, and tranquillitie: Burgomaſters and great Oneyers, ſuch as can hold in ſuch as wil ſtrike ſooner then ſpeak, and ſpeak ſooner then drinke, and drinke ſooner then pray, and yet (zoundes) I lie, for they pray continually to their Saint the Common-wealth, or rather not pray to her, but pray on her, for they ride vp and downe on her, and make her their bootes.

Cham. What, the Common-wealth their bootes? will ſhe hold out water in foule way?

Gad. She will, ſhe will, Iuſtice hath liquord her: we ſteale as in a Caſtle cockſure: we haue the receite of Fernſeede, wee walke inuiſible.

Cham. Nay by my faith, I thinke you are more beholding to the night, then to Fernſeed, for your walking inuiſible.

Gad. Giue me thy hand, thou ſhalt haue a ſhare in our purchaſe, as I am a true man.

Cham. Nay, rather let me haue it, as you are a falſe theefe.

Gad. Go to, *homo* is a common name to al men: bid the Oſtler bring my gelding out of the ſtable, farewell, ye muddy knaue.

Exeunt.

Enter Prince, Poynes, and Peto, &c.

Poin. Come ſhelter, ſhelter, I haue remoou'd Falſtalffes horſe, and he frets like a gum'd Veluet.

Prince. Stand cloſe.

Enter Falstalffe.

Falſ. Poynes, Poynes, and be hang'd Poynes.

Prince. Peace ye fat-kidneyd raſcal, what a brawling doeſt thou keepe?

Falſ. What Poynes, Hal?

Prin. He is walkt vp to the top of the hill, Ile go ſeeke him.

Falſ. I am accur'ſt to rob in that theeues companie, the raſcal hath remooued my horſe, and tyed him I know not where, if I trauell but foure foote by the ſquire further afoote, I ſhal breake my winde. Well, I doubt not but to die a faire death for all this, if I ſcape hanging for killing that rogue, I haue forſworne his company hourely any time this xxii. yeares, and yet I am be-

witcht

C 3

SCENE DEPICTING THE GADSHILL ROBBERY, AS PRINTED IN THE 1599 QUARTO OF *THE HISTORIE OF HENRY THE FOURTH* (PART OF THE FOLGER SHAKESPEARE LIBRARY COLLECTION).

The Historie

witch it with the rogues companie. If the rascall haue not giuen me medicines to make me loue him, ile be hang'd. It could
not be elfe, I haue drunke medicines, Poynes, Hal, a plague
vpon you both, Bardoll, Peto, ile starue e're ile rob a foote tur-
ther, and t'were not as good a deede as drinke to turne true-
man, and to leaue these rogues; I am the veriest varlet that euer
chewed with a tooth: eight yeardes of vneuen ground is threescore and ten miles afoote with mee: and the stonie hearted
villaines knowe it well inough, a plague vpon it when theeues
can not be true one to another. *They whistle.*
Whew, a plague vpon you all, giue mee my horse, you rogues,
giue me my horse, and be hang'd.

Prin. Peace ye fat guts, lie downe, lay thine eare close to the
ground, and list if thou can heare the tread of trauellers.

Falf. Haue you any leauers to lift me vp againe being downe?
blood ile not beare mine owne flesh so farre afoote againe, for
all the coine in thy fathers Exchequer: What a plague meane
ye, to colt me thus?

Prin. Thou lyest, thou art not colted, thou art vncolted.

Falf. I prethie good prince, Hal, helpe me to my horse, good
kings sonne.

Prin. Out you rogue, shall I be your Ostler?

Falf. Hang thy selfe in thine owne heire apparant garters: if
I be taine, ile peach for this; and I haue not Ballads made on you
all, and sung to filthy tunes, let a cuppe of facks be my poyfon:
when a iest is so forward, and afoote too, I hate it.

Enter Gadshill.

Gad. Stand.   *Falf.* So I do against my will.

Poi. O t'is our fetter, I know his voyce, Bardoll, what newes?

Bar. Case ye, case ye; on with your vizards, there's money
of the Kings comming downe the hill, t'is going to the Kings
Exchequer.

Falf. You lie, ye rogue, t'is going to the kings Tauerne.

Gad. There's inough to make vs all:

Falf. To be hang'd.

Prin. Sirs, you foure shal front them in the narrow lane: Ned
Poynes, and I will walke lower: if they scape from your encoun-

ter,

of Henry the fourth.

ter, then they light on vs.

Pero. How many be they of them?

Gad. Some eight, or ten.

Falf. Zoundes, will they not rob vs?

Prince. What, a coward, fir Iohn paunch?

Falf. Indeed I am not Iohn of Gaunt, your grandfather; but
yet no coward, Hal.

Prince. Well, we leaue that to the proofe.

Po. Sirra, Iacke, thy horse standes behinde the hedge, when
thou needst him, there thou shalt find him: farewel, & stand fast.

Falf. Now can not I strike him if I should be hang'd.

Prin. Ned, where are our disguises?

Poi. Here, hard by, stand close.

Falf. Now my masters, happy man be his dole, say I, euery
man to his businesse.

Enter the trauailers.

Trauai. Come neighbour, the boy shall lead our horses down
the hill, weele walke a foote a while, and ease our legs.

Theeues. Stand.

Trauel. Iesus blesse vs.

Falf. Strike, downe with them, cut the villaines throates: a
horeson Catterpillers, Bacon-fed knaues, they hate vs youth,
downe with them, fleece them.

Tra. O, we are vndone, both we and ours, for euer.

Fal. Hang ye gorbellied knaues, are ye vndone? no ye fatte
chuffes, I would your store were here: on Bacons on, what yee
knaues? yong men must liue, you are graunde iuers, are yee?
weele iure ye faith.

Here they rob them, and bind them.   Exeunt.

Enter the Prince and Poines.

Prin. The theeues haue bound the true men: no we coulde
thou and I rob the theeues, and go merily to London, it woulde
be argument for a weeke, laughter for a moneth, and a good iest
for euer.

Poines. Stand close, I heare them comming.

Enter the theeues againe.

Falf. Come, my masters, let vs share, and then to horse before
day: and the Prince and Poines bee not two arrant cowardes,
there's no equitie stirring, ther's no more valour in that Poines,
then in a wilde ducke.

Prin.

The Historie

Prin. Your money.
Pois. Villaines.

As they are sharing, the Prince and Poines
set vpon them, they all runne away, and
Falstaffe after a blow or two runs away
too, leauing the bootie behinde them.

Prin. Got with much ease. Now merrily to Horse: the theeues
are all scattered, and possest with feare so strongly, that they dare
not meete each other, each takes his fellow for an officer, away
good Ned, Falstaffe sweates to death, and lards the leane earth
as he walkes along, wer't not for laughing I should pittie him,

Poines. How the rogue roar'd.   Exeunt.

Enter Hotspur solus, reading a letter.

But for mine owne part my Lord, I could be well contented to bee
there, in respect of the loue I beare your house.

He could be contented: why is he not then? in the respect of
the loue he beares our house. He shewes in this, he loues his owne
barne better then he loues our house. Let me see some more.
The purpose you vndertake is dangerous,

Why that's certaine, t'is dangerous to take a cold, to sleepe,
to drinke, but I tell you (my Lord foole) out of this nettle danger, we plucke this flower safetie.

The purpose you vndertake is dangerous, the friends you haue named vncertaine, the time it selfe vnsorted, and your whole plot too
light, for the counterpoyse of so great an opposition.

Say you so, say you so. I say vnto you againe, you are a shallow cowardly hinde, and you lye: what a lacke-braine is this? by
the Lord our plot is a good plot, as euer was laid, our friends true
and constant: a good plot, good friends, & ful of expectation: an
excellent plot, very good friends, what a frostie spirited rogue is
this? why, my Lord of Yorke commends the plot, and the gene-
rall course of the Action. Zounds and I were now by this rascall, I could braine him with his Ladies fanne. Is there not my
father, my vncle, and my selfe, Lord Edmond Mortimer, my
Lord of Yorke, and Owen Glendower? is there not besides the
Dowglas? haue I not all their letters to meete me in armes by the
ninth of the next month? and are they not some of them set forward alreadie? what a pagan rascall is this, and infidell? Ha, you
shall see now in very sincerite of feare and cold heart, wil he to
the King, and lay open all our proceedings. O, I could deuide
my

of Henry the fourth.

my selfe, & go to buffets, for mouing such a dish of skim milke
with so honorable an action. Hang him, let him tell the king, we
are prepared: I will set forward to night.   Enter his Lady.

How now Kate, I must leaue you within these two houres?

Lady. O my good Lord, why are you thus alone?
For what offence haue I this fortnight bin
A banisht woman from my Harries bed?
Tell me, sweet Lord, what is't that takes from thee
Thy stomake, pleasure, and thy golden sleepe?
Why dost thou bend thine eyes vpon the earth?
And start so often when thou sitst alone?
Why hast thou lost the fresh bloud in thy cheekes?
And giuen my treasures and my rights of thee
To thicke ey'd musing, and curst melancholy?
In thy faint slumbers, I by thee haue watcht,
And heard thee murmur tales of yron wars,
Speake tearmes of mannage to thy bounding steed,
Cry courage to the field. And thou hast talkt
Of sallies, and retyres of trenches, tents,
Of pallizadoes, frontiers, parapets,
Of basilisks, of canon, culuerin,
Of prisoners ransome, and of souldiours slaine,
And all the currents of a heddy fight,
Thy spirit within thee hath bin so at war,
And thus hath so bestird thee in thy sleepe,
That beds of sweat haue stood vpon thy brow
Like bubbles in a late disturbed streame,
And in thy face strange motions haue appeard,
Such as we see when men restraine their breath,
On some great sudden haste. O, what portents are these?
Some heauy busines hath my Lord in hand,
And I must know it, else he loues me not.

Hot. What ho, is Gilliams with the packet gone?
Ser. He is, my Lord, an houre ago.
Hot. Hath Butler brought those horses from the Sheriffe?
Ser. One horse, my Lord, he brought euen now.
Hot. What horse, Roane? a cropeare, is it not?
Ser. It is my Lord.

D

Hot.

LESSON 3 "What a Plague Have I to Do with a Buff Jerkin?"

Actors in Rehearsal

PLAY SECTIONS COVERED IN THIS LESSON

1.1 King Henry IV hears reports of wars and rebellions.

LINES: King, 75; Lancaster, 0; Westmoreland, 32; others in the court, 0

1.2 The tavern crew jokes and plans a robbery.

LINES: Falstaff, 86; Prince Hal, 89; Poins, 48

1.3.127–313 The rebels meet.

LINES: Hotspur, 110; Northumberland, 16; Worcester, 60

WHAT'S ON FOR TODAY AND WHY

Today, acting groups accost their first scene. Let the students have at it and don't wince at mispronunciations or skewed interpretations. If students are to run the show, teachers had best get out of the way. However, as students read scenes through and discuss problems with language, they can use the teacher and other resources to answer questions, so you will want to have on hand a classroom library of resources. Some suggestions:

- A variety of editions of the play. Students will probably each have a copy of the New Folger edition, which reflects the excellent scholarship of Barbara Mowat and Paul Werstine. A collection of others is useful since text, glosses, and scholarly viewpoints expressed vary from edition to edition. The Oxford, edited by David Bevington, is a fine resource, as is the Signet, with Maynard Mack's useful introduction.
- *The Variorum Editions of Shakespeare*, a series begun by Howard Horace Furness, which compares editions before 1904 and gives a variety of critical responses to performances of the play. Variorum editions are often available in libraries, particularly college and university libraries. If these aren't a possibility, the Arden editions, famous for their thorough notes, are good substitutes.

- *The Norton Facsimile of the First Folio,* prepared by Charlton Hinman (currently out of print but available in many libraries), which presents the 1623 First Folio edition.
- *Shakespeare Lexicon and Quotation Dictionary,* by Alexander Schmidt, a two-volume set recommended by Stephen Booth as the best "Shakespeare dictionary."
- *Harvard Concordance to Shakespeare,* by Martin Spivak, a great help for finding when and where certain words occur in the play.
- *Oxford English Dictionary,* as complete an edition as you can afford, which can give students the definitions of words as people used them in Shakespeare's time and before.

To give students specific directions to use throughout the unit, duplicate Handout 4: Preparing Scenes for Performance.

WHAT TO DO

1. Power Play

Talk about log entries from the homework assignment. Ask students what they surmise about the distribution of power in *Henry.* Who has it? Who wants it?

2. Acting Company Rehearsal

Send students to their corners of the room with scripts (books) and Handout 4: Preparing Scenes for Performance. To solidify expectations, distribute Handout 5: Evaluation of Student Scenes. While they are rehearsing, write the homework assignment on the board.

3. Homework

About ten minutes before class is over, reconvene students to answer questions about the scenes in rehearsal and to tell them how you will evaluate their performance.

Distribute Handout 5: Evaluation of Student Scenes. If you plan to use this evaluation, let students preview it today. This is useful for evaluating the scenes in all five acts of the play. It can be used by the teacher alone, or you can ask the acting groups to do a group evaluation of one another.

Then give them homework assignments:

- Assignment 1: Practice your lines on whoever will listen. Do them in front of a mirror and add gesture, inflection, stress, pause. Get together with scenemates if possible. Directors for a day should write up notes about the entire scene to use at "final" rehearsals the next day (movement, line delivery, gesture suggestions, for example). Emphasize these directions as often as needed to ensure good performances over the course of the unit.

• Assignment 2: Think about a character you play in this scene. (Some students will play more than one.) In logs, write a few sentences about what this person is like. What does she hope to accomplish in the scene? Then think about your upcoming performance. Are there words (yours or others) you don't understand? Note those, and ask or look up before performing.

HOW DID IT GO?   Do your students take the log seriously? Do you plan to read logs from time to time? If so, use them as a measure of how well students comprehend the play, how involved they are with the people and the issues. Was the rehearsal total chaos? Just right—if actors and directors kept their minds on the production.

ॐ

HANDOUT 4

PREPARING SCENES FOR PERFORMANCE

During this unit, you will present a series of scenes from *Henry IV, Part 1*. You and your group will prepare a scene and perform it with scripts in hand. You will go through all the steps that actors do except memorizing lines.

1. Choose a director. Rotate. Use a different director for each scene.

2. As we did with the robbery scene in Lesson 2, read through the scene. Ask and answer questions about characters, plot, language, and staging. Use your teacher and the classroom library as resources. Ideally, everyone in the scene should understand every word spoken.

3. For each character in your scene, choose a trademark hat or prop. As the unit progresses, the character might be played by a number of actors, but if the character always appears on stage with the same hat or prop, it will be easy for the audience to recognize him or her.

4. Cast the scene. Assign a speaking part to each member of the group. It's okay to divide the longer speeches among actors. Just make sure the trademark hat or prop gets passed around. Likewise, it's okay for some members to play more than one part.

5. Cut the scene. If there are lines or phrases that cloud rather than clarify the business of the scene, cut them. But make sure all cast members work from the same script. This may mean that you make photocopies of your scene and use them rather than the books for scripts.

6. Use props, costumes, or other means to make your scene as clear as possible. For example, because so many characters drifted in and out of their scene, one group of students made pillow-case doublets—old pillow cases with holes cut for head and arms to avoid suffocation. They decorated the doublets with simple, bold, heraldic designs and the character's name.

7. Talk about how best to present this scene to the rest of the class, keeping in mind that they have not read the scene or done any preparation for it. If the scene is hard to understand, for example, the company may want to add an introduction or dumb show, or summarize it before or after.

8. Get on your feet and do the scene for a productive rehearsal.

9. Present it to the class.

ॐ

HANDOUT 5

EVALUATION OF STUDENT SCENES

Evaluator's Name: _____

Presentation Title: _____

Players: _____

Theme or Idea—20 points

It is clear that the acting group has a unifying idea or theme, and this idea helps the audience to see the scene in a clearer and/or more interesting way.   _____ (10)

Acting company members have used cuts, narration, special effects and/or other techniques to make sure the presentation expresses the unifying idea or theme.   _____ (10)

Performance—80 points

Players speak loudly and distinctly so they can be heard.   _____ (10)

Players deliver their lines so that the emotion and subtext come across.   _____ (10)

Players use appropriate movement, interpreting the lines physically whenever possible.   _____ (10)

Props and costumes are simple and imaginative and contribute to the audience's understanding of the scene.   _____ (10)

The set is simple but suggests the acting company's theme and reinforces the audience's understanding of the scene.   _____ (10)

The players demonstrate energy and enthusiasm.   _____ (10)

The players use the twenty minutes allotted for their presentation efficiently, moving smoothly through setup, performance, strike, and questions from the audience.   _____ (10)

Players cooperate. The group knows what to do and works together well.   _____ (10)

Total Group Score: _____/100

Comments:

Individuals to Be Commended:

LESSON 4 "It Jumps with My Humor"

Performing Act 1

ॐ _____

PLAY SECTIONS COVERED IN THIS LESSON

1.1 King Henry IV hears reports of wars and rebellions.

LINES: King, 75; Lancaster, 0; Westmoreland, 32; others in the court, 0

1.2 The tavern crew jokes and plans a robbery.

LINES: Falstaff, 86; Prince Hal, 89; Poins, 48

1.3.127–313 The rebels meet.

LINES: Hotspur, 110; Northumberland, 16; Worcester, 60

ॐ _____

WHAT'S ON FOR TODAY AND WHY

Shakespeare wrote to be performed, so do it. Give acting groups twenty minutes to rehearse. Then quiet the set and turn the spotlight on Act 1, scene 1. Depending on how efficient and experienced students are, this lesson could take two days. Don't rush it. Ask for heroic concentration and communication.

WHAT TO DO

1. Rehearsal

Send acting companies to their corners to perfect their performances. While they labor, write the homework assignment on the board.

2. Performance

If you plan to evaluate student scenes with Handout 5, ask each director to fill out the top portion of the form to give to you before the scene starts. If groups will evaluate one another, make sure they have copies of the form and time to complete it.

Set the stage. Introduce the play. Have the Rebels and Pub Crawlers take seats and turn their attention on the Courtiers. Rotate through the scenes. After each performance, pause and let actors answer questions from the house. Before the last performance, summarize for the class the opening of 1.3:

Henry IV meets with his former supporters in rebellion—Northumberland, Worcester, and Hotspur—to ask why Hotspur hasn't surrendered, in the feudal tradition, the prisoners he's taken in the continuing border wars. Hotspur explains that he was originally put off by the King's foppish messenger, then further refuses until the King ransoms his brother-in-law, Edmund Mortimer, from Owen Glendower. Henry refuses, calling Mortimer a traitor because he has married Glendower's daughter while being held prisoner. (Also, Shakespeare got this Mortimer, Roger Mortimer, mixed up with another Mortimer, Edmund Mortimer, who was a true claimant of the throne, so Henry didn't want Mortimer on the loose.)

3. Evaluation

Ask students about their level of understanding. Are they following the plot? Do they have a fair idea of who the people are? Would it help to look at their illustrated cast lists or their summaries during the performance? Do readers need to slow down, use more gestures, pause more often, speak more clearly?

4. Homework (Day 1)

In logs, ask students to summarize in a few sentences the scenes they saw performed. Also, ask them to read again Hal's last speech in 1.2 and tell what they think of Hal. Does the fact that he is calculating make him less likable? He says he will "imitate" the sun and become a true prince. How does the word "imitation" resonate in this play?

5. Homework (Day 2)

Ask students to summarize in their logs the scenes performed today. Then ask them to reread Hotspur's "honor" speech (1.3.199–212) and comment on the rivalry between Hal and Hotspur. Ask: What is your definition of honor? Can you invent a metaphor for it?

HOW DID IT GO?

Based on your observations during the performances and on the evaluation session, how do students respond to the scenes in performance? If they were fun and intelligible and the questions were genuine, the technique was successful. If not, give actors a pep talk.

5 "The Tenor of Thy Kinsman's Trust"

A Shaken Kingdom

WHAT'S ON FOR TODAY AND WHY

The main idea to leave with students at the end of this lesson is that even though Henry IV is a strong and able king, he could lose his power at any minute because of the way he took the throne. It is important to their understanding of the play that students realize Henry's claim to the crown is disputable. As a usurper with Richard's blood on his hands, Henry is a part of the general disorder of his kingdom, a disorder reflected in the robbers of the Boar's Head and in the rebels' camp.

To convey this idea, you will construct a genealogy chart and give them essential comments on the historical background—loosely transcribed from one Tom Eslick, a teacher at Proctor Academy, Andover, NH, created while at the Folger Teaching Shakespeare Institute. Don't nod off. I know the following "script" doesn't look brief, but it doesn't take too long, and I've found it crucial to understanding the play.

WHAT TO DO

1. Log Exchange

While you are putting up a blank genealogical chart for Edward III on an overhead transparency or on the board (Handout 6), ask students to exchange logs, write a response to one another, and re-exchange. Ask for recommended pieces to be read aloud, if you wish.

2. Genealogy Chart

Use the completed genealogical chart on Edward III and the accompanying script for yourself. Give students the blank chart (Handout 6). Fill in the blanks on the board or overhead and have students fill in as you explain who's who. Use the following text if it is helpful—I need it every time:

> Once upon a time there was a king named Edward III who was very good at producing offspring. To be specific, he fathered twelve children, seven of whom were boys. (The principle of legitimacy extended only to sons of kings and their heirs at the time.) Two of the boys died early—the second and the seventh sons, both named William—which leaves only five boys for us to keep track of.

Take a look at the Edward III genealogy handout. I hope filling in the names helps you to keep them straight. On the extreme left side of the paper fill in the box with the name of Edward III's firstborn son: Edward, called The Black Prince. Peter Saccio, Shakespeare historian, says this is because he wore black armor; but not at birth, I assume.

Since the second son, William, died early, the next box is the third son: Lionel of Antwerp. [It is convenient here to explain that titles often indicate place of birth as well as distinguishing traits; this becomes important when students find Henry IV's titles include Bolingbroke, Hereford, and Lancaster.]

In the third box fill in John of Gaunt. (Gaunt is the Anglicized word for Ghent in Flanders or Belgium.) In the fourth box enter Edmund of York, and in the fifth, Thomas of Woodstock (Gloucester). There we have Edward III's five sons.

Now there are only two more boxes to fill in. In the box underneath Edward, The Black Prince, place his son's name, Richard of Bordeaux (Richard II). In the box underneath John of Gaunt write Henry Bolingbroke (Henry IV). These are some of the principal characters in Shakespeare's tetralogy of history plays—*Richard II, Henry IV, Part 1, Henry IV, Part 2*, and *Henry V*. Let's consider the political situation that developed when Richard II took the throne.

Study the chart and read the first three items on the fact sheet. When Edward, The Black Prince, died, his father named Richard next in line of succession. A year later, Edward III died, leaving Richard king of England. Unfortunately, Richard was only 10 years old, too young to rule a country, so he was manipulated by his older uncles until he became an adult. Not surprisingly, he was a spiteful and capricious king.

3. How Henry Gained the Throne

Entertain questions and discussion about the genealogy chart. Then talk about how Henry IV came to power: that he was Henry Bolingbroke, the brassy lord who accused another nobleman of treason against King Richard; that Bolingbroke was in the throes of a fight-to-the-death duel with this nobleman when the king banished them; that Northumberland and other rebel lords brought Bolingbroke back to England and put him on the throne as Henry IV.

Ask: How would Henry IV react to the news that lords are rebelling? Why would he be particularly upset to learn that Northumberland and Northumberland's son are among the rebels?

4. Genealogy Chart II

Now that your students have mastered the information given so far, do a second genealogy chart with them so they can refine their understanding of relationships within the rebel camp and the court.

Tell them to read the information on Handout 7: Tawdry Background Details while you sketch another genealogical chart for *Henry IV, Part*

1. Copy the blank chart for Handout 7 on the board or put a transparency of it on the overhead and whiz through this:

> By looking at the charts you just did, you can fill in the third son of Edward III, Lionel of Antwerp; the fourth son, John of Gaunt; and his son, whom we can now call Henry IV.
>
> Lionel of Antwerp had a daughter named Phillipa, so you can enter her name under his. After you have entered Phillipa, place the name of her husband, Edmund Mortimer, in the box to the left of hers, linked by the double line denoting marriage.
>
> Now let's look at the children of this marriage. Follow the vertical line down from Phillipa and Edmund to the horizontal line to the left. Follow it to their firstborn child, Kate, Lady Percy. Kate is married to Henry Percy, Hotspur. If you follow the vertical line up and to the right, you will reach Hotspur's father, whose name is (you guessed it) Henry Percy (Earl of Northumberland). Henry (Northumberland) Percy's older brother is Thomas Percy (Earl of Worcester), so place it to the left.
>
> Your chart should now have nine boxes filled in, so be of good cheer. These will become cherished documents before we've finished studying the play.
>
> Before we fill in the remaining boxes, look at the tawdry detail that begins "Family alliances and wars." The second child of Edmund Mortimer and Phillipa was a son named Roger Mortimer (fourth Earl of March). This earl was the legitimate claimant to the throne while Richard was still king, but he was assassinated, leaving his son Edmund Mortimer (fifth Earl of March) the next in line of succession. So to the box right of Kate Mortimer, add Roger Mortimer, and beneath him his son Edmund, legitimate claimant to the throne.
>
> Shakespeare confused this Edmund as heir apparent with his uncle by the same name, Sir Edmund Mortimer. Shakespeare used the historian Holinshed as his source, and Holinshed was wrong. The confusion, however, is merely interesting historical data; it doesn't affect the play's drama.
>
> So, in the box to the right of Roger Mortimer, write Sir Edmund Mortimer, who married the daughter (the lady sings in Welsh) of Owen Glendower. She is known only as Lady Mortimer in the play. Her name goes in the box connected with the double line to Sir Edmund Mortimer's, and her father's name, Owen Glendower, goes above her.
>
> Hold on to these. You'll need them for reference.

5. Homework

Based on the information they acquired in the genealogy charts, ask students to write about Henry IV in their logs: what are his fears, his problems, his triumphs?

HOW DID IT GO?

No doubt about it, students are now overloaded with information. Let them process it according to their own learning styles. If they picked up only one idea, let it be that King Henry IV's position is precarious.

HANDOUT 6

GENEALOGY I

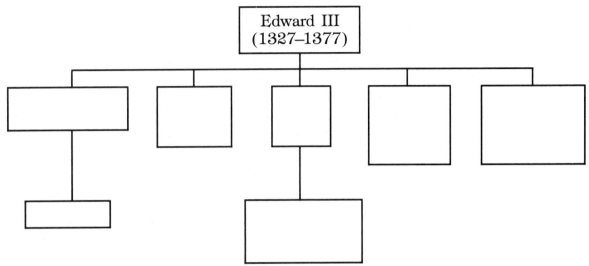

Fact Sheet

- In the 14th century in England, the crown passed from father to first son, to second son, and so forth; then to the father's oldest brother, second oldest brother, and so on. The principle of legitimacy decreed that none of the younger sons could inherit until the line of the oldest was extinct. Daughters were to work on their embroidery and not worry their pretty heads about thrones.

- Edward III is the villain of this piece because he had so many sons for us to keep up with—seven, in fact. Two of them—both named William, incidentally—died, making our task somewhat simpler.

- Edward, The Black Prince, was set to be the next king after Edward III. However, he died a year before his father. King Edward named The Black Prince's son Richard to succeed him to the throne.

- When Edward III died in 1377, only three of his sons remained: John of Gaunt, Edmund of Langley (York), and Thomas of Woodstock (Gloucester). The Black Prince's son, Richard, age 10, was named king.

- The situation in England was chaotic when Richard II took the throne—war in France, the Black Death, and a peasant revolt. Because he was so young, his uncles ran the country. As he grew older, the situation worsened. Richard got control of the kingdom and banished his uncle Gloucester to Calais, where he died. But Richard II lost control when he banished Henry Bolingbroke only to have a group of powerful noblemen return him to England. This group of rebels, aided in no small degree by Harry Percy (Northumberland), forced Richard to step down from the throne and give it to Bolingbroke, even though Richard II had ruled that Lionel of Antwerp's descendants were next in line. Bolingbroke became Henry IV. Richard II was executed.

HANDOUT 7

HENRY IV, PART 1: TAWDRY BACKGROUND DETAILS

Richard II, briefly stated: Henry Bolingbroke accuses Thomas Mowbray, who had escorted the banished Gloucester to Calais and was on hand looking suspicious when Gloucester died, of treason. Bolingbroke and Mowbray are to have an old-fashioned combat to the death to settle the dispute, but just as they are about to fight, King Richard II intervenes, declares both parties guilty, and banishes them both—Bolingbroke for ten years (reduced to six) and Mowbray for life. John of Gaunt soon dies (but not before uttering a patriotic speech about the sceptered realm), and King Richard boldly seizes his estate to finance his war against Ireland. This worries Harry Percy (Northumberland), who reasons that if the king can take Gaunt's estates what about his own? Northumberland sympathizes with John of Gaunt's banished and now disinherited son, Henry Bolingbroke, and seeks to return him to England. Bolingbroke sees his return as a chance not only to regain his inheritance but also to gain the throne. With the help of the rebel lords, Bolingbroke forces Richard's deposition and orders his imprisonment. Soon after, a toady takes it on himself to kill Richard to gain favor with King Henry IV.

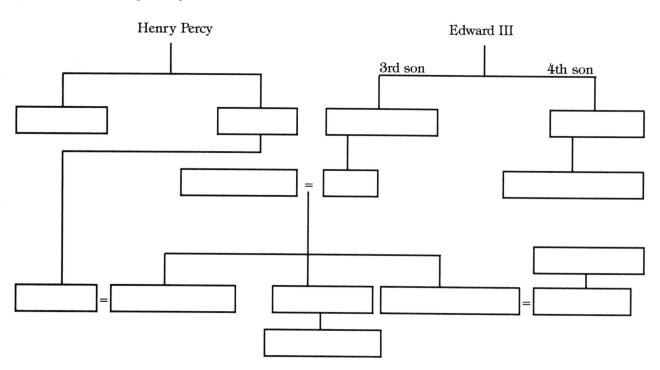

Fact Sheet

1. Much of Henry IV's reign was occupied with the suppression of revolt. The Welsh and Scots saw this internal strife as an opportunity to advance their own national ambitions.

2. Phillipa married Edmund Mortimer who died in Ireland in 1381. By that time he had had a son, Roger Mortimer, who became the 4th Earl of March. This Earl succeeded while Richard II was still king, and was the legitimate claimant to the throne. In 1398, Roger Mortimer was assassinated. Richard immediately recognized Edmund Mortimer, 5th Earl of March as the next in line (the great-grandson of the third son, Lionel—8 years old at his father's death). Henry IV kept the Earl and his brother under custody throughout his reign.

3. Who is the Mortimer defeated by the Welsh? Sir Edmund Mortimer, the legitimate claimant's uncle. Shakespeare was confused because Holinshed was. Otherwise, why, we might ask, in this time of inner turmoil, would Henry IV give an army to a rightful heir? But for the purposes of Shakespeare's view of history, it makes good sense not to ransom Mortimer since he feels he is the direct heir.

4. Hotspur is really 38 years old, two years older than the king himself, but Shakespeare makes him a young man to be a dramatic foil for Hal.

र्के

TEACHER'S GUIDE TO HANDOUT 6

GENEALOGY I

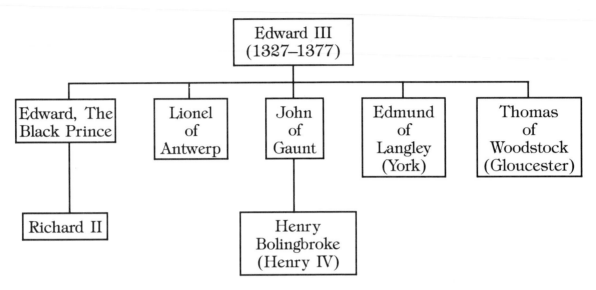

Fact Sheet

- In the 14th century in England, the crown passed from father to first son, to second son, and so forth; then to the father's oldest brother, second oldest brother, and so on. The principle of legitimacy decreed that none of the younger sons could inherit until the line of the oldest was extinct. Daughters were to work on their embroidery and not worry their pretty heads about thrones.

- Edward III is the villain of this piece because he had so many sons for us to keep up with—seven, in fact. Two of them—both named William, incidentally—died, making our task somewhat simpler.

- Edward, The Black Prince, was set to be the next king after Edward III. However, he died a year before his father. King Edward named The Black Prince's son Richard to succeed him to the throne.

- When Edward III died in 1377, only three of his sons remained: John of Gaunt, Edmund of Langley (York), and Thomas of Woodstock (Gloucester). The Black Prince's son, Richard, age 10, was named king.

- The situation in England was chaotic when Richard II took the throne—war in France, the Black Death, and a peasant revolt. Because he was so young, his uncles ran the country. As he grew older, the situation worsened. Richard got control of the kingdom and banished his uncle Gloucester to Calais, where he died. But Richard II lost control when he banished Henry Bolingbroke only to have a group of powerful noblemen return him to England. This group of rebels, aided in no small degree by Harry Percy (Northumberland), forced Richard to step down from the throne and give it to Bolingbroke, even though Richard II had ruled that Lionel of Antwerp's descendants were next in line. Bolingbroke became Henry IV. Richard II was executed.

र्के

ॐ

TEACHER'S GUIDE TO HANDOUT 7

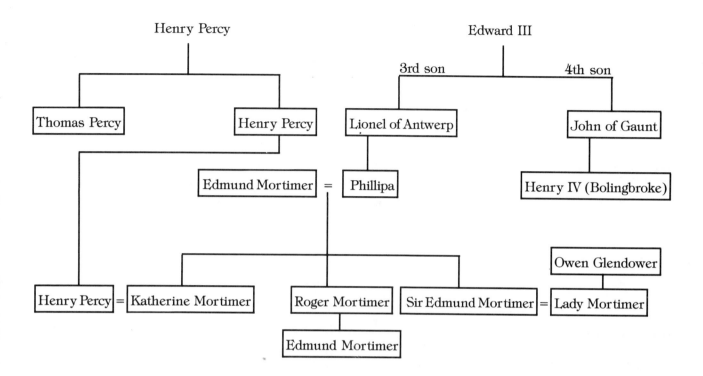

Fact Sheet

1. Much of Henry IV's reign was occupied with the suppression of revolt. The Welsh and Scots saw this internal strife as an opportunity to advance their own national ambitions.

2. Phillipa married Edmund Mortimer who died in Ireland in 1381. By that time he had had a son, Roger Mortimer, who became the 4th Earl of March. This Earl succeeded while Richard II was still king, and was the legitimate claimant to the throne. In 1398, Roger Mortimer was assassinated. Richard immediately recognized Edmund Mortimer, 5th Earl of March as the next in line (the great-grandson of the third son, Lionel—8 years old at his father's death). Henry IV kept the Earl and his brother under custody throughout his reign.

3. Who is the Mortimer defeated by the Welsh? Sir Edmund Mortimer, the legitimate claimant's uncle. Shakespeare was confused because Holinshed was. Otherwise, why, we might ask, in this time of inner turmoil, would Henry IV give an army to a rightful heir? But for the purposes of Shakespeare's view of history, it makes good sense not to ransom Mortimer since he feels he is the direct heir.

4. Hotspur is really 38 years old, two years older than the king himself, but Shakespeare makes him a young man to be a dramatic foil for Hal.

ॐ

LESSON 6 "Disorder, Horror, Fear, and Mutiny"

The Blood on Henry's Hands

WHAT'S ON FOR TODAY AND WHY

To continue with the theme of disorder and violence surrounding Henry IV, students will consider how two speeches from *Richard II* anticipate the mood of Henry's reign as illustrated by lines from *Henry IV, Part 1.*

WHAT TO DO

1. Richard II

Explain that Henry IV's troubles were predicted in the first play of the Henriad, *Richard II.* Hand out copies of Carlisle's speech (*Richard II*, 4.1.121–149) and Richard's (*Richard II*, 5.1.55–68) (Handout 8). Take the passages one by one. Read aloud a couple of times. Define words if necessary. Paraphrase. Answer the questions in the handout. Discuss the predictions. Judging from what he learned in Act 1 of *Henry IV, Part 1*, is there disorder, horror, fear, and mutiny in Henry IV's kingdom? Is it as bad as the field of Golgotha? Has the love of wicked men turned to fear? Did that fear turn to hate? And did that hate turn to danger and death?

2. How Bad Is It?

To show the magnitude of danger and death, return to *Henry IV, Part 1.* Point out that although Henry says, "The edge of war . . . shall no more cut his master," this play is full of violence and butchery. To illustrate, give them Handout 9, which traces the repetition of violent terms. To experience the bloody images, let them be read aloud, perhaps with the teacher or designated narrator reading the introduction and transitions and students taking turns reading the quotes. Then answer the questions raised in the handout.

3. Children's Poems

Distribute Handout 10: A Child's Version of the Henriad, which presents children's poems about Richard II, Henry IV, and Henry V. These make fun choral reading if you have time. If not, tell students to read them at home. Then have students react to them in their logs. Do they illuminate the plays?

HOW DID IT GO?   Did students expand their perspective of King Henry IV, the causes for his unrest, the motive for his drive, his need for a pilgrimage to atone?

ે

HANDOUT 8

PROPHECIES OF DOOM

William Shakespeare wrote four plays which scholars call the Henriad. The series starts with *Richard II*, in which Henry Bolingbroke is banished, then later crowned as Henry IV. Next is *Henry IV, Part 1*, then *Henry IV, Part 2*, both about the time when Henry IV was on the throne struggling with insurrections and an errant son, Prince Hal. The series ends with *Henry V*, when Prince Hal is King Henry V and leads an English army to France.

We saw in Act 1 of *Henry IV, Part 1* that Henry is troubled with rebel armies forming in the North, in Wales, and in Scotland, with some of the most admirable men in his court joining the revolution. Looking back to the play before this in the Henriad, we see predictions that if Henry is named king, England will degenerate into tumultuous wars, corruption, bloodshed.

Read carefully these predictions. Then answer the questions they raise.

Passage One: A group of nobles comes to depose Richard II. Knowing he is outpowered, he gives up his crown, which goes to Bolingbroke, also known as Herford and later as King Henry IV. The loyal Bishop of Carlisle predicts:

> What subject can give sentence on his king?
> And who sits here that is not Richard's subject? . . .
> My Lord of Herford here, whom you call king,
> Is a foul traitor to proud Herford's king,
> And if you crown him, let me prophesy,
> The blood of English shall manure the ground,
> And future ages groan for this foul act.
> Peace shall go sleep with Turks and infidels,
> And in this seat of peace tumultuous wars
> Shall kin with kin and kind with kind confound.
> Disorder, horror, fear, and mutiny
> Shall here inhabit, and this land be call'd
> The field of Golgotha and dead men's skulls.
> O, if you raise this house against this house,
> It will the woefullest division prove
> That ever fell upon this cursed earth.
> Prevent it, resist it, let it not be so,
> Lest child, child's children, cry against you "woe!"
> —*Richard II*, 4.1.121–149 (*The Riverside Shakespeare*)

1. Paraphrase the first two lines.

2. List the horrible things that will happen if Henry is crowned king.

3. For how long will the horrible things go on?

4. How does this affect Prince Hal?

Passage Two: Richard II addresses the men who betrayed him and sought to put Henry on the throne:

> Northumberland, thou ladder wherewithal
> The mounting Bullingbrook ascends my throne,
> The time shall not be many hours of age
> More than it is, ere foul sin gathering head
> Shall break into corruption. Thou shalt think,
> Though he divide the realm and give thee half,
> It is too little, helping him to all;
> He shall think that thou, which knowest the way
> To plant unrightful kings, wilt know again,
> Being ne'er so little urg'd, another way
> To pluck him headlong from the usurped throne.
> The love of wicked men converts to fear,
> That fear to hate, and hate turns one or both
> To worthy danger and deserved death.
> —*Richard II,* 5.1.55–68 (*The Riverside Shakespeare*)

1. What nobleman does Richard II mention by name? What part does this person play in the overthrow of Richard? What part does that person play in *Henry IV, Part 1?*

2. What foul sins will happen when Henry is on the throne?

3. When will the sins start? In *Henry IV, Part 1*, 1.1, Henry IV talks of going on a pilgrimage. Connect that with the sins mentioned in this passage.

4. Look at your genealogy charts and the information listed on them. Why does Richard II say Bolingbroke is "unrightful"?

5. Use what you know to make an intelligent guess: Are there people in Henry IV's court who were present for one or both of these prophecies? What effect does that have on Henry IV's power?

&

HANDOUT 9

A USURPER'S SHAKEN WORLD: A PATTERN OF IMAGES

In class discussion and in Handout 8: Prophecies of Doom, we have seen predictions of bloodshed, death, destruction during the reign of Henry IV. To what extent are these present in the play? Here is a list of violent images we encounter in *Henry IV, Part 1,* as pointed out by Maynard Mack. Can you add to the list?

Do you see patterns? Do the violent images become more frequent or intense? Do they center around particular people or places? What do you notice about the presence of violence?

Images of Violence in *Henry IV, Part 1*

In Henry's opening speech, he explains how England is recovering from the "furious close of civil butchery" (1.1.13).

"So shaken as we are, so wan with care" (1.1.1).

His realm's peace is "frighted . . . pants to breathe" (1.1.2).

"No more the thirsty entrance of this soil / Shall daub her lips with her own children's blood" (1.1.5–6).

Henry assures the court that "The edge of war . . . No more shall cut his master" (1.1.17–18) and that he will keep his pledge to journey to Jerusalem.

Almost immediately, however, Henry is informed that his realm's troubles continue. In the West, a thousand of Mortimer's men have been "butcherèd" and mutilated (1.1.42–46). In the North, ten thousand Scottish corpses were seen "balked in their own blood" (1.1.69).

These images of violence continue throughout the play:

"guns, and drums, and wounds" (1.3.57)

"many a good tall fellow destroyed" (1.3.64)

"bloody noses and cracked crowns" (2.3.98)

"a garment all of blood" (3.2.140)

men offered up "hot and bleeding" to "the fire-eyed maid of smoky war" (4.1.120–21)

Falstaff's recruits tossed dead into a pit: "Tut, tut, good enough to toss; food for powder" (4.2.66–67)

The maimed sent to the town's end "to beg during life" (5.3.40–41)

HANDOUT 10

A CHILD'S VERSION OF THE HENRIAD

Eleanor and Herbert Farjeon compiled a collection of children's poems about English monarchs and published them in *Kings and Queens* (London: J.M. Dent and Sons, Ltd., 1983). Here are the entries for Richard II, Henry IV, and Henry V.

Henry V
1413

Henry was a wild boy,
Fond of fun and fooling;
When he was the Prince of Wales
He made a hash of schooling;
Rollicking with tosspots,
Trying daddy's crown on,
Henry was the sort of boy
Fathers always frown on.

Henry was a brave man,
Fond of martial phrases;
When he was the English King
He won his country's praises;
Bucking up his soldiers,
Urging rank and file on,
Henry was the sort of man
Women always smile on.

Richard II
1377

Bend down your head,
King Richard the Second!
Bend down your head
And put on the crown!
The people are singing
Good luck to King Richard!
The joy-bells are ringing
All over the town.
Bolingbroke's banished,
The rebel has vanished,
Richard is up,
And Bolingbroke's down!

Bow down your head,
King Richard the Second!
Bow down your head
And put off the crown!
The people are wailing
Bad luck to King Richard!
And mock at him trailing
His chains through the town.
His dog as he lingers
Licks Bolingbroke's fingers,
Bolingbroke's up,
And Richard is down!

Henry IV
1399

Bolingbroke, Bolingbroke, what will you do?
The Kingdom of England is split into two!
Harry the Hotspur, the flame of the north,
Is chafing to vanquish you, Henry the Fourth,
Douglas of Scotland is arming his clans
To fight you and beat you and baffle your plans!
Owen Glendower, the Wizard of Wales,
Is marshaling demons and devils with tails!
Richard's poor zany, a wandering elf,
Is claiming, men say, to be Richard himself!
And Harry, your son, sits in taverns and sings,
And cares not a straw for the glory of kings,
Bolingbroke, Bolingbroke, what will you do?

'I'll do a king's duty and see the thing through!
I'll show this young Hotspur, so bristling and bold,
What happens to lords who scoff at my sway
I'll strike at the Douglas who scoffs at my sway
And slit up his bagpipe for ever and aye!
'Glendower in Wales I'll besiege and beset—
I was never afraid of a bogeyman yet!
'The wandering zany is nothing to dread—
Let him say what he chooses, King Richard is dead!
'And my son, who has driven a thorn through my heart,
Will learn in good season to take the King's part!'

LESSON 7 "He Frets like a Gummed Velvet"

Setting Student Assignments

&

PLAY SECTIONS COVERED IN THIS LESSON

2.3 Hotspur reads a letter saying the rebellion is too dangerous, hears the anxious questions of his wife.

LINES: Hotspur, 73; Lady Percy, 48; Servant, 3

2.4.116–337 Falstaff gives his account of the Gad's Hill robbery.

LINES: Prince Hal, 86; Poins, 10; Falstaff, 116; Hostess, 5; Bardolph, 14; Peto, 5; Gadshill, 0; Francis, 0

2.4.338–570 The tavern crew hears news of civil war; Hal and Falstaff play King Henry and Prince Hal; Hal protects Falstaff.

LINES: Prince Hal, 61; Poins, 1; Falstaff, 122; Hostess, 8; Bardolph 2; Sheriff, 8; Carrier, 1; Peto, 9

&

WHAT'S ON FOR TODAY AND WHY

Now that students have a fairly solid historical footing, they will review Act 1 and take a short quiz. Finally, they will organize for the second round of scene performances.

You might skip 2.1, since it does not advance the plot, and 2.2, the Gad's Hill robbery we did in Lesson 2, but be prepared to recap it or have students enact it again when performances begin.

WHAT TO DO

1. Reacting to the Homework Assignment

Ask for volunteers to read their log entries about the children's poems. Invite comments. Collect logs to read.

2. Act 1 Quiz

As a class, or in small groups, review for five minutes the main events and characters students have met in *Henry.*

Then administer this brief quiz: Briefly identify the following characters in one or two sentences each: Falstaff, Hal, Hotspur, Richard II, Henry IV.

3. Organizing for Act 2 Performances

Appoint new directors and give the scene assignments for each group:

- Rebels: 2.3—Lady Percy with Hotspur
- Pub Crawlers: 2.4.116–337—Falstaff and company's account of robbery
- Court: 2.4.338–570—News of civil war; Falstaff and Hal's play

Explain that because there is no court scene in Act 2, Courtiers will do a tavern scene. They can rehearse in the court space and perform in the tavern space.

Help students with the letter Hotspur will read (in 2.3) from an unknown author who says he will not join the rebellion because it is too risky.

Students will need some discussion to set in their minds the political and military situations and to sort out which characters are with the king and which are rebelling against him. Get out the illustrated chart and review who is in what camp.

Finally, send students to their groups to cast their scenes.

4. Homework

Tell students to read their assigned scenes at least twice and to bring to class questions about language and ideas for staging.

HOW DID IT GO?

To judge the extent of students' involvement in the unit, use qualitative evidence: observe how they behave in rehearsal, read their log entries and quiz answers. Or use the direct method: ask them.

L E S S O N 8 "For It Is Worth the Listening To"

Act 2 in Rehearsal

PLAY SECTIONS COVERED IN THIS LESSON

2.3 Hotspur reads a letter saying the rebellion is too dangerous, hears the anxious questions of his wife.

LINES: Hotspur, 73; Lady Percy, 48; Servant, 3

2.4.116–337 Falstaff gives his account of the Gad's Hill robbery.

LINES: Prince Hal, 86; Poins, 10; Falstaff, 116; Hostess, 5; Bardolph, 14; Peto, 5; Gadshill, 0; Francis, 0

2.4.338–570 The tavern crew hears news of civil war; Hal and Falstaff play King Henry and Prince Hal; Hal protects Falstaff.

LINES: Prince Hal, 61; Poins, 1; Falstaff, 122; Hostess, 8; Bardolph, 2; Sheriff, 8; Carrier, 1; Peto, 9

WHAT'S ON FOR TODAY AND WHY

Today students will rehearse in their acting groups. Because they are more experienced and know how to use the classroom library to answer questions, the teacher should be less in demand and, with luck, can spend most of the period reading students' logs.

WHAT TO DO

1. Rehearsal

Do not dally. Hasten to acting companies for planning and rehearsal.

2. Homework

Ask students to perfect their work for Act 2 by practicing gestures, expression, and projection.

HOW DID IT GO?

What did the acting groups accomplish? If they are set, plan to start staging Act 2 tomorrow. If they are unsure and unprepared, repeat this lesson. Maybe you can get all of the logs read and the quizzes graded. Return these as soon as you can.

LESSON 9 "Thou Wilt Not Utter What Thou Dost Not Know"

Act 2 on Stage

ॐ _____

PLAY SECTIONS COVERED IN THIS LESSON

2.3 Hotspur reads a letter saying the rebellion is too dangerous, hears the anxious questions of his wife.

LINES: Hotspur, 73; Lady Percy, 48; Servant, 3

2.4.116–337 Falstaff gives his account of the Gad's Hill robbery.

LINES: Prince Hal, 86; Poins, 10; Falstaff, 116; Hostess, 5; Bardolph, 14; Peto, 5; Gadshill, 0; Francis, 0

ॐ _____

WHAT'S ON FOR TODAY AND WHY

Today students should present some fine performances. Student actors should understand the relationship between Lady Percy and Hotspur in 2.3 and the camaraderie among the tavern crew in 2.4. To give more time to the "play extempore" (2.5.338–570), do only the 2.3 and 2.4 today and let the little play within the play have a day of its own.

Remember to pause after performances, so that acting groups can answer questions, comment—whatever.

As with the first round of scenes, have evaluation forms prepared so that you and/or your student acting groups can assess student performances while they are in progress.

WHAT TO DO

1. Introduction and Setup

Return logs and quizzes and discuss. Then send students to their acting companies. Give them five minutes to organize before starting the scenes. Distribute evaluation forms. Begin with a brief recap of 2.2, the Gad's Hill robbery, or act it again if you have time. It will be clearer and better.

2. Performance and Discussion of 2.3

Have Rebels perform 2.3. After performance, make sure students understand the significance of the letter Hotspur reads from one who will not join his rebellion because its outcome is too uncertain. He will be deserted by more than this one.

Encourage discussion of the relationship between Kate and Hotspur. Why is Kate "unworthy" of his confidences, according to Hotspur? How did student actors portray their relationship? Could different choices in inflection, body language, and gestures make their relationship seem more loving or playful?

Let student actors answer questions from the audience.

3. Performance and Discussion of 2.4

Have Pub Crawlers perform 2.4.116–337. Ask the actors to answer questions from the audience. It will be obvious that there is a difference between what went on in the robbery and what Falstaff claims went on.

4. Homework

Ask students to summarize in their logs the scenes performed. Give them Handout 11: "To Lucasta, on Going to the Wars." Tell them to write a comparison of the thesis of this poem to the Percys' conversation in 2.3.

HOW DID IT GO?

Actors' energy level, audience questions, and log and quiz answers should give you some idea of their comprehension level.

❧

HANDOUT 11

"TO LUCASTA, ON GOING TO THE WARS"

Tell me not, sweet, I am unkind,
That from the nunnery
Of thy chaste breast and quiet mind
To war and arms I fly.

True, a new mistress now I chase,
The first foe in the field;
And with a stronger faith embrace
A sword, a horse, a shield.

Yet this inconstancy is such
As thou too shalt adore;
I could not love thee, dear, so much
Loved I not honor more.

—Richard Lovelace (1649)

❧

LESSON **10** "We Shall Have a Play Extempore"

More Act 2 on Stage

ॐ

PLAY SECTION COVERED IN THIS LESSON

2.4.338–570 The tavern crew hears news of civil war; Hal and Falstaff play King Henry and Prince Hal; Hal protects Falstaff.

LINES: Prince Hal, 61; Poins, 1; Falstaff, 122; Hostess, 8; Bardolph, 2; Sheriff, 8; Carrier, 1; Peto, 9

ॐ

WHAT'S ON FOR TODAY AND WHY

After a discussion of Richard Lovelace's poem, students will perform 2.4.338–570. Afterward, if you can locate a video version of *Henry IV, Part 1*, cue up the portion to be staged today. Showing more might discourage your actors, but seeing how professional actors and directors stage the scene can reinforce our concepts and inspire future performances.

Three versions of *Henry IV, Part 1* are available, each of which has its own strengths. Ideally your school media specialist will purchase all of them.

• *Chimes at Midnight,* Orson Welles's famous 1965 production, is an amazing visual masterpiece, but the sound track is flawed. The least complete of the three productions, *Chimes* is mostly Welles's compilation of the Falstaff-Hal scenes from *Henry IV, Part 1* and *Henry IV, Part 2,* plus a few from *Richard II* and *Henry V.* The Act 2 tavern scene students have been working on starts about twenty-seven minutes into the tape and runs seven minutes. The film includes a wonderful Boar's Head Tavern—Falstaff with a pot on his head, and lots of barking dogs. It is available from Facets Multimedia (1-800-331-6197).

• In the 1979 BBC version, this scene starts about one hour and fifteen minutes into the tape and runs twelve minutes and thirty seconds. Anthony Quayle plays Falstaff and David Gwillim plays Hal. This video has rowdy cheering and laughter and a fine cushion, and is available from The Writing Company (1-800-421-4246).

• The English Shakespeare Company's "Wars of the Roses" production of *Henry IV, Part 1* features British football hooligans, women in leather, skinheads, and punk hairdos. Students will hear Bardolph punctuating lines with his trombone, Gadshill playing a flute for the sheriff, and parts of Falstaff's speech accompanied by a flute. It is real Shakespeare and the most complete rendering of the scene, with few lines cut. It runs seventeen minutes and can be found about one hour and five minutes into the tape. Barry Stanton plays Falstaff, and Michael Pennington plays Hal. This is available from Films for the Humanities (1-800-257-5126), also a source for the English Shakespeare Company's productions of *Henry IV, Part 2* and *Henry V*.

Together, the three productions complement each other and give students bold ideas for scene concepts.

Because the log assignment is lengthy, you may want to make copies of it for students to take home. To prepare for the homework assignment, write the log questions on the board.

WHAT TO DO

1. Lucasta

Lead a discussion based on the work students did in their logs. Give particular attention to the Lovelace poem. Invite a reading, various comments.

2. Performance of 2.4.338–570

Have Pub Crawlers perform 2.4 only from 338 to 499. Stop when Hal says, "I do. I will." Let the actors answer questions from the audience.

Now resume and finish the performance. Again take questions from the audience.

3. Video of 2.4

If you have a video version, show just 2.4 and discuss directors' choices in both film and classroom versions.

4. The Sun in a New Light

If you like, ask students to return to Hal's "sun" speech, 1.2.202–224. Read it in unison. Ask: In light of what went on in Act 2, what do you think was in Hal's mind as he spoke these words?

5. Homework

Tell students to prepare for a quiz on Acts 1 and 2. Ask them to summarize in their logs the scene they saw today. Tell them to answer in their logs these questions:

· How many robberies have taken place or are being planned thus far in this play?
· How does the theme of robbery cut across the three groups of characters?
· Explain the line "coward(ice) upon instinct" (2.4.284). Under what circumstance, for example, might it be defensible?
· Describe your response to Falstaff's version of the robbery. Are these "lies" or humorous hyperbole?

HOW DID IT GO? The level of questions and discussion will let you know whether students understand what's up. Ask directors about level of cooperation.

LESSON 11   "A Time for Frighted Peace to Pant"

Workshop Day

WHAT'S ON FOR TODAY AND WHY

To bind together the loose ends and to give students a chance to pursue their long-term writing and activity projects, have a workshop day. The only formal activities will be a quiz on Acts 1 and 2 and a teacher-led discussion of the homework.

WHAT TO DO

1. Quiz

Give open-book quiz on Acts 1 and 2 (Handout 12). Correct together, and collect those and logs.

2. Conferences

Ask students to write on a slip of paper what they have chosen to do for their long-term writing and activity assignments. Then give them time to work on them. As they do, conduct one-minute conferences with each student. They hand you their choices, and you troubleshoot and double-check their intent and understanding of expectations.

HOW DID IT GO?

The quizzes and logs will indicate progress.

HANDOUT 12

OPEN-BOOK QUIZ ON ACTS 1 AND 2

Identify and explain the context for each of the following quotes. Who says it to whom, and under what circumstances?

1.   O, that it could be proved
   That some night-tripping fairy had exchanged
   In cradle-clothes our children where they lay,
   And called mine "Percy," his "Plantagenet"!

2. Where shall we take a purse tomorrow, Jack?

3.   I'll keep them all.
   By God, he shall not have a Scot of them.

4. Strike! Down with them! Cut the villains' throats!
   Ah, whoreson caterpillars, bacon-fed knaves . . .

5.   In faith,
   I'll know your business, Harry, that I will.

6. Why, hear you, my masters, was it for me to kill the heir apparent?

7. Banish not him thy Harry's company, banish not him thy Harry's company. Banish plump Jack, and banish all the world.

&

LESSON **12** "I Speak Not This in Estimation . . . But What I Know Is Ruminated, Plotted, and Set Down"

Speech Explication

WHAT'S ON FOR TODAY AND WHY

Speech explication gives students another taste of the kind of close reading Shakespearean scholars and actors do. Moving concentration from a kingdom to small units of language, this activity helps students discover a universe in a word. Then, as these universes begin to cluster and echo, students return to the world of the stage with new sounds in their ears.

Speech explication calls for strong focus and first-rate resources. Besides the editions, concordance, and *Oxford English Dictionary* listed in Lesson 3, I consult

- George J. Becker, *Shakespeare's Histories* (Frederick Ungar, 1977)
- Graham Holderness, *Shakespeare's History Plays Richard II to Henry V* (Macmillan, 1992)
- Scott McMillin, *Shakespeare in Performance: Henry IV, Part One* (Manchester University Press, 1991)
- Jeanne Addison Roberts, "Prince Hal as a Model for Professional Women," in *The Agnes Scott Alumnae Quarterly*, Summer 1974 (available by request from the Folger Shakespeare Library)
- electronic versions of the plays (Shakespeare on Disk or Word-Cruncher, for example) for help in locating words and phrases
- and the marvelous articles in Part One of this volume.

Today students will explicate one speech together. Each will be assigned a second speech from the wide-sweeping list of explications in Handout 13, which includes seventeen speeches that span all the plays of the Henriad and cumulatively give the history of Henry V from boy to king to father. Students will do the explications over the course of the unit and present them to the class near the end.

To illustrate how close reading and acting complement each other, show, if you can locate it, Ian McKellan's videotape *Acting Shakespeare* in which he describes the scholarship an actor needs to do to perform Macbeth's "Tomorrow" soliloquy. This video is no longer available for purchase, but there may be a copy floating around your library or English Department.

Duplicate Handout 13 and Handout 14.

WHAT TO DO

1. Introduction to Close Reading

Tell students that actors and scholars alike use scholarship to look for accurate ways to read Shakespeare's words. If you have the Ian McKellan videotape clip, show it. If not, give a brief explanation of close reading. Show students the research materials they will need. Augment your classroom library or have resources put on reserve in your school library and give students a bibliography.

2. Speech Explication 1

Distribute Handout 13: Speeches for Explication. Tell students that these speeches trace Hal from wild youth to king. Ask the class to choose one speech for close reading. Give them Handout 14: Speech Explication. Work through the explication process with them.

3. Speech Explication 2

Assign each student one speech from those remaining on Handout 13 to do on their own. The speeches vary in length and difficulty, so you may want to assign them selectively or to pairs of students, depending on the strengths and size of your class. Tell them they will have time to do the assignment over the course of the unit.

HOW DID IT GO?

Close reading is more pleasurable for some students than others. You will make some converts to scholarship, and everyone will learn a bit more about the language.

ৰ

HANDOUT 13

SPEECHES FOR EXPLICATION

Here are selected speeches spanning the Henriad. For each speech you choose to explicate, follow the steps in Handout 14.

Can no man tell me of my unthrifty son?
'Tis full three months since I did see him last.
If any plague hang over us, 'tis he.
I would to God, my lords, he might be found.
Inquire at London, 'mongst the taverns there,
For there, they say, he daily doth frequent,
With unrestrained loose companions,
Even such, they say, as stand in narrow lanes
And beat our watch and rob our passengers,
Which he, young wanton and effeminate boy,
Takes on the point of honor to support
So dissolute a crew.

—Henry IV to his court at the end of *Richard II*, 5.3.1–12
(The Riverside Shakespeare)

Yea, there thou mak'st me sad, and mak'st me sin
In envy that my Lord Northumberland
Should be the father to so blest a son,
A son who is the theme of Honor's tongue,
Amongst a grove the very straightest plant,
Who is sweet Fortune's minion and her pride;
Whilst I, by looking on the praise of him,
See riot and dishonor stain the brow
Of my young Harry. O, that it could be proved
That some night-tripping fairy had exchanged
In cradle-clothes our children where they lay,
And called mine "Percy," his "Plantagenet"!
Then would I have his Harry and he mine.

—Henry IV to his court, beginning of *Henry IV, Part 1*, 1.1.78–90

Thou art so fat-witted with drinking of old sack, and unbuttoning thee after supper, and sleeping upon benches after noon, that thou hast forgotten to demand that truly which thou wouldst truly know. What a devil hast thou to do with the time of the day? Unless hours were cups of sack, and minutes capons, and clocks the tongues of bawds, and dials the signs of leaping-houses, and the blessed sun himself a fair hot wench in flame-colored taffeta, I see no reason why thou shouldst be so superfluous to demand the time of the day.

—Hal to Falstaff, *Henry IV, Part 1*, 1.2.2–13

Marry then, sweet wag, when thou art king, let not us that are squires of the night's body be called thieves of the day's beauty. Let us be Diana's foresters, gentlemen of the shade, minions of the moon, and let men say we be men of good government, being governed, as the sea is, by our noble and chaste mistress the moon, under whose countenance we steal.
                    —Falstaff to Hal, *Henry IV, Part 1*, 1.2.24–31

An old lord of the Council rated me the other day in the street about you, sir, but I marked him not, and yet he talked very wisely, but I regarded him not, and yet he talked wisely, and in the street, too.
                    —Falstaff to Hal about Chief Justice, *Henry IV, Part 1*

Thou didst well, for wisdom cries out in the streets and no man regards it.
                    —Hal to Falstaff, *Henry IV, Part 1*, 1.2.89–95

I know you all, and will awhile uphold
The unyoked humor of your idleness.
Yet herein will I imitate the sun,
Who doth permit the base contagious clouds
To smother up his beauty from the world,
That, when he please again to be himself,
Being wanted, he may be more wondered at
By breaking through the foul and ugly mists
Of vapors that did seem to strangle him . . .
So when this loose behavior I throw off
And pay the debt I never promisèd,
By how much better than my word I am,
By so much shall I falsify men's hopes;
And, like bright metal on a sullen ground,
My reformation, glitt'ring o'er my fault,
Shall show more goodly and attract more eyes
Than that which hath no foil to set it off.
I'll so offend to make offense a skill,
Redeeming time when men think least I will.
                    —Hal, *Henry IV, Part 1*, 1.2.202–224

PRINCE   Thou art violently carried away from grace. There is a devil haunts thee in the likeness of an old fat man. A tun of man is thy companion. Why dost thou converse with that trunk of humors, that bolting-hutch of beastliness, that swollen parcel of dropsies, that huge bombard of sack, that stuffed cloakbag of guts, that roasted Manningtree ox with the pudding in his belly, that reverend Vice, that gray iniquity, that father ruffian, that vanity in years? Wherein is he good, but to taste sack and drink it? Wherein neat and cleanly but to carve a capon and eat it? Wherein cunning but in craft? Wherein crafty but in villainy? Wherein villainous, but in all things? Wherein worthy, but in nothing?

FALSTAFF   I would your Grace would take me with you. Whom means your Grace?

PRINCE   That villainous abominable misleader of youth, Falstaff, that old white-bearded Satan.

FALSTAFF   My lord, the man I know.

PRINCE   I know thou dost.

FALSTAFF   But to say I know more harm in him than in myself were to say more than I know. That he is old, the more the pity; his white hairs do witness it. But that he is, saving your reverence, a whoremaster, that I utterly deny. If sack and sugar be a fault, God help the wicked. If to be old and merry be a sin, then many an old host that I know is damned. If to be fat be to be hated, then Pharaoh's [lean] kine are to be loved. No, my good lord, banish Peto, banish Bardolph, banish Poins, but for sweet Jack Falstaff, kind Jack Falstaff, true Jack Falstaff, valiant Jack Falstaff, and therefore more valiant being as he is old Jack Falstaff, banish not him thy Harry's company, banish not him thy Harry's company. Banish plump Jack, and banish all the world.

PRINCE   I do, I will.

> —Hal and Falstaff, *Henry IV, Part 1*, 2.4.462–499

Do not think so. You shall not find it so.
And God forgive them that so much have swayed
Your Majesty's good thoughts away from me.
I will redeem all this on Percy's head,
And, in the closing of some glorious day,
Be bold to tell you that I am your son. . . .

> —Hal, *Henry IV, Part 1*, 3.2.134–139

Thou hast redeemed thy lost opinion
And showed thou mak'st some tender of my life
In this fair rescue thou hast brought to me.

> —King Henry to Hal, *Henry IV, Part 1*, 5.4.48–50

What, old acquaintance, could not all this flesh
Keep in a little life? Poor Jack, farewell.
I could have better spared a better man.
O, I should have a heavy miss of thee
If I were much in love with vanity.
Death hath not struck so fat a deer today,
Though many dearer in this bloody fray.
Emboweled will I see thee by and by;
Till then in blood by noble Percy lie.

> —Hal to "dead" Falstaff, *Henry IV, Part 1*, 5.4.104–112

(Hal has tried on his dying father's crown when his dad comes to and scolds him.)

HAL   I never thought to hear you speak again.

K. HENRY   Thy wish was father, Harry, to that thought:
   I stayed too long by thee, I weary thee.
   Dost thou so hunger for mine empty chair
   That thou wilt needs invest thee with my honors
   Before thy hour be ripe? O foolish youth,
   Thou seek'st the greatness that will overwhelm thee.

> —*Henry IV, Part 2*, 4.5.91–97 (*The Riverside Shakespeare*)

(A few moments later.)

K. HENRY   [O my son,]
   God put [it] in thy mind to take it hence,
   That thou mightst win the more thy father's love,
   Pleading so wisely in excuse of it!

> —*Henry IV, Part 2*, 4.5.177–180 (*The Riverside Shakespeare*)

This new and gorgeous garment, majesty,
Sits not so easy on me as you think.
Brothers, you [mix] your sadness with some fear:
This is the English, not the Turkish court,
Not Amurath an Amurath succeeds,
But Harry Harry. Yet be sad, good brothers,
For by my faith it very well becomes you.
Sorrow so royally in you appears
That I will deeply put the fashion on
And wear it in my heart. Why then be sad,
But entertain no more of it, good brothers,
Than a joint burden laid upon us all.
For me, by heaven (I bid you be assur'd),
I'll be your father and your brother too.
Let me but bear your love, I'll bear your cares.
Yet weep that Harry's dead, and so will I,
But Harry lives, that shall convert those tears
By number into hours of happiness.

   —Hal, now Henry V, *Henry IV, Part 2*, 5.2.44–61 *(The Riverside Shakespeare)*

I then did use the person of your father,
The image of his power lay then in me,
And in th' administration of his law,
Whiles I was busy for the commonwealth,
Your Highness pleased to forget my place,
The majesty and power of law and justice,
The image of the King whom I presented,
And strook me in my very seat of judgment;
Whereon (as an offender to your father)
I gave bold way to my authority,
And did commit you.

   —Chief Justice to Hal, now Henry V, *Henry IV, Part 2*, 5.2.73–83
          (The Riverside Shakespeare)

You are right justice, and you weigh this well,
Therefore still bear the balance and the sword,
And I do wish your honors may increase,
Till you do live to see a son of mine
Offend you and obey you, as I did. . . .
     You did commit me;
For which I do commit into your hand
Th'unstained sword that you have us'd to bear. . . .
     There is my hand.
You shall be as a father to my youth,
My voice shall sound as you do prompt mine ear,
And I will stoop and humble my intents
To your well-practic'd wise directions.

   —Hal to Chief Justice, *Henry IV, Part 2*, 5.2.102–121 *(The Riverside Shakespeare)*

I know thee not, old man, fall to thy prayers.
How ill white hairs becomes a fool and jester!
I have long dreamt of such a kind of man,
So surfeit-swell'd, so old, and so profane;
But being awak'd, I do despise my dream.
Make less thy body (hence) and more thy grace,
Leave gormandizing, know the grave doth gape
For thee thrice wider than for other men.
Reply not to me with a fool-born jest,
Presume not that I am the thing I was,
For God doth know, so shall the world perceive,
That I have turn'd away my former self;
So will I those that kept me company.
When thou dost hear I am as I have been,
Approach me, and thou shalt be as thou wast,
The tutor and the feeder of my riots.
Till then I banish thee, on pain of death,
As I have done the rest of my misleaders,
Not to come near our person by ten mile.
                    —Hal, now Henry V, to Falstaff, *Henry IV, Part 2,* 5.5.47–65
                                        (*The Riverside Shakespeare*)

But if the cause be not good, the King himself hath a heavy reckoning to make, when all those legs, and arms, and heads, chopp'd off in a battle, shall join together at the latter day and cry all, "We died at such a place"—some swearing, some crying for a surgeon, some upon their wives left poor behind them, some upon the debts they owe, some upon their children rawly left. I am afeard there are few die well that die in a battle; for how can they charitably dispose of anything when blood is their argument? Now, if these men do not die well, it will be a black matter for the King that led them to it. . . .
                    —Michael Williams, a soldier on the battlefield, to Hal, now Henry V,
                              Henry V, 4.1.134–145 (*The Riverside Shakespeare*)

Upon the King! let us our lives, our souls,
Our debts, our careful wives,
Our children, and our sins lay on the King!
We must bear all. . . .
                         What infinite heart's ease
Must kings neglect, that private men enjoy!
And what have kings, that privates have not too,
Save ceremony, save general ceremony?
And what art thou, thou idol Ceremony? . . .
I am a king that find thee; and I know
'Tis not the balm, the sceptre, and the ball,
The sword, the mace, the crown imperial,
The intertissued robe of the gold and pearl,
The farced title running 'fore the king,
The throne he sits on, nor the tide of pomp
That beats upon the high shore of this world—
No, not all these, thrice-gorgeous ceremony,

Not all these, laid in bed majestical,
Can sleep so soundly as the wretched slave;
Who, with a body fill'd and vacant mind,
Gets him to rest, cramm'd with distressful bread,
Never sees horrid night, the child of hell;
But like a lackey, from the rise to set,
Sweats in the eye of Phoebus, and all night
Sleeps in Elysium. . . .

—Hal, now Henry V, to himself, *Henry V,* 4.1.230–274
(The Riverside Shakespeare)

Thus far, with rough and all-unable pen,
Our bending author hath pursu'd the story,
In little room confining mighty men,
Mangling by starts the full course of their glory.
Small time; but in that small most greatly lived
This star of England. Fortune made his sword;
By the world's best garden he achieved,
And of it left his son imperial lord.
Henry the Sixt, in infant bands crown'd King
Of France and England, did this king succeed;
Whose state so many had the managing,
That they lost France, and made his England bleed;
Which oft our stage hath shown; and for their sake,
In your fair minds let this acceptance take.

—Chorus, *Henry V,* Epilogue *(The Riverside Shakespeare)*

&

HANDOUT 14

SPEECH EXPLICATION

For each speech you choose to explicate, make an entry in your log. Identify it by quoting the first line and listing the line numbers.

Step 1:

Choose a speech to explicate.

Answer this question in your log: What makes this a good speech for close reading?

Step 2:

Read the speech aloud at least three times.

Step 3 (if possible):

Find the speech in the *First Folio Facsimile* to see what it might have looked like in 1623, about seventeen years after Shakespeare wrote it. Read it carefully. Compare with your edition. Have words or lines changed? If there are some interesting changes, note them in your log.

Step 4:

Return to the speech in the New Folger edition. Make a list of any words you do not understand. Check the footnotes for definitions. Then compare with the footnotes in one or two other editions, the Variorum, or Schmidt's *Lexicon and Quotation Dictionary.* If the definitions differ, note this in your log.

Look up these words and any words remaining on your list in the *Oxford English Dictionary.* Remember that the beauty of the *OED* is that it gives a series of definitions in chronological order so that it is possible to find out what definition people in Shakespeare's time ascribed to this word. Add these definitions to your log.

Step 5:

Note recurring images you find in this speech. For example, do you see a repetition of food words, or blood words, or fat jokes, or hand references? If you see a word or image repeated, look it up in the *Harvard Concordance* if possible. This will identify other places where it occurs in *Henry IV, Part 1* and other plays.

Find these speeches. Notice who said them and under what circumstances. If there is a connection worth mentioning, make a note of it.

Step 6:

Paraphrase the speech.

Answer, in a sentence or two: What does the speech lose in your paraphrase of it? (Be as specific as possible.)

Step 7:

Answer these questions:

- Is it important who speaks the speech? Explain.
- What (in the speaker) motivates the speech?
- What does the speech reveal about the speaker?
- Comment on how you imagine this speech performed.

Step 8:

Memorize the speech, making the most effective performance you can.

What did you learn about the speech by memorizing it?

Step 9:

What is the best question you still cannot answer about the speech?

Step 10:

Write an outline to help you when you are explicating and performing this speech in class.

LESSON 13 "O, Then the Earth Shook"

Rehearsing Act 3

28

PLAY SECTIONS COVERED IN THIS LESSON

3.1.1–197 Rebels plan how they will divide the kingdom.

LINES: Mortimer, 42; Hotspur, 81; Glendower, 57; Worcester, 17

3.1.198–276 Mortimer and his wife conduct a love scene, he in English, she in Welsh; Hotspur and Lady Percy have a heart-to-heart talk.

LINES: Mortimer, 20; Glendower, 21; Lady Mortimer, unspecified and in Welsh; Hotspur, 28; Lady Percy, 10

3.2 King Henry scolds Hal, then gives orders to march when Blunt brings news of English rebels joining the Scots.

LINES: King, 134; Prince Hal, 44; Blunt, 7

3.3 Falstaff accuses Mistress Quickly of robbing him. Hal gives Falstaff a command of foot soldiers.

LINES: Falstaff, 122; Bardolph, 12; Hostess, 41; Prince Hal, 44; Peto, 0

28

WHAT'S ON FOR TODAY AND WHY

Students will gallop to the north of England for plans of war as they organize to perform scenes from Act 3. Because the court scene is brief and contains only two actors, Courtiers will divide. One group will do a rebel scene, one where we see a man and wife who speak two different languages. Actors might choose to substitute a contemporary Spanish or French love song, which should be easier than Welsh to obtain. Photocopy Handout 15: Rebels' Map of England for the rebels to use in 3.1.

WHAT TO DO

1. Act 3 Assignments

Assign new directors for these scenes in Act 3:

• Rebels: 3.1.1–197
• First Courtiers: 3.1.198–276
• Second Courtiers: 3.2
• Pub Crawlers: 3.3

2. Rehearsal

Give groups the remainder of the period for rehearsal. Confer with the rebels about distributing the map (Handout 15) as part of their performance. If the listeners have the map in hand, and if the actors read Mortimer's speech slowly and well, the audience can mark the map according to the lines of division spelled out in the text.

Also inform the Courtiers that you are going to offer four possible subtexts for their scene (see Lesson 14) so they can prepare for these interpretations.

3. Homework

Tell students to rehearse their lines, improvise costumes and props, and generally refine their performances. Explain (again) that the success of the study will depend on their involvement in the staged scenes. This will be the third performance—surely it will reflect the mature scholarship and heightened enthusiasm of veteran actors.

HOW DID IT GO?

By now the actors should be carrying the unit. Students should need little direction. Teachers should feel somewhat useless. Read logs. Take a nap.

HANDOUT 15

REBELS' MAP OF ENGLAND

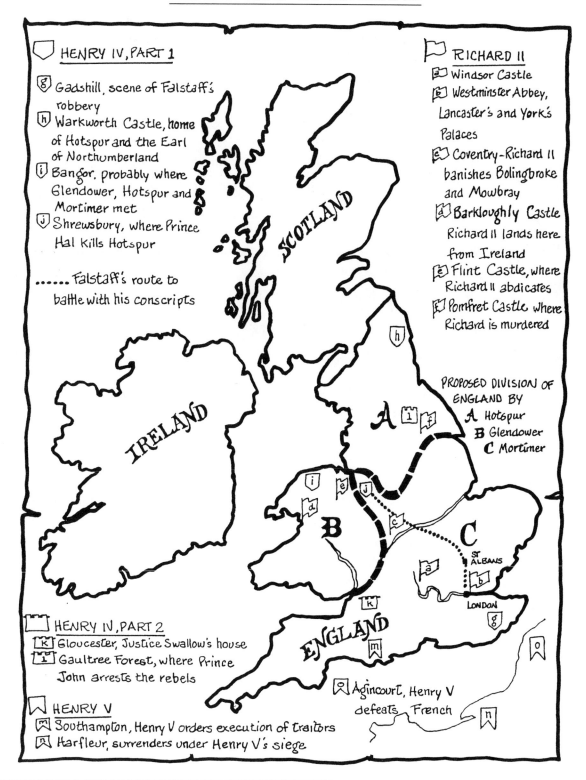

HENRY IV, PART 1

g Gadshill, scene of Falstaff's robbery

h Warkworth Castle, home of Hotspur and the Earl of Northumberland

i Bangor, probably where Glendower, Hotspur and Mortimer met

j Shrewsbury, where Prince Hal kills Hotspur

...... Falstaff's route to battle with his conscripts

RICHARD II

a Windsor Castle

b Westminster Abbey, Lancaster's and York's Palaces

c Coventry-Richard II banishes Bolingbroke and Mowbray

d Barkloughly Castle Richard II lands here from Ireland

e Flint Castle, where Richard II abdicates

f Pomfret Castle where Richard is murdered

PROPOSED DIVISION OF ENGLAND BY
A Hotspur
B Glendower
C Mortimer

HENRY IV, PART 2

k Gloucester, Justice Swallow's house

l Gaultree Forest, where Prince John arrests the rebels

HENRY V

m Southampton, Henry V orders execution of traitors

n Harfleur, surrenders under Henry V's siege

o Agincourt, Henry V defeats French

LESSON 14

"In a New Channel, Fair and Evenly"

Act 3 in Performance

❧ ——————————

PLAY SECTIONS COVERED IN THIS LESSON

3.1.1–197 Rebels plan how they will divide the kingdom.

LINES: Mortimer, 42; Hotspur, 81; Glendower, 57; Worcester, 17

3.1.198–276 Mortimer and his wife conduct a love scene, he in English, she in Welsh; Hotspur and Lady Percy have a heart-to-heart talk.

LINES: Mortimer, 20; Glendower, 21; Lady Mortimer, unspecified and in Welsh; Hotspur, 28; Lady Percy, 10

3.2 King Henry scolds Hal and gives orders to march when Blunt brings news of English rebels joining the Scots.

LINES: King, 134; Prince Hal, 44; Blunt, 7

❧ ——————————

WHAT'S ON FOR TODAY AND WHY

After a brief run-through by all groups, Rebels and First Courtiers will perform 3.1 for others. I think it is important to note how Shakespeare makes Hotspur so vibrant, giving him lines like "I had rather live / With cheese and garlic in a windmill far / Than feed on cakes and have him talk to me / In any summer house in Christendom" (3.1.166–169), which makes his death at the end more painful. We also have a new scene between Hotspur and Kate to talk about. Are students' perceptions of their marriage changing? Scene 2 is the "real" confrontation between Hal and his father that he practiced for with Falstaff. Bolingbroke could hold forth when he was wound up, and this scene is no exception. It helps to keep the students' interest if you assign groups four "parental chewing-out themes" to identify.

WHAT TO DO

1. Rehearsal

Make this short—ten minutes maximum.

2. The Rebels Divide England

Have the Rebels present 3.1.1–197. It is fun to have Glendower move through the audience to hand out copies of the map of the proposed division of England (Handout 15). Discuss Hotspur's teasing of Glendower. Is it deserved? Does it, as his uncle Worcester says, "leave behind a stain / Upon the beauty of all parts besides"?

3. The Lady Speaks in Welsh

Ask First Courtiers to perform 3.1.198–276. How do students feel about Hotspur's treatment of Kate in this scene?

4. Subtext in Your Face

Before Second Courtiers do 3.2, write the following on the board:

· You've let me down. Your little brother has taken your place.
· If I had behaved the way you do, I'd have got nowhere.
· By being polite and low-key, I got people on my side.
· You're going to turn out just like your no-good uncle Richard.

Divide nonperforming class into four groups and assign each a theme to listen for. At the end of the performance, ask them to indicate the lines that express the idea.

5. Performing 3.2

Ask Second Courtiers to perform. Then ask them to lead a discussion about each of the subtexts written on the board. Which are valid? Are some more valid than others? What lines support each?

6. Homework

Ask students to write in their logs a summary of each scene presented today. Then ask them to write a new speech about a father or mother admonishing a son the way it *should* be done.

Remind them that readable drafts of written projects will be due for peer conferences in three more lessons. Pub Crawlers should prepare for staging 3.3.

HOW DID IT GO?
Companies have been evaluated three times with the same form. Is it generating improvement? If not, adjust.

A discussion of the four subtexts should indicate levels of understanding of the play. Ask for questions about words and lines if you think they're a problem.

LESSON **15** "Am I Not Fallen Away Vilely Since This Last Action?"

Over the Hump

🙶

PLAY SECTION COVERED IN THIS LESSON

3.3 Falstaff accuses Mistress Quickly of robbing him. Hal gives Falstaff a command of foot soldiers.

LINES: Falstaff, 122; Bardolph, 12; Hostess, 41; Prince Hal, 44; Peto, 0

🙶

WHAT'S ON FOR TODAY AND WHY

Now that students know what they're doing with scene preparation and performance, and now that almost all of the assignments are started and the "between the acts" activities completed, the unit will pick up speed as it moves from Act 3 toward the end. Today students will perform the final scene of Act 3 and organize for Act 4. Cut 4.4. It introduces two new characters and is a throwaway; possibly Shakespeare needed it to buy time so that other actors could get into battle dress. The rest of the class can be spent in discussion, research of assigned speeches, preparation for tomorrow's quiz on Acts 1–3, rehearsal for Act 4, help with writing or activity projects.

WHAT TO DO

1. Admonishments

Collect the parent scoldings students did for homework. Display them in the classroom.

2. Performing 3.3

Ask Pub Crawlers to perform 3.3. Discussion questions might include

- Is Falstaff's treatment of Mistress Quickly reminiscent of Hotspur's treatment of Kate?

- Falstaff describes himself as living "out of all order, out of all compass" (3.3.21). At Shrewsbury in Act 4, Sir Walter Blunt accuses Hotspur of standing "out of limit and true rule . . . against anointed majesty" (4.3.45–46). In what ways are Hotspur and Falstaff alike?

· Hal has just promised his father, "I shall hereafter, my thrice gracious lord, / Be more myself" (3.2.94–95). Is his promised reformation evident in 3.3?

· Compare Hal's last lines in the scene with Falstaff's. What is the effect on an audience of juxtaposing these lines?

3. Organizing for Act 4 Performances

Assign new directors; announce scenes. Note that remaining action of the play is at Shrewsbury. Ask Courtiers to do a Rebel scene.

· Rebels: 4.1, Hotspur abandoned
· Pub Crawlers: 4.2, Falstaff and conscripts
· Courtiers: 4.3, Blunt offering Hotspur amnesty

4. Projects

Give students the rest of the period to work on projects. Confer with those who need help.

5. Homework

Tell students to study for a quiz on Acts 1–3 and rehearse lines in Act 4.

HOW DID IT GO?

Assignments should be shaping up, discussion lively, performances relaxed and well rehearsed.

LESSON 16 "I Did Never See Such Pitiful Rascals"

Calm Before the Battle

🙠 _____

PLAY SECTIONS COVERED IN THIS LESSON

4.1 Hotspur learns that he has been abandoned by his father and Glendower, so he will have to fight the king's forces alone.

LINES: Hotspur, 79; Douglas, 12; Messenger, 6; Worcester, 22; Vernon, 25

4.2 The prince rides to war in style while Falstaff struggles with his motley foot soldiers.

LINES: Falstaff, 64; Bardolph, 3; Prince Hal, 8; Westmoreland, 8

4.3 Blunt delivers to Hotspur the king's offer of amnesty.

LINES: Hotspur, 73; Worcester, 4; Douglas, 4; Vernon, 20; Blunt, 20

🙠 _____

WHAT'S ON FOR TODAY AND WHY

Students will take a quiz on Acts 1–3 and rehearse before performing Act 4. Quizzes for Acts 4 and 5 will be incorporated into an essay test after the reading is complete.

WHAT TO DO

1. Quiz

Give an open-book quiz on the following:

· Bardolph
· Poins
· Mistress Quickly
· Glendower
· Worcester

Identify each character in a sentence or two of your own; then find a quote—something said to or by the character—that reveals something about the character.

2. Rehearsal

Rehearse Act 4 scenes for the remainder of the period.

3. Homework

Tell students to work on their lines and projects.

HOW DID IT GO?

Do you have students who are not meeting their responsibilities or need extra help with this unit? This would be a good time to schedule individual conferences.

LESSON **17** "It Lends a Luster . . . to Our Great Enterprise"

Act 4 on Stage

ও

PLAY SECTIONS COVERED IN THIS LESSON

4.1 Hotspur learns that he has been abandoned by his father and Glendower, so he will have to fight the king's forces alone.

LINES: Hotspur, 79; Douglas, 12; Messenger, 6; Worcester, 22; Vernon, 25

4.2 The prince rides to war in style while Falstaff struggles with his motley foot soldiers.

LINES: Falstaff, 64; Bardolph, 3; Prince Hal, 8; Westmoreland, 8

4.3 Blunt delivers to Hotspur the king's offer of amnesty.

LINES: Hotspur, 73; Worcester, 4; Douglas, 4; Vernon, 20; Blunt, 20

ও

WHAT'S ON FOR TODAY AND WHY

In 4.1, at Shrewsbury, we see Hotspur abandoned. Neither his father nor Glendower will join him in battle, but his courage doesn't falter, although he says, "Doomsday is near. Die all, die merrily" (4.1.142). In 4.2, Falstaff comments on his conscripts to Hal: "good enough to toss; food for powder, food for powder . . ." (4.2.66–67). In 4.3 we return to the edgy rebel camp where Hotspur receives Sir Walter Blunt and an offer of amnesty from the King. In short, the smell of blood is in the air, and today's performances should reflect the pre-battle anxieties.

WHAT TO DO

1. Rehearsal

Allow for a brief rehearsal. Set up the part of the room you have designated for Shrewsbury—probably somewhere in the middle.

2. Performance

Run the scenes quickly, but take questions after each performance, as always. If there are not too many questions between scenes, you should be able to complete Act 4 in one day.

3. Food for Powder

Ask: Traditionally, who has been "food for powder" in war? At the risk of being thought Marxist, you may want to use Siegfried Sassoon's poem "Base Details" as a comparison. Ask students why they think Hotspur doesn't take the king's offer immediately. Might he later?

4. Homework

Remind students to summarize scenes in their logs. Tell them that tomorrow is writing-conference day, so they are to bring to class readable drafts of their papers. Some students may need to complete the play before they can complete papers, particularly if they need direct quotes, but since everyone should know the story and have seen or acted in four acts, all papers should be well under way.

HOW DID IT GO?

Ask for questions, observations. Are actors putting heart into their performances? By now, they should be showing the motive and the cue for passion.

LESSON **18** "Thou Shalt Find Me Tractable to Any Honest Reason"

Writing Conferences

WHAT'S ON FOR TODAY AND WHY

Group writing conferences serve several purposes. Students hear themselves read their own papers and often discover places to edit; they receive praise and criticism from their classmates; they hear specific references or examples to support an argument.

WHAT TO DO

1. Peer Writing Conferences

Put students in groups of three or four to listen to their classmates read their papers. Ask them to follow the old formula of "Praise, Question, Suggest" after each student has read and ask the writer to take notes on the conference. Notes and original draft must be handed in with the final paper—due at end of unit. You may choose to sit in on each of the groups for a bit. When everyone has been heard, you may ask for groups to choose a best piece for reading to the class.

2. Homework

Tell students to revise papers. Review specifications and due dates.

HOW DID IT GO?

Everyone should have some kind of paper in hand, and after today you'll know whom you have to haunt.

LESSON 19 "I Saw Young Harry with His Beaver On"

Battlefield Plans

❧ _____

PLAY SECTIONS COVERED IN THIS LESSON

5.1 Worcester goes to Henry, receives offer of amnesty.

LINES: King, 47; Prince Hal, 29; Worcester, 47; Falstaff, 19; Vernon, 0

5.2 Worcester and Vernon lie to Hotspur about the king's offer, fearing "he will suspect us still" and let off the younger (misled?) Hotspur.

LINES: Worcester, 35; Vernon, 21; Hotspur, 40; Douglas, 6; Messenger, 1; Second Messenger, 1

5.3 The battle. Douglas kills Blunt, mistaking him for the king. Hotspur corrects him. Hal asks Falstaff for a sword; instead, Falstaff gives him a pistol that turns out to be a bottle of sack.

LINES: Blunt, 7; Douglas, 15; Hotspur, 9; Falstaff, 25; Prince Hal, 9

5.4 The battle continues. Hal saves his father and kills Hotspur. Falstaff pretends to be dead, then takes Hotspur's body and pretends to have killed him.

LINES: Westmoreland, 1; Douglas, 8; Hotspur, 17; Falstaff, 39; Prince Hal, 78; King, 19; Lancaster, 6

5.5 The King sentences Vernon and Worcester to death but allows Hal to spare Douglas. All exit.

LINES: King, 26; Worcester, 3; Prince Hal, 15; Lancaster, 2; Westmoreland, 0

❧ _____

WHAT'S ON FOR TODAY AND WHY

Today we get started on Act 5 performances. The scenes take place in Shrewsbury; in 5.3 and 5.4 all groups come together for a big battle. For the battle, assign speaking parts and one or two directors to orchestrate it. Most important are the moments when Hal saves his father and the fight between Hal and Hotspur.

If you have access to video versions, this is the place to use them. The sequence in *Chimes at Midnight* is ten minutes long, and it makes a good comparison to the BBC version. Of course, students like acting the fight—I just don't allow anything sharp—and I have them perform *before* viewing the films.

WHAT TO DO

1. Act 5 Assignments

Assign scenes and directors for Act 5, all at Shrewsbury:

- Courtiers: 5.1. Suggest that the group cut repetitive material about the rebel cause and discuss why it is repeated.
- Rebels: 5.2
- All Groups: 5.3 and 5.4. The battle: All groups fight; assign speaking parts and one or two directors; it is *very important* that actors with speaking parts rehearse well.
- Pub Crawlers: 5.5. Most of the tavern crew stayed at home, so ask them to lower themselves and play courtiers.

2. Rehearsal

Send all groups to their corners to rehearse. You might need to work with the directors of the battle scene to plan special effects and avoid bloodshed.

3. Homework

Ask students to practice for performance of Act 5, to revise papers, and to work on assigned speech explications and activity projects.

HOW DID IT GO?

The language, the staging, the character objectives—all should be coming easier as students prepare.

LESSON 20   "Come, Let Me Taste My Horse"

Performing Act 5

઩_____

PLAY SECTIONS COVERED IN THIS LESSON

5.1 Worcester goes to Henry, receives offer of amnesty.

LINES: King, 47; Prince Hal, 29; Worcester, 47; Falstaff, 19; Vernon, 0

5.2 Worcester and Vernon lie to Hotspur about the king's offer, fearing "he will suspect us still" and let off the younger (misled?) Hotspur.

LINES: Worcester, 35; Vernon, 21; Hotspur, 40; Douglas, 6; Messenger, 1; Second Messenger, 1

5.3 The battle. Douglas kills Blunt, mistaking him for the king. Hotspur corrects him. Hal asks Falstaff for a sword; instead, Falstaff gives him a pistol that turns out to be a bottle of sack.

LINES: Blunt, 7; Douglas, 15; Hotspur, 9; Falstaff, 25; Prince Hal, 9

5.4 The battle continues. Hal saves his father and kills Hotspur. Falstaff pretends to be dead, then takes Hotspur's body and pretends to have killed him.

LINES: Westmoreland, 1; Douglas, 8; Hotspur, 17; Falstaff, 39; Prince Hal, 78; King, 19; Lancaster, 6

5.5 The King sentences Vernon and Worcester to death, but allows Hal to spare Douglas. They exit.

LINES: King, 26; Worcester, 3; Prince Hal, 15; Lancaster, 2; Westmoreland, 0

઩_____

WHAT'S ON FOR TODAY AND WHY

Acting groups will run through their scenes and get directors' tips before performing. Students should feel the poignancy of Hotspur's desertion by his father and Glendower; the wretchedness of Falstaff's remarks about, and leadership of, his men; the joy of Hal's redemption; the pain of Hotspur's death; the humor of Falstaff's resurrection. The acting and discussion will probably take two days. Prepare Handout 16: Group Performance Evaluation. This is a good way for students to evaluate themselves and the members of their group; it was devised by Alice Kotake, a teacher at Mililani High School, Mililani, Hawaii.

WHAT TO DO

1. Courtiers' Performance

After a rehearsal for all groups, begin with the Courtiers' performance of 5.1.

- Note that Falstaff, Hal, and King Henry are together for the first time. Are their behaviors predictable?
- Does Worcester's line describing King Henry's growing "by our feeding to so great a bulk" intentionally (or unintentionally) connect him to Falstaff?
- What heroic gesture does Hal make? Compare Falstaff's "catechism" in 5.1.128–142 on honor to that of Hotspur in 1.3.199–212. Who's right?

2. Rebels' Performance

Have the Rebels perform 5.2. Here are some questions to ask the players at the end of the scene:

- Despite Worcester's many accusations of King Henry's faithlessness, he returns to Hotspur and lies to him about the king's offer. Why?
- This is only one example of the betrayal of the younger generation by the older in this play. What others can you think of? (Some people think all wars are such betrayals.)
- Just as Worcester has been "infected" by his suspicion, Hotspur seems to doubt the courtesy of Hal's challenge to him in single combat. Must one character rise in stature at the expense of another in plays? In life?

3. Evaluations

Distribute Handout 16. Create a thoughtful atmosphere so that students can take some time to evaluate themselves and the other members of their acting group.

4. Close Reading

If time remains, have students work on assigned close-reading speeches. They will be presented the day after performances are finished.

5. Homework

Ask students to summarize in their logs the scenes performed today and write about their changed perspectives of Hal, Hotspur, King Henry, and Falstaff.

Remind them of writing and activity projects. Finally, tell actors with assigned lines in the battle scene to practice them several times aloud.

HOW DID IT GO?

Ask for questions, comments. Evaluations will tell you about student involvement, and the thoroughness and accuracy of work in acting groups.

HANDOUT 16

GROUP PERFORMANCE EVALUATION

Your Name	Member	Member	Member	Member

Criteria: 1 (low)–10 (high)

1. Attendance
   Was present at all scheduled meetings

2. Punctuality
   Came on time to all meetings

3. Positive attitude
   Helped the group move toward success

4. Responsibility
   Fulfilled all obligations: (list and check off below)

   ☐ _____
   ☐ _____
   ☐ _____
   ☐ _____
   ☐ _____
   ☐ _____
   ☐ _____

5. Teamwork
   Worked as a group member

Total: 50

Reactions: On the other side of this page, please write two brief paragraphs. Use the first to identify and explain your positive comments and the second to list and explain your suggestions and to ask questions.

Teacher's signature _____

LESSON 21   "Die All, Merrily"

The Battle: Epic in Performance

WHAT'S ON FOR TODAY AND WHY

Even if you have films, it is fun for your student actors to have one shot at the Battle of Shrewsbury. So let them have one run-through, and to underscore King Henry's "counterfeiting" by dressing many of his knights in his colors, wind them all up in the same ribbons or bandannas.

WHAT TO DO

1. Staging the Battle

Give the field of Shrewsbury to the directors and let the battle begin. After the performance, discuss the notion of imitation or counterfeit:

· May royalty be assumed at will, with a costume? May it be cast off at will?
· Prince Hal eventually became a popular king. Was his valiant behavior enough to overcome the stain of the Bolingbroke usurpation?
· Falstaff counterfeits death in 5.4 after leading all his poor recruits to death or maiming—"for the town's end, to beg during life" (5.3.40–41)—and has some more remarks about the kind of honor Sir Walter Blunt has won in death (5.3.34–35). He also pretends to have killed Hotspur, a lie Hal lets him get away with. Why?

2. Viewing the Battle

If you have videos at hand, your students would no doubt enjoy comparing battles by professional companies to their own.

3. Homework

· Ask students to compare Hal's eulogy for Hotspur in logs:

> Fare thee well, great heart.
> Ill-weaved ambition, how much art thou shrunk!
> When that this body did contain a spirit,
> A kingdom for it was too small a bound,
> But now two paces of the vilest earth
> Is room enough . . .
>
> (5.4.89–94)

with his for Falstaff (when he thought him dead):

> Poor Jack, farewell.
> I could have better spared a better man.   (5.4.105 – 106)

What do these eulogies reveal about Hal?

· Ask students to read the last scene of the play and summarize it.

HOW DID IT GO?   The performance should have been fun and moving. And students should feel satisfied. They have thought about and spoken and listened to hundreds of lines of Shakespearean text. They have been kings and soldiers and booze hounds and barmaids in courts, in taverns, and on battlefields. Their many parts have made a whole.

LESSON 22   "Doomsday Is Near"

Project Workshop

WHAT'S ON FOR TODAY AND WHY

Students have three projects to wind up: the writing project, the activity project, and the speech explication project. Today students will have to complete and fine-tune their work, and confer with you if necessary.

WHAT TO DO

1. Logs

Talk about log entries. Hear comments about the eulogy comparisons and the play in general. Ask

- What person in the play do you know best?
- With whom do you identify?
- What did you learn about yourself in doing *Henry IV, Part 1*?

2. How goes the field?

Give students the remaining time to perfect writing, activity, and explication projects. Tell students to be prepared to present their activity projects tomorrow. Hear oral projects over the next two days; other projects are due tomorrow. Begin hearing speech explication projects day after tomorrow.

3. Homework

Whatever it takes to be prepared.

HOW DID IT GO?

How valuable were the log assignments in this unit? Were they routine busywork, or did they lead students to pleasurable interaction with the text? If you like, ask students to answer these questions in one last log entry.

LESSON 23 "To Hear This Rich Reprisal"

Oral Project Presentations, Essay Exam

WHAT'S ON FOR TODAY AND WHY

Today students who chose oral or performance activity projects will present them. Then the close reading analyses of the speeches will begin. An essay test will follow. Altogether, this work will take two days.

WHAT TO DO

1. Activity Projects

Ask students to volunteer (or have them sign up) for the oral activities; ask students who hand in other projects to tell the class briefly what they did.

2. Speech Explication

Students present their speech explications. Do the speeches in the order they appear on Handout 13. Leave time for questions after each presentation. Working through these seventeen speeches will serve as a good review for the essay test.

3. Essay Exam

Give students this essay question, which is based on the free-response question of the 1990 Advanced Placement Literature and Language Exam:

> *Henry IV, Part 1* depicts conflicts between a parent (or parental figure) and a son. Write an essay in which you analyze the sources of the conflict and explain how the conflict contributes to the meaning of the work.

> Have students do this exam in class or as a take-home.

4. Homework

Remind students that final writing activity papers are due the next day or two.

HOW DID IT GO?

To evaluate the work of individuals and/or teams, assess their presentations and the essay response.

LESSON 24 "The True and Perfect Image of Life Indeed"

Making a Scene: *Henry IV, Part 1* Festival

As with the *Hamlet* unit, end with a festival of scenes from *Henry IV, Part 1*. Students can work in any group they like and do any scene they like. It must be memorized and run about ten to fifteen minutes. Allow four or five days for rehearsal and one or two days for the festival.

My students often choose to meet for additional rehearsals outside class, usually at my house. You may structure this activity as much or as little as you like. I sometimes assign one act to each of five groups; their task is to choose a central scene or a medley of scenes. Sometimes I let groups choose scenes from any part of the play, collapse the action of the entire play, or follow a single character (my last year's sophomore class had four Falstaffs; one Falstaff merely stepped behind a screen to remove the velcro "fat suit" and hand it to the next one).

There is no single right way to hold a Shakespeare festival. My only rule is that student groups perform for one another using Shakespeare's language. You may embellish as you see fit with costumes, music, and food (cider and doughnuts are always a hit).

If you want grading guidelines, the most logical course of action is to use Handout 5, as you did for the earlier scene performances.

WHAT TO DO

1. Forming Acting Companies

Assign students to groups or let them form new acting companies. After students are assembled in groups, they will need to choose a director and cast parts. Give them about twenty minutes to do this. If they have been thinking about what scenes they'd like to do during the unit thus far, this task will be much easier.

2. Specifications for Performance

Review expectations. Tell the students when and where they will perform. Suggest they arrange rehearsals outside class.

3. Rehearsals

Allow rehearsals to get under way while you read writing projects and essay tests. At the end of the four (or three or five) rehearsal days, set the order of performances and answer any last-minute questions.

4. Festival

Celebrate your Shakespeare festival. You may want to invite parents or other classes if your actors are willing. Collect group evaluations.

5. *Henry V*

If you like, follow up the festival by showing Kenneth Branagh's *Henry V.*

HOW DID IT GO?   You and your students should have a splendid time.

"I Have Had a Most Rare Vision": Teaching Shakespeare with Video

MICHAEL LoMONICO
FARMINGDALE (N.Y.) HIGH SCHOOL

The Folger team has created *Shakespeare Set Free* to prove with passion one simple but mighty idea: Shakespeare wrote scripts. To know them, perform them. We work at it. We get students on their feet with swords in hand shouting, "Strike, down with them, cut the villains' throats!" No doubt about it—performance is the most important teaching strategy for a successful *Hamlet, Henry IV, Part 1,* or any Shakespeare unit.

And the perfect complement to performance is video. Most teachers I know use video. How they use it is another matter. I always wince when I hear a teacher say that he has an easy week because he is showing *Hamlet* or *Romeo and Juliet* to his classes. You've seen him, sitting in back of the room grading papers in the dark, or in the case of one teacher in my school, sitting at his desk in front of the room, unable to see the screen but able to see that the students stay awake.

The show-the-movie-at-the-end-of-unit technique is a holdover from the days of the 16-millimeter projector. Any teacher who has been in the business for more than ten years will remember what that was like: reels the size of pizzas (and about as easy to handle), each containing about forty minutes of scratchy film; threading nightmares in which nervous thumbs tried to shove slippery celluloid through tiny doors and lenses, following an intricate series of arrows; sound that was out of sync or garbled; dramatic moments ruined when the film would kink, go off the track, clog, or break.

Once, during a showing of *To Kill a Mockingbird* in my room, the take-up reel actually fell off the projector, spewing film over the floor, much to the amusement of my supportive students. Often the film ran overtime; perhaps they put forty-three minutes on the reel, or I lost time with one of the previously mentioned mishaps. Students who had waited for three or four days to see if Hamlet or Macbeth died at the end had to leave to get to sixth period because of a math test. "Just wait a minute," I remember shouting as they ran out of the room. "You're going to miss the best part."

Rarely did a school own a copy of a feature film, and renting from a distributor was expensive. Teachers needed to reserve the film long in advance of showing it (in our school, we always selected dates for the "indispensable" films a year in advance), so the films never arrived at an opportune time in the teaching of the play. Also, the film had to be returned to the distributor within five days, forcing the teacher to work within a rigid schedule. So if teachers got their hands on a good film and they got it working on the projector, they naturally showed every second of it.

Then came the videocassette revolution. Most schools acquired VCRs—several years after the last kid on the block had one—and teachers were excited about being able to show films in this newly accessible and convenient way. Since the revolution, however, I have noticed that most teachers, especially the more experienced ones, use videotapes nearly the same way they used 16-millimeter film.

As I walk down the hall in my school, I notice that most show the film in forty-minute segments for three or four days in a row and that they rarely talk over the film. The only real advantages of videotape for them are that it is easier to load and rewind and that they can pick up a cassette from their media center or video store rather than going through the hassle of ordering. So what we have gained with this new technology is some convenience for the teacher but not much instructional innovation.

The real advantages of video in the classroom are these:

1. *Accessibility.* Many versions of Shakespeare's plays are now available for as little as $19.95. Several years ago, when I first asked our head librarian to order a second version of *Macbeth,* she was taken aback and informed me that we already owned one. It took a long explanation to convince her to indulge my folly, and now we own several versions of many plays I teach. I also share my personal collection with students.

2. *Portability.* After long battles with my school librarians, I was able to convince them that students could be trusted to sign out a videotape overnight or over a week-end, just like at a video store. Now my students can watch a Shakespeare play at home in a group and report back to the rest of the class. They have done this with multiple versions of the same play, especially *Hamlet, A Midsummer Night's Dream,* and *Macbeth.* We now have copies of several other plays in the library, and I assign these to my students to view at home. They really like the BBC *Titus Andronicus.*

3. *Flexibility.* Film on a reel is a linear medium. To show it, the projector operator must start at the beginning and go to the end. Videotape and now laser disks allow the teacher to scan to a specific scene or line or word with relative ease. Once students have performed a scene, for example, the teacher can show a three-minute video version and let the young actors compare their production decisions to professional ones.

In talking to teachers around the country, I have discovered many who have created lessons that take full advantage of the superiority of the new media in teaching Shakespeare. Incorporating their ideas and my own, I have developed a short list of video methods that propel students right into the play:

One Scene Many Ways

I select any scene from the play and cue it up on two or three or four videos. This may be a scene they have just read or even acted out, but sometimes I like to select a scene they have not read. I usually distribute a handout with short identifications of each version by actor, producer, or director (like Olivier, Jacobi, Kline, and Gibson) and some space for students to write comments. Some like to follow along in the text, so I sometimes hand out a copy of the scene.

After watching each clip, students have five minutes to write about what they have seen without discussion. After the last version, we begin the discussion. I insist that they not say which one they liked best but talk about the differences and speculate about the actors' and director's intentions in the scene. Usually they cannot hold it in, and eventually I relent and let them vote on their favorite. Despite my explanations, I still occasionally have a student ask, "OK, but which version is the right one?" My goal is to show students that there is no "correct" way to do Shakespeare, that all actors and directors bring their own interpretations to the scene.

Video to Go

This project involves letting the students view a Shakespeare play on video at one of their homes. A recent survey pointed out that although most adolescents preferred watching TV alone in their rooms, they prefer to watch videos in a group. With this in mind, I let my students sort themselves into groups of four or five. They must watch the film as a group in one or two sittings. They assign and rotate roles such as recorder (keeping a log of the entire process), reader (following the text, identifying characters, and noting cuts in the text), typist, and caterer. After viewing the video, they prepare a class presentation in which they analyze such elements as camera work, costumes, music, and acting.

The Whole Play—But Not at the End

Consider these two true statements: (1) One of the best Shakespeare videos available at this writing is Kenneth Branagh's *Henry V.* (2) One of the obstacles to teaching *Henry IV, Part 1* is getting faces to go with all the names of people. Solution: Show *Henry V before* starting the *Henry IV, Part I* unit. Students will get swept into the character of Hal; they will meet many of the people from the court and the tavern; they will see what happens to rebels; and they'll see how Hal develops. If necessary, use a video guide and stop the VCR often to explain who's who and what's happening.

Video is excellent for teaching Shakespeare to our students because he wrote plays, and students come to us true video veterans with thousands of hours of TV and movie watching under their belts. So get the remote control working to freeze frames to analyze relationships (a modern equivalent of *tableaux vivants*). Rewind a critical moment and show it in slow motion. Talk about why Gertrude looks younger than Hamlet in the Olivier version (she was). Ask the class which Falstaff looks more realistic and which Hal acts more like they imagined him. Let the students tell you why their production of the robbery at Gad's Hill was better than the BBC's—or why Amanda's version of "To be or not to be" was better than Mel Gibson's.

By using these techniques, you and I can teach students much more about Shakespeare's plays. Moreover, because the viewers are also actors, their ownership of the plays will be complete.

More Bullets

⅋

NANCY GOODWIN
CLINTON (OKLA.) HIGH SCHOOL

Believe me, teachers, there are days in the midst of the best of units that I go searching for more ammunition.

The goals are right. The students are motivated. I am teaching my heart out. But for reasons I have never figured out in my twenty years in the classroom, things go flat. Where is that jolt of energy? Where is that activity that will make the blood rush again?

As Peggy O'Brien told you in the Introduction, the units in *Shakespeare Set Free* were designed by a team of expert teachers, then edited to their present state. Those artful words cover months of strain and sweat as editors chose from many great activities the ones that fit the unit best. Result: great stuff lying on the cutting-room floor—the very firepower I need. Here are my favorites.

"To Be" with Drums

Sue Peters told how in her Arizona classroom she would ask a student to bring a trap set to class. She would pass out copies of the all-time favorite *Green Eggs and Ham*, by Dr. Seuss. She would get the students on their feet, get the drummer drumming, and ask everyone to recite *Green Eggs and Ham* as they moved free-form around the classroom. Then she would give them copies of Hamlet's "To be or not to be" soliloquy and do the same thing. Then she would go to the board and write in large letters, *Shakespeare has a beat.*

All of this happened *before* the *Hamlet* unit, so students carried to Shakespeare's text an iambic pentameter undercurrent they could feel in their bones.

One day circumstances converged to create the perfect moment for me to try this. The drummer's younger brother had early-morning detention, so I commuted his sentence in exchange for his lugging the drum set to the vocal music room. I gave out the scripts, sent Matt to the drums, and let the students take over. Soon we were all carried away on the beat of Shakespeare's words. The impromptu performance piece they created follows.

TO BE OR NOT TO BE: A CHORAL READING
Arranged by students of Clinton High School

Arrange participants like a chorus—standing in a semicircle. Divide into three sections. Assign solo parts. Accent the words in bold.

ALL: (whisper rhythmically) To **DIE** (pause a beat), to **SLEEP** (pause a beat), to **sleep**— per**chance** to **dream** (pause 2 beats). (repeat this phrase 3 times)
SECTION ONE: To **be** or not to be, **that** is the **ques**tion.
SECTION TWO: To **be** or not to be, **that** is the **ques**tion.
SECTION THREE: To **be** or not to be, **that** is the **ques**tion.
SECTION ONE: Whether (da-**da**-da-da)
SECTION TWO: Tis nobler
SECTION THREE: In the mind
SECTION ONE: To suffer
ALL: (start at a very high pitch, descend to a low pitch) The slings and arrows of outrageous fortune
SECTION ONE: Or (da-**da**-da-da)
SECTION TWO: (louder) Or (da-**da**-da-da)
SECTION THREE: (louder) Or (da-**da**-da-da)
ALL: (louder) Or?
ALL: (whisper, keep repeating during solos) To **DIE** (pause a beat), to **SLEEP** (pause a beat), to **sleep**—per**chance** to **dream** (pause 2 beats).
(all solos delivered as if at protest march)
SOLOIST ONE: To take arms!
SOLOIST TWO: Against!
SOLOIST THREE: A sea of troubles!
SOLOIST FOUR: And by opposing!
SOLOIST FIVE: (very loud) End them!
SECTION ONE: (Loud to normal) Ennnnnnnd them
SECTION TWO: (softer) Ennnnnd them
SECTION THREE: (very soft) Ennnnnnnnd them
ALL: (whisper rhythmically) To **DIE** (pause a beat), to **SLEEP** (pause a beat), to **sleep**— per**chance** to **dream** (pause 2 beats). (repeat this phrase 3 times, softer and slower each time)

The Question of Questions

At one time the *Hamlet* unit included some journal work in which several days before the unit the teacher would ask students to answer in their logs some very piercing personal questions. Not until *Hamlet* unfolded would they see the purpose of these questions, but by then students had already reacted to the situations with honesty and anxiety. Extremely effective prereading writing. I've never seen this fail to work in a classroom of seniors. The problem is that the questions raised in *Hamlet* are not polite:

• Imagine that you are a child in a happy family—a father who has a prosperous and respected business, parents who love each other and love you. How do you feel?

• Imagine that you are away at college or in the service or off working for a year, and you come home to find that your father is dead. How do you feel?

• Imagine further not only that your father is dead but that your mother has moved a new man into her bedroom. How do you feel about this man? How do you feel about your mother?

- Imagine that this new man has taken over your father's business, the business you were trained to run. How do you feel?
- Imagine that you learn that your father did not die naturally, that the new man murdered him. How do you feel? What if your mother helped him? How do you feel?
- What would you do to rectify this situation? List as many solutions as possible.

We cut these pre-*Hamlet* questions. But no doubt about it—they are a powerful jolt, so when I have a class who trusts me, I sometimes sneak them in anyway, and when I do, I insist that students be brutally honest. The purpose, after all, is to tear away the shield of polite countenance and get to the horror of the play. However, I never read what students write; in fact, sometimes I have them tear out the pages and throw them away as soon as they're written. If students will use writing to get primal emotions to the surface, that is enough.

Students are often puzzled about Hamlet's feelings for Ophelia. Why does he treat her so cruelly—putting on a crazy act in her closet, telling her to get herself to a nunnery, insulting her with nasty language at the play? What is he thinking? It's easy for students to conclude that Hamlet is disturbed and not himself or that he doesn't love Ophelia and is trying to ditch her, but it is not so easy for students to think about the possibility that he loves her and is acting for her own good.

I don't know that this conclusion is the best subtext, but because it's the hardest for students to consider, I add these questions to the exercise:

- Imagine that you love someone very much and that you have got yourself in so much trouble that you see that there is no way out—there will be a bad ending for you and all your closest associates. What would you do?
- Imagine that you can't tell anyone about the trouble and that you decide you have to protect the person you love by getting him or her out of your life. How would you do it?

Images

We talk so much about performance that I sometimes forget that Shakespeare's play also takes place in my head. So when I teach *Hamlet*, I always stop and take one of my favorite speeches, "What a piece of work is a man," and focus on how the words affect the mind. It's amazing, isn't it, that Shakespeare scratched some marks on a paper four hundred years ago and that today those marks make pictures come to life on the stage in my head. Ah, yes . . . I give you this lost lesson, Shakespeare's Imagery.

WHAT'S ON FOR TODAY AND WHY

Shakespeare's language is rich with words that produce pictures in the mind. Because these pictures flash by so quickly, we can help students enjoy a stronger visual effect by slowing down and focusing on the images. When we talk about images, we do not mean anything fancy or esoteric. We mean the pictures that appear on the screen in our heads when we hear or see certain words. When we hear the word "elephant," we cannot help ourselves—we "see" an elephant. Most of us do not "see" anything when we hear the word "with." Visual images vary with individuals, and we are not suggesting that everyone has to "see" every image in the passage we have isolated. But it is interesting to notice how different images work in a passage. Are there words and phrases that invoke images in most everyone? Are there images that are seen in more detail than others? Are there words and phrases that produce conflicting images—some see one thing, others another?

In this lesson we will turn on our inner eyes and look for images while we hear the words from *Hamlet,* 2.2.318–326.

Teachers will need to locate a recording of the Broadway musical *Hair.*

WHAT TO DO

1. Working with Images

Talk to the class about the power of words to create mental pictures. Give them some examples. Ask them to say words that produce mental pictures: "pilgrim," "fork," "bus," "clock." Ask them to point to where they "see" these items. Most will point to a space a few inches in front of their forehead. Then they will laugh because this seems at once so right and so ridiculous.

Talk about this mental stage. Test its powers. Can students "see" split-screen images there—Marilyn Monroe on one side and Elvis Presley on the other? Can the two turn and talk to each other? Can students see a meadow? Can they see a tower? Can they put the tower in the meadow? Can they play out a narrative there—start with one person—say, themselves on a certain occasion like a birthday or the prom—and move into a scene with more people and a story?

Again ask them to point to the mental stage. Now ask them to move it around their head and stop it by their right ear. At this point, some students will be giving you the same look the Native Americans gave Columbus. Others will be dazed and scared. Allay their fears and proceed.

2. What a Piece of Work

Read to students *Hamlet,* 2.2.318–326 ("I have of late" to "congregation of vapors"). Or play an audiotape, such as the one featuring Kenneth Branagh. Tell students that Hamlet is talking to two old school friends. Then read the passage again, very slowly, and have students note any word or phrase that causes a picture to pop into the stage in their heads. Ask which words and phrases produced mental pictures. Compile the list on the board or overhead projector. By discussion or a show of hands, determine which words and phrases produced the most pictures.

Are there words like "canopy" that produced different pictures in different minds? Are there words like "wherefore" or "not" or "the" that produce no pictures? Ask: What is the effect of all this? Do patterns emerge? Does power emerge?

Then read or hear 2.2.327–334 ("What a piece of work" to "you seem to say so").

3. The Musical Version

Ask students to look at this passage in the text. Have them put their fingers on the line "I have of late. . . ." Play "What a Piece of Work Is Man" from the sound track of the musical *Hair*. Swim away with the images.

HOW DID IT GO?
If you helped students to "see" more pictures in Shakespeare's language, the lesson was perfect.

Holinshed's Chronicles

There is so much historical background material in the *Henry* unit that we were afraid you'd revolt if we added more, but *Holinshed's Chronicles* (1587 edition) is a gem. It is included in many editions, including the signet classic of *Henry V.* If you plan to show *Henry V*, give students the first few pages of the Henry V section of the chronicles ("Henry, Prince of Wales, son and heir to King Henry the fourth, born in Wales at Monmouth on the river of Wye" to "but also the whole realm of France, as heir to his great-grandfather, King Edward the Third"), a good dictionary, their genealogy chart, a list of directions, and a group of congenial peers with whom to conspire, and a good time will be had by all. Directions:

- List the most important information about Henry V.
- List the most interesting information about Henry V.
- Make a diagram of his immediate family—father, mother, sisters, brothers.
- Explain the incident with Paris Balls.
- Compare Holinshed's version of Hal to Shakespeare's.

The BBC's Falstaff

Kenneth Branagh's *Henry V* is one of the all-time best Shakespeare videos. I work it into many units, and I would never do *Henry IV, Part 1* without it. I also use *The Merry Wives of Windsor*, one of the best productions in the British Broadcasting Company's Shakespeare series. Queen Elizabeth I, Jeanne Roberts tells us in *Shakespeare's English Comedy: Merry Wives of Windsor*, found Falstaff one of the most entertaining characters in all of drama, so she asked Shakespeare to write another play with Falstaff, one in which the audience would see Falstaff in love. Thus, probably in 1597, Shakespeare interrupted his work on *Henry IV, Part 2* to write *The Merry Wives of Windsor*. The BBC production stars Richard Griffiths as Falstaff, Prunella Scales as Mistress Page, and Judy Davis as Mistress Ford. There are many scenes showing Falstaff as the foolish lover. Whether you use an excerpt or two or show the entire play, your students will find much pleasure in the post-Henriad Falstaff.

So there they are. The extra bullets. I toss them on the table, yours to use if the moment arises. Go to the showdown armed and dangerous.